Just A Few Lines...

the unseen letters and memorabilia of

Brian Close

By David Warner

Edited by Ron Deaton

GREAT NORTHERN

Great Northern Books
PO Box 1380, Bradford,
West Yorkshire, BD5 5FB

www.greatnorthernbooks.co.uk

ISBN: 978-1-912101-02-3

Design by David Burrill

CIP Data
A catalogue for this book is
available from the British Library

For Vivien for caring for Brian

ACKNOWLEDGEMENTS

The seeds for this book were sown a couple of months after Brian Close's death in September, 2015, when I paid a call upon his widow, Vivien, and she mentioned that she had started looking through Brian's wardrobe and had gathered together a bin-liner full of his neckwear, ties, dickie bows and the odd cravat. She said she had it in mind to dispose of them – either by simply throwing them away or at best offering them to a charity shop. She seemed to think they would be of no interest to anybody! Needless to say I suggested that they should be referred to members of the Yorkshire Cricket Foundation's Archives Committee where their significance could be properly assessed.

Shortly afterwards, I became aware that she had in her possession a tremendous amount of cricket memorabilia which had either been accumulated by her late husband over the years or passed on to her by the family of Brian's best friend, John Anderson, who had saved scores of letters and other fascinating items either sent or given to him by the great man during his early Yorkshire and England days.

I quickly realised that so wide was the range of memorabilia that there was scope for at least one book on this unique collection and from that moment on Vivien could not have been more generous with her time or more diligent in helping to assemble and pass on the material. Without her willing assistance the project would never have got off the ground.

I am equally indebted to Ron Deaton, a leading expert on Yorkshire cricket memorabilia, who readily agreed to edit this book and has spent countless hours doing so. Either at his home or mine or at Vivien's he has meticulously gone through everything with a toothcomb and his help and advice have been invaluable. Having worked in newspapers all my life, I know what makes a good sub editor and I marvel at his qualities.

The assembling of *Just A Few Lines* has taken a good chunk of the last four years out of Ron's life and my own but we have enjoyed every minute of it and the experience has added, for us, a new dimension to Brian's life.

Throughout the writing of the book, I have received every encouragement and assistance from Yorkshire County Cricket Club with its current Chairman, Robin Smith, fully supportive every step of the way. Despite the demands on his time in an ICC World Cup and Ashes summer, which has seen Emerald Headingley play host to both events, he never hesitated for a second in my request for a Foreword and I greatly appreciate his interest.

Thanks and gratitude are due, also, to the Yorkshire Cricket Foundation, the official charity and community arm of Yorkshire CCC. The Foundation's Heritage Manager, Paul Goodman, was ever helpful in making the Brian Close Collection, housed in the Emerald Museum at Headingley, available whenever items were required for copying or photographing, and all my fellow members of the Foundation's Archives Committee, particularly Chairman Chris Hardy and Brian Sanderson, were readily on hand when help was needed.

Furthermore, I am indebted to Brian's former Yorkshire colleague, Ken Taylor, a distinguished artist, for letting me reproduce his splendid painting of Brian on the front cover of the book, and to author Stephen Chalke for supplying me with a sharp image of the work.

Finally, I would like to thank David Burrill, of Great Northern Books, for his keen interest from the start and for his patience in allowing me to get on with the book at my own pace.

CONTENTS

FOREWORD

So much has been written about Brian Close that even cricket aficionados would say that there is surely little now to add: schoolboy cricket and football prodigy, youngest ever England selection, played for England in 22 Tests over four successive decades, best win ratio of any England captain ever, unfairly sacked by Yorkshire (about which the protests of Yorkshire supporters are heard even now), loved a flutter on the horses, hair-raising driver and, through it all, the most likeable and popular of men.

I first met Brian in 1984 when I became the Club's solicitor and he was a member of the Yorkshire General Committee and Cricket Chairman, and what a privilege that was. As with all Yorkshire schoolboys of the 1950s, Brian had for me been something of a god, worshipped from afar; yet now I was speaking with him and he was treating me as an equal!

Over the following years I saw him often. I played golf with him and even cricket. He was the opposing captain in a charity cricket match. We lost! There were no airs or graces about Brian, just simple human empathy and kindness, and right to the end I continued to enjoy his company at Headingley when he would pop into the office for a chat whether or not there was a match in progress on the field.

Nobody but Brian would have been allowed to disturb the Club's operational efficiency so regularly, but Brian was different. Everybody loved to see him, from the Chairman down!

But my knowledge of Brian is now shown to be seriously incomplete by David Warner's insightful book. Far from the uncomplicated, rumbustious character we had all assumed him to be, Brian is revealed, through his correspondence with a schoolboy friend (happily preserved and made available to Yorkshire by Vivien, Brian's widow) as a thoughtful, literate and profoundly intelligent man.

We learn, for instance, that at Aireborough Grammar School he was encouraged to aim for university and a possible career in medicine, a path from which he was deflected only by his cricketing skills which had propelled him into the England side at the age of 18 years and 149 days.

I am sure there are many more worthy to contribute this foreword, and I feel immensely honoured to have been selected for the task. This book re-writes Brian Close's early life story and gives to all cricket lovers a fresh analysis of a man who was widely admired, and remains so, and whose place in Yorkshire's and England's cricketing history, already assured, will be enhanced by David Warner's fresh insight.

Robin Smith
Chairman. Yorkshire County Cricket Club
March 1, 2020

INTRODUCTION

The great and the good of English cricket packed into St Chad's Parish Church at Headingley on September 30, 2015, for a service of thanksgiving for the life of Brian Close CBE.

Family friend and cricketing colossus, Sir Ian Botham, was among those who attended to pay moving tributes, along with Colin Graves, Chairman of the England and Wales Cricket Board, and Bryan Stott, a team-mate of Brian's during Yorkshire's post war glory days starting in the late 1950s.

Few in the church – if any at all – were unaware that Brian had led Yorkshire, Somerset and England with great distinction and that throughout his career he had been unflinchingly brave to the point of foolhardiness.

They knew, also, that Brian was a multi-talented sportsman who excelled at practically everything he turned his hand to, whether it be cricket, soccer, golf or a host of other sports and pastimes.

He often got into scrapes with authority on the way but his sheer love of sport and his competitiveness were never for a moment doubted.

Dennis Brian Close was born in Rawdon on February 24, 1931, and he died a few miles away at his Baildon home on September 14, 2015, having spent most of his 84 years immersed in both sport and *The Sporting Life* which was never far from his side.

This book is not intended to serve as a statistical reminder of Brian's action-packed career which has been thoroughly recorded already. Instead, it focuses on a surprising aspect of his life that few people had any knowledge of at all – his prolific letter writing, particularly as a young man.

By the time Brian had become England's youngest Test cricketer at the age of 18 years and 149 days – a distinction he still holds – he was somehow finding time in the middle of a crowded life to correspond regularly with 20 or so close relatives and acquaintances.

Opposite page: Brian Close, right, with his best friend, John Anderson

Over a hundred of these letters were penned during an eight-year period to his schoolboy friend, John Anderson, from nearby Horsforth, and they traced in remarkable detail his development as a young footballer with Leeds United, Arsenal and Bradford City and his early days with Yorkshire and England.

Perhaps unknown to anyone else, these letters were stored away by John and following the deaths of both the writer and the recipient they were handed over to Brian's widow, Vivien, by John's younger sister, Jill, along with a treasure trove of memorabilia which was built up by John via Brian.

Following consultations between Vivien and the archives section of the Yorkshire Cricket Foundation, the charitable arm of Yorkshire County Cricket Club, the letters and a significant quantity of other memorabilia were added to items already in the Foundation's ownership to form the Brian Close Collection. Several of Brian's letters open up with the words "Just a few lines" ... hence the title of the book.

It is doubtful whether there exists a comparable collection of letters from 70 or so years back which have been written by such a distinguished sportsman. In addition to adding flavour to important events of the time they also provide a colourful account of Brian's inner feelings on his difficult tour of Australia in 1950-51 and the part he played in MCC's controversial A tour of Pakistan in 1955-56 which was almost called off by the MCC following the soaking of a home umpire in what became a huge diplomatic incident.

Although things rarely went right from a cricket angle for Brian on the 1950-51 tour of Australia, the letters clearly show that this did not prevent him from having a splendid time socially, and who can blame him? Brought up in a big family and on the breadline in the austere years before and after the Second World War, Brian as a handsome 19-year-old suddenly had a sparkling new world of plenty opened up to him Down Under – and, boy, did he make the most of it.

From his schoolboy years, Brian regularly visited John at his home and in some ways he clearly regarded the Andersons as part of an extended family. He perhaps felt an obligation to write regularly to John, even when it meant having to put pen to paper at all sorts of unsociable and inconvenient times.

Brian obviously valued John's friendship but he was not obsessed with him in the same way that perhaps John was with Brian. Right up to the end of their days, Brian was never far away from John's thoughts.

Many of the letters are reproduced in full with only the odd spelling mistake or other minor error corrected but because of the sheer volume of letters others have been edited, particularly those written while he was staying in London and on Arsenal's books.

Also, it will come as no great surprise that writing in his late teens and early twenties to a trusted friend, Brian readily refers to his female acquaintances and admirers. The only reason why some of these references have been omitted is to avoid repetition and nothing to do with their perfectly acceptable content.

Where additional information has been added in Brian's letters it is contained within square brackets, i.e.: [February 20, 1956]. Where sentences or paragraphs have been taken out of the letters this is indicated by a series of dots, i.e. ....

Readers of this book will hopefully learn a little more of the Brian Close they knew, and a good deal more of the Brian Close which emerges through his youthful letters of so long ago.

CHAPTER ONE

CLOSE RECALL

Remembering Brian: His wife, Vivien – Margery Anderson, elder sister of John – school friend Audrey Brown (nee Newbould) – longstanding friend and acquaintance Dr Keith Howard, Chairman of the Emerald Group – school friend and Yorkshire team-mate Bryan Stott

Nobody knew Brian as well as his wife of 50 years, Vivien. They first bumped into each other in Bermuda in 1964 where Yorkshire were playing cricket on a post season tour and where Vivien, a BOAC air hostess, had flown in from London and was awaiting the return trip home. Her memories of Brian lead to a better understanding of him and shed light on aspects of his life that the public are generally unaware of. She says:

Brian's family came from Rawdon and lived in a council house. There was Harry and his wife, Esther, and their children Peter, Brian, Tony, Kenny, Alan and Mary, eight of them, and in what must have been an almighty squeeze in a council house, but then his father was only a weaver and his mother couldn't work, obviously. You can't work when you have got six kids can you?

After starting out at Littlemoor Primary School, Rawdon, he went to Aireborough Grammar School and he was a bright pupil, very clever. I have still got his school certificates along with a lot of photographs. He could do maths falling off a log. He was not at all artistic and didn't read books or anything like that but anything mathematical he was an absolute genius. He was encouraged at school to go to university and his original ambition was to be a doctor and, of course, one of the main things you need to become a doctor is maths but National Service and cricket and going to Australia meant that all that fell apart. He had a struggle within himself as to whether to become a doctor or make cricket and sport in general a priority. Nobody else in the family had done anything like it but his father was a good cricketer, a wicket-keeper.

He had too much talent for one person. He had the brains, he had the sporting ability, the looks, the body, the health, he had everything – which is all too much for one person.

He met John Anderson, who became a lifelong friend, while at school at Aireborough in the first year at 11. They started off together and were as thick as thieves. I didn't come on the scene until Brian was 34 or so. John and his sister, Margery, both got polio very badly and when Brian was writing to John they often discussed the polio. John was in the RAF and he was treated for polio. He lived for the rest of his life with the effects of polio and had to give up tennis although he was an outstanding table tennis player and champion.

Brian excelled at cricket, football, swimming, in fact at every sport at school. Brought up in very austere circumstances after the war, going on a Test tour to Australia as a 19-year-old was a tremendous experience for him. It must have been absolutely wonderful for him and I think his working class parents were deeply bemused by what was happening to their son. It would, perhaps, have been a help if he'd also had somebody else to guide him at that stage.

John and Brian did everything together as young men and John would have been immensely proud of Brian when he was chosen to go to Australia. He received very good support from John's family and was like a member of their family. I never knew John's father but I knew John's mother. I think his father was quite strict but John's mother and John's elder sister, Margery, were very good to Brian. The pair used to go to each other's house and when Brian went to theirs they would feed him and I think they had a whale of a time. They all went ballroom dancing and had a great time socially up in Yeadon. They had a good life the two of them, they enjoyed it.

Then I think John felt it a bit when Brian went to Australia because he obviously felt left behind, he was bound to, but Brian always maintained this contact and when I appeared on the scene one of the first people I met was John and I think in a way John begrudged me a bit because I took Brian away so to speak. They were never going to have the friendship they had because I came first which is understandable. But their friendship still continued and John's friendship did with me, also.

John was Brian's best man and our daughter Lyn's godfather and he used to come up every week and go for a drink and we remained very close, always.

I know this sounds melodramatic but when, towards the end,

Brian was going through all his cancer treatment for some unknown reason they didn't get in touch. Brian was very ill and John was very ill but I can remember going to see John when he was bedridden and he said: 'I just want to die. You know, if Brian isn't around I just want to die'. And he died very soon after Brian and he duplicated the Church service and the funeral and he even had a tea at Headingley after the service which was also at St Chad's like Brian's had been a few weeks earlier.

Regarding my own background I was born in London and moved to Devon when I was ten when the firm my father worked for moved lock, stock and barrel down to Devon to a little town called Ottery St Mary which is an idyllic place in East Devon. I took my 11-plus in a school there that had all of 11 pupils. I had a wonderful life there and stayed from 10 until 17 and then you realise that you either marry somebody local or leave. There was no alternative and I didn't want to marry anybody local, so I went to London when I was 17. I worked in the Home Office until I was 18 but then I didn't need my father's consent for everything so I au paired in France for a year because I knew I wanted to be an air hostess. I know this sounds stupid but in my summer holidays in Devon I used to work in Woolworth's on the coast and then I got little bottles of perfume, as cheap as chips, which had Paris, London and New York on them and that is what I wanted to do. So I thought, 'How can I do that?' I realised I needed language, needed to live away from home, be a certain size, a certain shape, and that is what I set out to get before I was 21 – which I did.

Then I became an air hostess with BOAC and first met Brian. The route of the plane I was on went London, Bermuda and the English girl, who was me, got off and the plane would pick up a South American girl and go on all the way down to Lima. So I was left all on my own in little Bermuda for a week, which was hard, and that was when the Yorkshire cricket team were there on their tour of Canada, America and Bermuda.

So I am just trotting along on the beach minding my own business and there is this group of lads all having lunch. I didn't think anything of it and they said would I like to join them? Freddie Trueman said would I go with him for a swim and I said what I said to all fellows, 'Are you married?' And he said, 'Yes'. There are plenty of pebbles on the beach without picking the married ones and then Brian came and said, 'Would you like to come for a swim?' and I said, 'Are you married?' and he said, 'No'.

And they had the Governor General invite them to a cocktail party that night, which all cricket teams do, don't they? And Brian said 'I can't come and collect you from your hotel but would you like to join us?' That's quite daunting to get a taxi to a Governor General's house when you don't know anybody, but I did and I had a very nice evening and Brian took me back to my hotel and he said – that very night – 'I am sorry, but I am going to marry you'. Absolutely amazing. And I said 'Don't be so stupid, you're not my cup of tea at all, and I am engaged to a pilot'.

But he wore me down, didn't he? He kept asking, again and again and again and I would say 'Don't write to me', but he used to send me records through the post whenever I came back to England from wherever I had been in the world. He just didn't give in and this went on from September until the New Year and I had come up to Yorkshire and was beginning to quite like him but he was nothing like anything I had mixed with before. I didn't know anything about Northerners and I didn't understand bloody this and bloody that but I agreed to come up here to a New Year's Party with him at the Craiglands Hotel in Ilkley and at midnight he said 'I am asking you to marry me for the last time'. And he got this diamond solitaire out which was exactly like the one I had on anyway and I had had far too much to drink and I said 'Yes'.

I didn't really know who he was or anything. I didn't realise, I hadn't a clue who he was until I read the papers the next day. All the time I had known him I was really unaware as to what he was. Why should I? I had never followed cricket, my parents had never heard of him and of course it was winter – and you don't play cricket in winter in England.

So he just ran his paint business or whatever it was. It makes me seem ridiculous but I was busy working and I had my fiancé, so why should I know about him?

I felt really sorry for my other fiancé, it was a bit cruel really but he was called Brian as well so that helped. They used to phone me and say 'Hi darling' and I wouldn't have a clue which it was, but eventually this Brian would put a 'bloody' in or 'bloody hell' and I would think 'Right, I've got that one on the line'.

That's not good is it? And I had fixed the wedding up to the original Brian, my pilot, so I didn't change the date, I just went and saw the vicar who I knew well – obviously, in a small town in Devon – and I said I am still getting married on that day but it is a different surname. When you see it in print it sounds awful, doesn't it? My poor parents!

We did 50 years together and I wouldn't say I never regretted it. I did regret it at times. When we came back off honeymoon I still didn't fully comprehend that he was well known and he said 'I am off to play cricket' and then he buggered off for about six weeks and left me in complete isolation because I knew nobody up here in Yorkshire at all, so it was a bit hard initially, it wasn't much fun.

But I supported him fully throughout our married life. He was easily led and even for all his travelling he was still quite gullible. He never saw bad in people ever and unfortunately I do, I always look for the bad and unfortunately 50 per cent of the time you find it but he never bad-mouthed anybody, ever. But I could see him doing the wrong things and heading for trouble and I thought 'Don't do that, Brian'. So I am just glad that I was there for him because we were like chalk and cheese really.

He was far cleverer than I was, far cleverer, but whereas he was clever and a mathematician I was well read and into literature and also artistic, so together we made a good combination. But I am glad I married him because I think he would have gone under. I am sure he would have gone under.

Brian wrote all these letters to John and I didn't even know they existed at the time and it was his sister who saved them after John had died and then passed them on to me.

It will surprise many that Brian was such a prolific letter writer. He didn't read – other than *The Sporting Life*. He didn't read books at all, *Readers Digest* was about his limit, but he could write pages and in wonderful English and very distinctive. His letters were a joy to us all. I have still got letters from when he went with Derrick Robins to South Africa. They are very good. And from when he went out to Trinidad and when he got sacked by England he went out to Freeport with Peter Smith. Pages and pages of properly constructed letters, very descriptive of who he had met, where he had been. And when he went to Ceylon, as it was then, he was there for a month and The British Council worked him to death going to schools and colleges and everything but the letters were incredible, telling what school he had been to, what match he had played in, who he had met, everything, just incredible.

But he could talk the hind leg off a donkey and he could write like he spoke but he didn't read. Strange isn't it?

It has been an interesting life we have had together and I don't like the way people took advantage of him which they did. And nobody guided him. He could have done so much more and been so much more in his achievements and in a materialistic sense. He was not materialistic and he never bothered about money, I wish he had. I think young cricketers today are guided, they have somebody to point them in the right direction but he was open to any charlatan that wanted to take advantage of him and he wasn't worldly-wise enough. He was from a good family but his father was just a mill worker, God bless him, and he didn't know the ways of the world, so he learned everything the hard way which is the best way, isn't it? And, whatever, he was admired by all who watched cricket. I never really understood cricket and I am sorry even now I don't understand it.

*   *   *

Margery Anderson, whose last address was in Rawdon, lived in the family home with John and their parents in Victoria Crescent, Horsforth. They moved to Bradford for two years and their children were in prep school for Bradford Grammar School. The family moved back to another address in Victoria Crescent. Margery recalled those early days in an interview for this book. Sadly, she passed away on October 25, 2019, aged 91.

Brian and John would meet for the first time at Aireborough Grammar School. They were roughly the same age and in the same class. I didn't take much notice of their friendship while they were at school. Brian hadn't time to be coming down to our house then and probably couldn't have afforded it even though it would only have been a penny or so for the bus drive.

John was invalided out of the RAF after six weeks and he rather liked it when he got there. My grandfather, who was a doctor, said he will never be accepted because he's had rheumatic fever as a child. He went for an examination and they weren't satisfied, obviously, and so he went for a second time and he was sent into the RAF. Well, his heart was affected with the rheumatic fever and so grandpa said they won't take him. But in getting him out of the RAF – I think it was the square bashing there that affected him – he was sent to Catterick in an RAF ambulance so that they could sort him out before the official getting rid of him and who should he see there but Brian Close. And so, of course, John would have been delighted to see him. Brian was at the hospital because he was injured and John was there before being invalided out of the RAF.

So they were there together but I don't know how long for. Brian was back in the Army and John was officially discharged from the RAF. He got a small pension, I don't know how much it was. Afterwards he was able to play tennis to a good standard but after getting polio he wouldn't go near Rawdon Tennis Club again but he started playing table tennis and he would come home and tell me about it. He played for the Gas Board and he would come home and say we are going down a league or going up and it was a sort of yo-yo thing.

When Brian started to visit us at home, only Brian came and none of his brothers or his sister. Just Brian was enough for my father. He would come home and there was Brian, sitting there, probably in his chair. He came night after night at one stage. He and John were very friendly but Brian wasn't treated as one of the family by my father. My mother liked him but she always played up to young men but some of my boy friends who came she was quite rude to. She would give Brian a warm welcome but would look daggers when my boy friends came.

John thought he would like to be like grandfather Anderson who had nine children and never had to work because someone left him a lot of money. At 18 or 19 he didn't have a job but father was suggesting things and making him apply for things. In the end John went to the Gas Board, so daddy must have pushed him into it and he was in it right up to retirement and he did extremely well.

We both got polio at the same time when I was 23. I came home from having lunch with my boyfriend at the time and we went for a walk in the afternoon and had a bit of tea. He was going into Leeds to get his train back to Oxford and when I walked in home there was only John there and I said 'Oh, I do feel awful, I think I am going to bed'. He said: 'I don't feel very well, either'. The next morning mother sent for the doctor and they thought I had got flu. John did have a bit of trouble with his leg. The doctor came and he thought John had got a stiff leg. He came on two days to see us and on the second visit I couldn't move ... and John's leg had gone completely. Jill, our younger sister, was wandering about our bedrooms as a four-year-old carrying hot water bottles for us. The doctor sent for the specialist immediately and in the afternoon we were sent to Seacroft Hospital.

We went off in the same ambulance, mustn't that have been terrible for our parents? Jill was kept in a pram with no exercise at all but fortunately she didn't get it or she would have grown up all deformed as well.

Daddy was disgusted with Brian because Brian never contacted, sent a letter or visited and it turned out he said he was frightened he might get it which was true, but he should have written.

[Brian did write but the family must not have been aware of that at the time. His correspondence shows that he wrote four undated letters to Mrs Anderson and at least one of them mentions 'visiting' John and telling her not to worry. Two of the letters are addressed FROM "Catterick Military Hospital" confirming that it catered for not only Army personnel. The hospital was a hutted complex to the north of the camp. The site is now a housing estate.]

But until Vivien told me I was unaware that Brian had written a letter at all to John, never mind a whole lot.

Oh yes, they did continue to meet up and instead of our house being cluttered it was Vivien's! I think John was quite upset when Vivien came along because she took Brian away from John. That was definitely so.

In the early stages of his career with all the publicity of going to Australia, John and mother were glued, when we got television, whenever Yorkshire or England were playing. I would say, 'Has Brian done anything?' but I only had a passing interest.

*   *   *

It is now almost 80 years since Audrey Brown (nee Newbould) and Brian were in the same class together and she reminisced:

Although we started at Aireborough Grammar School in September, 1941, and were in the same form until 1948 I don't remember much about Brian until we were in the fifth form and taking School Certificate. As it was the science form there were not many girls in S5.

When we were taking Higher School Certificate in 1948 there were only two girls in the sixth form. Brian was very helpful to me in the physics lessons.

Although Brian was well known for his sporting prowess he was very intelligent and in the A stream throughout his school life. Looking through some old school magazines he is mentioned many times, having won athletic and swimming championships. One magazine mentions his Performances of Merit for the School cricket team: six wickets for three runs (v Harrogate), six wickets for 10 runs (v Hanson), five wickets for 23 runs (v Bingley), five wickets for 19 runs (v Hanson), four wickets for eight runs (v Salts). And a batting average of over 100.

He was Fairfax house captain (1946-47), receiving a batting and bowling PE award. He was well known for the distance he could throw a cricket ball. One incident I remember when we were in the fifth form was that he left the room on some pretence and his coming back with the result of some horse race – so he was interested in betting then!

In the magazine it mentions he was a member of the Autumn Potato Camp that the boys attended at Wrangle (Lincolnshire) at the end of the War in 1945.

*   *   *

Dr Keith Howard OBE, is Chairman of the Bingley-based Emerald Group which provided the Yorkshire Cricket Foundation museum at Headingley and in 2018 acquired the naming rights of the stadium which is now known as Emerald Headingley. He recalls:

 I regard myself as a friend and acquaintance who has known Brian for over 70 years and first came into contact with him in our early days when I was playing my first competitive game of cricket for Horsforth Hall Park in the Airedale and Wharfedale Junior League at the age of ten or 11 and Brian was playing for the opposing side, Rawdon.

The occasion remains in my mind quite vividly. I was asked to go in last man and I went in indicating to the rest of the team that I would be seeking to score a boundary off this last ball which proved not to be the case. I took guard as best I could and it turned out Brian Close came in to bowl and I heard the rattle of stumps as I was bowled for zero which was a memory I don't particularly wish to dwell on but it was an indication of the standard of my batting generally. That is a recollection which has stayed with me all my life.

I knew John Anderson pretty well because I lived at Victoria Walk and he lived at Victoria Crescent. And I knew his sister Margery very well and the memories of their illnesses send shudders through my body. Margery and I served on the political committee at Pudsey. I was chairman of the Pudsey Division Conservative Association during much of the 1970s and she was a regular and very conscientious committee member. John was in the category of a friendly associate and despite the fact that I lived nearby he was not one of the lads. He, like Margery, contracted polio and she suffered even more than he did. I admired her for her strength of will and character.

I lived for quite a few years in the vicinity and the reason I didn't get to know John well was that the large majority of the lads of our age went to Aireborough Grammar School and I went to Leeds Grammar School so our paths didn't cross all that frequently.

A good friend of mine was Ian Pullan and he ended up by being one of the groomsmen at my wedding. I knew him until he died seven or eight years ago. He acted as a link between me and Aireborough Grammar School so I heard quite a lot of Brian Close and the ways in which he was developing and I was duly impressed by it all. I knew of the way in which his school friends viewed him, particularly through the trip to Australia. I heard plenty from Ian Pullan and his friends about the trip and also that his scholastic achievements were quite impressive particularly in the quantitative side that would very obviously have led to him going to university if he had wanted.

My sister, Valerie Luty, who is younger than me, also went to Aireborough Grammar School and I got another line, therefore, into the development of this chap with the wonderful achievements and temperament throughout the years.

I played soccer for the local side during my schoolboy days in Horsforth Hall Park and Ian Pullan and I came up with the idea that we ought to have a cricket match between Leeds Grammar School and Aireborough Grammar School. These took place over a couple of years when we were 15 or 16 and we took them extremely seriously as young boys do. I remember walking with a leather kit bag full of cricket gear and I thought I would have the chance of revenge for my earlier dismissal of so many years ago.

We then diverged, as boys do, and I went to university and Brian went to play cricket which seemed to be the sensible choice albeit that in those days he was known for having a good brain. It was a few years before he and I came into contact again. It was the occasion of the Yorkshire nets in 1948 and the purpose was to select a Yorkshire Federation side for their Southern tour. It was a Yorkshire age group side and I went there as an opening bowler on the recommendation of Herbert Sutcliffe because he brought a side to play Leeds Grammar School. So imagine this net with two or three young lads vying for a place on this Yorkshire Federation tour and I was competing with another pace bowler and bowling against Brian Close. So we had three people bowling to him. Each of us would bowl and this dark-haired chap I didn't know came in to bowl against Brian Close. His wickets were splattered all over the place by this dark-haired bowler and the selector was Arthur Mitchell. His comment when Brian's stumps went flying was 'Tha'll do, lad' and I thought, 'That's ended my chances,' which proved to be the case because the chap with dark hair was Freddie Trueman! So Freddie Trueman was bowling to Brian Close with me in attendance and surprise, surprise, they decided to choose Freddie. It was a very sensible choice, particularly as I had been born in Lancashire, a fact which came out later on!

Yorkshire said they would recommend me to Old Trafford if I chose but that showed I was no good because Yorkshire wouldn't recommend anybody they thought might cause them problems in the future.

On one occasion when Herbert Sutcliffe brought a team to the school I opened the bowling to him and he despatched my first delivery to the clock tower but I varied my length a bit for the next and he was caught at square leg.

Brian and I didn't meet up again for quite a number of years after he had made his name and reputation in first-class cricket but when I became President of Scarcroft Cricket Club I realised a chap I could invite to our President's Day in the '70s would be Brian. So I invited him and he came and played and demonstrated his abilities. Seeing him close to hand he had all the left-hander's skill and artistry. It was a privilege to see at first hand that Brian's skill had not declined in any way and his classic left-hander's shots stayed very much in my mind.

Vivien accompanied him on one occasion but it didn't help to reduce the volume of liquor. Both enjoyed themselves and he came the following year and would have continued coming but he had got into this period of having his hip problems, as I did.

I met Brian at places like Park Avenue and on one occasion he spent the whole of the match with his head in the racing pages of the *Daily Mail*, he seemed more interested in the racing results than the cricket!

Both of us were pretty keen on physical fitness. By this time Brian had had one or two operations and so had I. I remember the steam room at the Hollins Hall Hotel Spa which Brian would take over entirely with his particular exercises and his legs shooting out all over the place and not bothering about anybody else.

I also remember his intense commitment and his unwillingness to give in to anything. Once, he had just had a new hip the day before and he was going to a cricket match for somebody or other in the next five or six days. It was just unbelievable.

In later years I passed him in a morning and we became very friendly towards the end. I like to think I was friendly with Brian and with Vivien too.

I played cricket for 60 years. I damaged my ankle playing rugby at Keighley and that really did for me as a fast bowler until it came back about 30 years later and I took up opening bowling again and bowled into my 70s. I was playing for Scarcroft in the Wetherby League. I also used to play in the Yorkshire Council until I damaged my ankle.

My big claim to fame was that I was the first wicket for Bob Appleyard when he came back following his season out with tuberculosis. Yorkshire put out a full XI to play Leeds University at Weetwood and I actually stayed in a couple of overs batting at No 7 against Freddie Trueman before a new bowler came on and bowled me – it was Bob.

I went to considerable lengths in going to Headingley to try and get the scorecards of the two years I played against them but to no avail, they weren't kept. I got four for 16 one year and four for 27 the other year. Bryan Stott was in that Yorkshire side, and we often have a word together.

Bob and I became very good friends in later years. I thought he was Yorkshire's outstanding bowler since the war.

It seems quite remarkable that I should be at the Brian Close Collection Show and Tell presentation at Emerald Headingley in March, 2018. I couldn't have dreamt all those years ago that this would happen with me there. I was duly impressed and felt then that it would be appropriate for someone to write a book about his letters and other memorabilia. The occasion linked with my association with the Yorkshire Taverners and on one of their away days at Lord's Brian came with us and I asked him to give a talk about himself and his exploits. I had this strange view of him of being the outstanding physical specimen in Yorkshire. He was remarkable.

I remember that during his Army time he was drafted to box for his Regiment and he said that he had never lost a bout and I can well imagine it because he was a wonderful physical specimen despite his future intake of cigarettes and alcohol! Sooner or later it had to take its toll but he held on for a long while.

* * *

Yorkshire batsman Bryan Stott was not only a close friend of Brian's but he played under his captaincy at Aireborough Grammar School and he also ended his first-class career under his captaincy in the 1963 season, by which time he had scored 9,168 runs for the county with 17 centuries.

Born in Yeadon, a stone's throw from Brian's birthplace of Rawdon, for whom they both played league cricket for a while, Bryan probably witnessed the development of his friend – who was over three years older – more than any other contemporary, and although he knew him better than most he was completely unaware of Brian's talent for letter writing until he first cast eyes upon some of his letters almost 70 years after they were first penned. He remembers Brian like this:

I knew Brian Close for longer than most people and I can recollect meeting him for the first time at Rawdon Cricket Club. I was a ten-year-old and my father had moved from Yeadon Cricket Club to Rawdon after a serious illness and

Brian was already there at Rawdon CC. He was a brilliant cricketer even then and so it was a bit of hero worship to a certain extent. I played with him in the juniors at Rawdon and then he went to Yeadon and carried on with his career. I joined him at Yeadon later on. Even in those early days he was a big strapping lad and a far better cricketer than anyone else. Then, of course, I went to Aireborough Grammar School and Brian was still there and I played football and cricket with him in the school team. He was just an amazing sportsman, really, and I got on well with him. I thought he was a real grand lad and I enjoyed his company very much right from those early days.

I also knew his best friend, John Anderson, who was also at Aireborough Grammar School at the same time as Brian and in his form. John unfortunately contracted polio at the time of that terrible epidemic. It affected him a lot and stopped him doing most sports but he was always keenly interested in sport right up to his death shortly after Brian's.

So you could see they were a good pair together – Brian who could play all sports and John his admiring pal. It is now apparent that Brian wrote to John religiously, particularly on the MCC tour to Australia. It was very interesting to read those letters only recently. When Brian came back from that tour I arranged to play a round of golf with him at Rawdon Golf Club and we talked about the tour.

It had certainly not been a happy tour at all for Brian and he had had some really miserable moments. I think he was very much a loner because he had not been encouraged by the senior pros and I was delighted, therefore, when I read those letters to John and realised that this was completely different to what I knew had happened on the cricketing side and I could just picture him writing to John and telling him of things that were of interest to two friends. I could understand him wanting to cheer John up with the happier side of his trip, so that John was reading of happier events and not the more sorrowful ones.

It still came as a big surprise to me that Brian was such a prolific writer. Brian was constantly doing things in the dressing room like smoking a cigarette, making a cup of tea, filling crosswords in or picking winners but I had no idea he was such a great letter writer and probably it was an outlet for him on that trip because he definitely had some very lonely periods. I think that was partly because of some jealousy from the older professionals. Mind you, Brian was a bit of a tearaway in his own way but absolutely confident in his own ability and not big-headed in any way. A challenge was a challenge to take on and not be beaten and many of the players on that tour were fairly seasoned professionals but there were also a lot of amateurs and at that time the amateurs were a different breed, and different from a lot of the amateurs we came across later on. A barrier was still there at that point and a lot of the amateurs would not have taken kindly to Brian's approach and so he would have found it very, very difficult. I often wonder looking back, Brian was picked, I won't say on a whim because he had already done the double, but he was still in the Army and if you look at some of the professionals who were left at home and were not on that trip there were some very good cricketers among them. They had not made the trip and Brian had, so knowing professional cricketers in those early days there was a fair amount of jealousy quite likely coming from the older ranks. It was difficult to deal with for a young lad whose world was at his feet.

I am absolutely sure that Freddie Brown was not the right sort of person for Brian to have as his captain in Australia. My knowledge of Freddie Brown was that he was a very autocratic person and I certainly wouldn't have wanted to play under him, that's for sure. I think he was a very poor captain from my experience of when we played Northamptonshire and I certainly wouldn't have wanted to go on tour with Freddie Brown, definitely not.

The environment was not right for Brian out there and it was a great pity. While Yorkshire's secretary, John Nash, was Joint Manager on the tour he did not have too much time to spend with Brian but I am sure it would have helped if he had because John was such a nice chap. Then again, it would have been difficult for Len Hutton to have given him the assistance he required and it needed one of the other senior pros to room with him if at all possible and just guide him. And the captain could have arranged that if he had had the inclination. It could have been a disastrous tour for Brian and it was only his determination and fortitude that made it possible for him later on to pull himself back from the disappointments.

Yet when the opportunity came for him to become captain himself he had grown up very much. He quickly learned the tactics, he thought things through and he observed things that went on. He was a great thinker, was Brian, and he could weigh the opposition up. As far as wickets were concerned Raymond Illingworth was the greatest reader of pitches that I have ever known and he helped a lot from that point of view, but as a captain Brian's technical ability was his greatest asset.

You see, he was a very intelligent lad, Brian, with a good brain on him, and I think that once he had got over that experience of Australia and become the determined cricketer that he was, then that tour probably spurred him on to be the man that he was in the end.

I just had one year under Brian's captaincy of Yorkshire before I retired and I really enjoyed it. Going back a bit, when Billy Sutcliffe was captain Brian had tried to suggest things to him but he wasn't quite prepared to listen to him but when Ronnie Burnet took over he was prepared to listen to Brian and he appointed him as senior professional which is a very important position in the team. This was perfect for Brian because it gave him scope not only to advise Ronnie but also very gently and very quietly from gully or second slip or from wherever he was on the field to direct us by way of hand signals to where he thought we should be and where Ronnie hadn't put us!

But this was also where Jimmy Binks, our wicketkeeper, started to come into his own. As well as being a great wicketkeeper, Jimmy also had a very astute cricketing brain and he would convey to Brian what he had felt was very important information. And, of course, there was Raymond as well, so Ronnie had got three really experienced professionals to lean on but Brian was effectively the mouthpiece and senior pro.

And everybody got on so well. The team spirit in that side was just fantastic, so everybody contributed and it was a really great atmosphere. But after being told in 1962 that I was still only a Yorkshire player by one vote I thought it was time I went back to business full time.

Then Brian was appointed captain for 1963 and I had a long talk with my wife, Sheila, and we decided that would be my last season. I thought to finish my playing days under the same captain as I had started them was a lovely way to go. So at Lord's on the first day of the season, when Yorkshire were playing MCC, I took Brian out for dinner and told him I was going to finish at the end of the summer. We had a general chat about that situation and I just said play me anywhere you like, in the second team if necessary it won't matter. And I really enjoyed that year, I really did, because Yorkshire cricket had got a real meaning behind it and I had a huge admiration for Brian. I obviously regarded him as a great team-mate and friend as I also did later on when I was on the committee and Brian joined it during the Boycott problems. It was different on the committee because Brian didn't have quite the same control as he did on the cricket field, so it was a far more difficult period than playing! He was a great chap and I had a lot of affection for him. He wouldn't hurt a fly intentionally but he did some daft stuff, some daft stuff!! It was a great privilege when Vivien asked me to give a eulogy at his funeral.

CHAPTER TWO

SPORTSMAN OR SCHOLAR?

Spring 1948 and the world's his oyster – Only 17 and playing for Leeds United Reserves and in an England Youth Soccer International – Selected for Yorkshire Cricket Federation's Southern Tour – The start of Brian's letters to John Anderson – All the fun of the Fair – An early attack of migraine

As a schoolboy, Brian was seriously overburdened with both sporting ability and brains and during his final term at Aireborough Grammar School in 1948 he had two all-consuming passions. One was sport, both football and cricket, and the other was a desire to become a doctor. His exam results were good enough for his headmaster to encourage him to go to university and study medicine but he was already being pulled strongly in the direction of sport.

An early photograph shows him as a member of the 1944-45 Guiseley Juniors Football Club and the following season he was

Guiseley Juniors with shields and trophy. Brian is seated fifth from left

Brian captained Leeds United Stormcocks in this 4-1 victory over Leicester City Juniors

playing for Leeds United Juniors, wonderfully named Leeds United Stormcocks.

Now, at 17, he was rapidly making a name for himself on both fronts, first being selected for the Yorkshire Cricket Federation's Southern Tour, which included games against Middlesex and Sussex, and then, in the autumn, having just left school, being picked by England for the Youth International against Scotland at Aberdeen. It was a match which England lost, but only, according to Brian, because of the brilliance of Scotland's goalkeeper!

Federation cricket provided a valuable stepping stone in Brian's young days because it served as a direct link between school and league cricket and a possible place in the Colts XI. The establishment of the Yorkshire CCC Academy was still many years away and to be selected to play for the Federation was a landmark for those teenagers with serious ambitions to play cricket professionally.

It is while Brian is on the Federation tour that we first become acquainted with his great school chum, John Anderson, the correspondence between them continuing regularly for several years until Brian sent John a series of aerogramme letters from the controversial MCC A team tour of Pakistan in 1955-56. In all, Brian despatched over 100 letters to his friend who might well have sent even more in return.

Brian is sixth left standing in the England team for the Youth International against Scotland

John's letters do not appear to have survived the passage of time but Brian's, now part of the Yorkshire Cricket Foundation's collection of Brian Close memorabilia, shed previously unseen light on this great sportsman's early career. Few, if any, sporting stars of his generation will have left such a legacy.

And Brian's letters were not hurriedly scrawled notes. They were epistles often running up to 12 large sheets. Who would ever have imagined that this action-packed man would have spent so much of his precious time putting pen to paper – and in such a descriptive fashion? Brian, the hugely talented sportsman, the great captain, the fearless competitor, we all know, but Brian the wordsmith?

So it was, that on August 18, 1948, Brian wrote and sent off his first letter to John. It was postmarked Harrow, had stuck on the envelope a 2½d blue 1948 Olympic Games stamp and was addressed to John's home in Victoria Crescent, Horsforth.

Belmont School
Harrow
Wednesday, 9.0am

Dear John,

I hope you have had some fine weather up there. We have, with plenty of fun blown in. Last night we went into London and got lost. We got into town at about 10pm because we have to get three connections, two of which are tubes.

When we got out at Piccadilly Circus we walked past the Piccadilly Hotel and saw five Aussies: Toshack, Johnston, Miller, McCool and Tallon [England v Australia at The Oval, August 14, 16, 17, 18]. Some of the lads got their autographs. We walked further down the street and came to a terrific place with about half-a-dozen doormen stood in the doorway.

Anyway, since we were up to mischief we all walked in past them and trouped into a lift and went to the top floor. Here we went into the bathrooms, had a wash and were just about to go out when an attendant came up and said "2d each please". We nearly fainted and in the confusion two of us slipped out while the others paid.

We went on walking round the streets, calling in funfairs and walking in hotels, going up to the top floors and coming out of them again without doing anything. When we decided it was time to go back we caught the last tube to a place about five miles from where we live and then we had to get a taxi home.

Yesterday, when we were to play Buckinghamshire, we got 180 and then they got 80 for three. I got 44 and then was bowled with a full toss which I was trying to hit over the pavilion. Then, when they were in, one lad got 50 but he was missed five times, two of which were slap into their hands, anybody would think they were a lot of lame ducks. In my first over I had three catches missed in the slips, all of which went for fours, and then later I had two missed at short leg, one behind the wickets. Anyway, I finished up with one for 25.

The lad on their side who got 50 got a county cap for it (for being missed five times and never hitting one in the centre of his bat). In their side there are chaps up to 24 or 25.

While we have been down here we've had some smashing girls and plenty of fun. The place we are staying at is a school which has been keeping parties from schools who had been visiting the [Olympic] Games. Anyway, when we arrived we were placed next to a party from a Glasgow School (wee bonny lassies), we didn't half have some fun. There were about half-a-dozen

Scottish lads with them as well and we found out one who could play the pipes and then we paraded up and down the corridors at about 1.0-2.0 in the morning, wakening everybody.

Then we went raiding the girls' bedroom and had them screaming and dashing out into the corridors until two of their women teachers came, then we dashed back to the bedrooms and made ourselves scarce. When the row had quietened down we went into their room again and played cards and ate food until about four in the morning since they were going back to Glasgow that morning. Anyway, we finally got to bed at somewhere just before 5am but even then we didn't go to sleep. I don't know how we played cricket that day.

On Sunday when we were up at Newcastle we had a smashing time and left Newcastle at just after midnight and landed back home in time to get a wash, a shave and get packed up ready for off in the morning.

Anyway, I shall have to leave now because we are going to play Middlesex at Ealing and then after that we are going to Eastbourne. So cheerio and good luck until next time.

Yours sincerely

Brian

PS: We passed Wembley on the way to the cricket ground yesterday.

*　　*　　*

Brian's next letter was written, it says, from his home in Canada Terrace, Rawdon, at 8.0am on a Friday but with no exact date given. It was postmarked Eastbourne,1.30pm, August 20, which was also a Friday, and that is from where it was most likely written, Brian giving his home address as a guide as to where John should send his next letter.

Dear John,

I hope this gets to you before you go away because I don't have the address to which you are going, so you write to me first.

Since I wrote to you last, everything has been flying around in circles. On the Thursday morning I went and played a game of golf with a man called Robinson from Huddersfield and beat him by 3 and 2 for 5/-. On the Thursday morning we left Eastbourne about 10.0am for Hastings and landed at the cricket ground just before 11.0am.

It was a smashing cricket ground. It wouldn't hold many but the field was like a billiard table and all round the field there are hotels towering over the cricket field. It was the most beautiful and nicest ground I have ever seen, never mind played on.

Anyway, we got on playing, I opened for the first time and in 50 minutes we had 77 on the board of which I had 59. Then I got careless and tried to force a short ball away to the off and played on. By then it was only about 12.30pm so I went into the shopping centre of Hastings to look around without bothering to change. I went buying peaches, ice cream and everything, in fact I nearly bought all Hastings up.

Anyway, by lunch it had started raining and thundering and in half-an-hour it was like a duck pond, so there was no further play. We came home to Eastbourne by 5.0pm and had time for another round of golf but this time we didn't score as we both went round with two balls each. We came back to the Training College by 8.0pm for dinner or rather supper, and after we went to the Pier Ballroom and stayed there until 12.0pm. We had a smashing time, we got talking to about half-a-dozen girls from Liverpool, two from South Wales, near Cardiff, and a couple from Eastbourne, and we had quite a time. If I haven't mentioned it before the band was Harry Roy and his Band and it wasn't half good to dance to.

We had drinks (minerals, don't get me wrong) bought for us

The Yorkshire Federation team which played Sussex at Hove. Brian, who captained the side, is seated in the centre with Fred Trueman on his left

by loads of people in the dance and we chose our own dances and songs for the band to play. Anyway, we were all disappointed when it was time for the last waltz. We are going to paint the town red tonight, the last night, and then tomorrow we are going to London to look round the Houses of Parliament, etc, etc.

Anyway, I will close now else I'll be too late to go to Brighton. So cheerio and good luck until next time. Hope you are enjoying yourself up there as much as I am.

Yours sincerely

Brian

PS: Don't forget to write first to me.

* * *

Back home from the tour, Brian writes on August 25 to John in Ulverston, Lancashire, and fills him in with his adventures at the local fair. He has a great time, but shortly afterwards describes what are clearly symptoms of migraine, a condition which later threatened his budding career with Yorkshire. This was the last letter of 1948.

Dear John,

I received your letter this morning and by the sound of it you missed the boat on this cousin of yours. I got a letter from Margaret yesterday and she said they were having loads of photographs taken.

I am having a pretty dull time of it while you are all away enjoying yourselves. On the Monday morning and afternoon I played cricket with "Schneider" and a few more and then we went to the feast at night. It's a good one for once, there's the dodgems, a caterpillar, a dive bomber, Noah's Ark and another big roundabout, and what's good about it is that it's staying until the weekend so we'll be able to go on it on Saturday.

On Tuesday I went again up to the cricket field and as some lads were bowling at me all my eyes went blurred and I started feeling sick. Anyway, I went home and was as sick as a dog so I stayed in bed until about 6.30pm and then I wandered down to Elland Road to have a game of billiards and a talk. I was too poorly to train.

Oh, I forgot to tell you that while I was at the feast I had a go on the coconuts and with my first ball I aimed at a side one instead of the middle one and knocked it off. Next ball I knocked the middle one off, and hit a third which did not fall off. Anyway, for the trouble I got a fruit dish or something. I gave "Schneider" it to hold for me until later and at the end I forgot all about it and he walked off with it.

After the go on the coconuts I went on the skittles, similar but instead of the coconuts you had to knock five or six skittles over to win. Anyway, with my first ball I knocked the top two off, with the next I knocked the next two off and to win a prize I had to knock one of the remaining two over so I wound myself up and threw with all my might and honest if it had have hit the iron sheet at the back it would have either bust it or cracked it. Anyway, it hit one of the skittles full in the face and it never even rocked never mind fall over and they are only small skittles, about six inches high, the bottom two must have been nailed on.

I have done nothing today so far but tonight I am going to watch Leeds United v Brentford and I'll back Leeds any day at home. [Leeds United 0, Brentford 0. Another 'loser' if Brian did back Leeds to win!]

On Tuesday I was talking to Mr. Crowther, [presumably C. Arthur Crowther, Leeds United secretary from 1935-1958] they have got me the job and I am going for an interview next week some time. It's smashing, as much time off for cricket and football said Mr. C. and no loss in pay so I'm sitting pretty.

All I'm waiting for in the results is to see whether I've passed in maths, the rest can go to hell for all I care.

Anyway, I'll close now because my tea's ready so cheerio and good luck, hope you are enjoying your holiday and keep your pecker up.... I'm looking forward to Saturday, another 100 and a nice time afterwards.

....Anyway, I'll see you on Friday night at the Glen so cheerio, write back soon.

Yours sincerely

Brian

PS: Excuse school paper, I ran out of my writing pad in writing to Margaret and Peter is out, and I don't know where my mum's is, the shops are shut and really this is the only paper which is at hand at the moment.

The young Brian has practised writing his signature several times on this copy of *Sport Weekly* magazine. Once perfected he went on to give his autograph in a clear hand many thousands of times during his lifetime

CHAPTER THREE

MAY 11 – JUNE 20, 1949

START OF MOMENTOUS SUMMER

The momentous summer of 1949, Part One: – Brian makes his Yorkshire debut en route to completing the Double – Meets Len Hutton for the first time – On the way to becoming England's youngest Test player – National Service call-up deferred – John in the RAF – Brian changes mind from RAF to Army – Plays in North v South Test Trial – Peeved at agreeing to play for Yeadon and getting nothing for it – Detailed description of his tour of London with Frank Lowson

Brian's correspondence with John in 1948 colourfully traced the first steps of a budding career but at that stage his experiences were probably little different to those of all the other talented teenagers around the country who had stepped on the rung of Federation cricket with their counties.

Now, however, he was in a class apart, jettisoned to fame within a few short months.

Yet at the start of the 1949 season, Brian still appeared to be heading more firmly in the direction of a soccer career rather than cricket. He was on the professional books of Leeds United, having played for the Stormcocks and the Reserves, yet the early games of the new cricket season saw him still playing for Yeadon in the Bradford League.

But he was being noticed by those who mattered, including the great Bill Bowes who was now a much respected cricket journalist with a Leeds newspaper. In his preview of the Yorkshire season he wrote: *Brian Close, the six-foot Rawdon lad, can be singled out for immediate mention. He looks to be a natural successor to Frank Smailes.*

He could be relied upon to bowl six or seven overs with the new ball, then revert to off-spinners and with the bat do anything that Frank ever did.

The call was not long in coming – as Bowes no doubt knew that it would. After Yorkshire had opened up against the New Zealanders at Bradford Park Avenue, Brian was told to travel to Fenner's for the game against Cambridge University where Freddie Trueman and Frank Lowson were also to make their debuts.

Even the possibility of cricket with Yorkshire had seemed a long way off during the winter when Brian should have begun his National Service but he reported for his medical in the February while carrying a soccer injury and his call-up was delayed, although the injury soon cleared. By mid-summer, Brian was firmly established in the Yorkshire side and the Club successfully sought the help of Bradford Central MP, Maurice Webb, in getting call-up deferred until the end of the season.

Webb's intervention meant that Brian was able to go on and complete the double in first-class matches of 1,098 runs and 113 wickets, 958 of the runs coming for Yorkshire and 105 of the wickets.

Brian's all-round prowess made him a teenage cricket sensation and were to result in him making his Test debut against New Zealand at Old Trafford on July 23. At 18 years and 149 days he was – and remains – England's youngest Test cricketer. The three-day Test ended in a draw and Brian claimed one wicket and was out for a duck, but he was praised in Wisden for following the correct policy of big hitting. It was an early example of the maxim that Brian held close to his heart for the rest of his life – that the interests of the team are far more important than personal achievement.

The Yorkshire team for his first match were to stay at the University Arms in Cambridge and it was from there that Brian was to write his first letter to John as a Yorkshire cricketer. It was postmarked Cambridge, 12.15pm, May 11, the first day of the match, and read:

Dear John,

Just a few lines to let you know I'm alright – we've had a smashing time.

I had a bit of a rush this morning and a tight squeeze to get everything in my suitcase and bag but anyway I managed to find

time to buy a jockstrap in Leeds before the bus came.

Frank Lowson and myself were introduced to all the press people 'Kilburn etc' and had our photographs taken right and left before we got going. We picked Freddie Trueman up at Barnsley and there were more photos this time with Norman Yardley. Anyway we got going and had a game of cards to while away the time and in next to no time we reached Grantham where we stayed for dinner. We didn't half tuck ourselves into the food as though we hadn't eaten for weeks, you ought to have seen what some of the lads (Alec Coxon in particular) ate.

Anyway we arrived at Cambridge and installed ourselves in the hotel, Frank and I are sharing a room with bathroom and everything. We unpacked and then walked along to the ground just in time to see Essex play a draw with Cambridge. What a pitch and what a wicket – the outfield is like a billiard board so you can judge what the wicket is like and the field is terrific in size.

Anyway we came back and had tea and then Frank and I went with Bill Bowes and Norman Yardley round touring the colleges bordering the river and Oh what a lovely district it is with its lawns, tennis courts and the colleges themselves were a sight to see. When it got reasonably dark we went in for a game of snooker in the hotel. Oh! of course I won, I beat him three times running, and then at nine-o'clock we retired to our room and I had a lovely hot bath and now here I am writing to you.

Tomorrow night I shall be going to see Alan Ladd in 'Whispering Smith' all being well. Anyway that's about all I can tell you for the time being. I'll write again on Thursday. So cheerio and good luck.

Yours

Brian

PS: My Oxford address is Royal Oxford Hotel, Oxford.

*   *   *

At the conclusion of the match, it was straight on to Oxford from where Brian was able to describe to John just what had happened over the past few exciting days and also to plan for a return trip home. From his hotel room Brian wrote:

Dear John,

I received the letter this morning, I've got lots to tell you since [your] last letter.

We had a marvellous time at Cambridge while we were there. We saw 'Scott of the Antarctic' on Wednesday and Fred Astaire and Judy Garland in 'Easter Parade' on Thursday.

With the playing point of view, on the second day when Norman [Yardley] declared, I bowled [John] Dewes with a beauty and then in the same over [Harry] Halliday missed [Hubert] Doggart in the slips in one of the simplest catches I've seen, right down his 'cake hole', and then the following over Trueman missed [Robert] Morris so that if I'd have had any luck at all I would have had three wickets for about ten runs that night.

I'll tell you something, before this trip I didn't really believe that a wicket could last for a week or even four days but the one at Fenner's was as good when we finished as it was when we started, honest there wasn't a mark or a scratch to say that a cricket ball had been bounced all over it for three solid days. I couldn't believe it.

We had marvellous weather, no clouds at all, not even a speck on the horizon for the whole three days. Living in the hotels is grand, especially when you have a very nice chambermaid to bring you a cup of tea and a paper up in the morning as we had at Cambridge. We didn't start getting pally with her until the day we left, and the one here is a bit too old.

Oxford is a much bigger town than Cambridge and loads of shops to look round, big sweet 'queues' but I'll see if I can find some for your mother – and you I suppose.

The match today was on a much more fair wicket than at Cambridge though not from the scenery. In this respect Cambridge was marvellous. I got D.B. Carr and if I'd had my catches taken I would have had about seven wickets [He got four in each innings]. The lad who got 50 for them [58, opener Murray Hofmeyr, a South African Rugby Blue] was missed three times in the leg trap off me and other catches were dropped, but anyway I was satisfied. Frank Lowson batted really well to get 50-odd not out [he finished with 66] as he did at Cambridge. Freddie bowled well today.

Tomorrow we are all going golfing at the invitation of the nearby club. On Monday I go in No 6 because Gerald Smithson has come in and he goes in No 5. Norman is No 7 and Ted [Lester] No 8.

I shall be coming home Tuesday night to play at Bradford on Wednesday so I might be seeing you before you go into the RAF, either in the morning if I'm not too tired or at night and we'll go somewhere on Thursday if you want to have a last flip as Norman says. He's a very nice chap and I get on very well with him.....

The University lads we play are quite decent – Dewes is a bit of a cocky blighter, Doggart's quite nice, van Ryneveld [Clive Berrange van Ryneveld, a future South African captain] is a very likeable chap, in fact they all are.

Anyway, I'll finish now 'cause I think I've exhausted my knowledge up to now but I'll find something else to tell you by Wednesday.

Yours

Brian

I am enjoying myself immensely, I hope you are having a good time, also.

*   *   *

From Oxford it was straight on to The Star Hotel in Wells ahead of Brian's Championship debut against Somerset the following day, and it is here that he meets Len Hutton for the first time. He pens his letter to John soon after arriving at the hotel. It is the last one before John goes into the RAF and he was somewhat surprised for various health reasons that John had passed the medical.

Dear John,

Thank you for [your] letter, I suppose you've seen I've gone to Somerset so I shall not see you before you go. Anyway, all the best and good luck while you're in.

I was very sorry to hear it but I suppose sooner you get in sooner you'll get out. I don't know what I shall do now with my time, that's if I have any when I'm not playing cricket but you'll write and let me know how you're going on each week and let me know your address.

By the way, tell your mother I'll come down on Sunday night to see you all and bring some sweets if I have the patience to queue. I haven't any yet but I fancy I shall be able to get some here. It looks a very nice town and we are going to look round the cathedral sometime.

How do you like it, I got [D.B.] Carr out twice [v Oxford University in The Parks, concluded earlier that day] and he's got a chance of 1,000 in May. I ended up top score as well eh! [36 in second innings in Yorkshire defeat] and caught two in the bargain. They were lucky everything ran for them.

The other night I went to see A. [Anton] Walbrook in 'The Queen of Spades' a real mad picture absolutely awful and one of the worst pictures I've seen.

We went for (Frank and I) a walk round the town and there looks to be quite a few decent women around so I might enjoy myself. Anyway I'll finish now and have some shut eye. Good luck and all the best in RAF.

Yours

Brian

Write to me at Yeadon when you get there. Hurry up and get some leaves.

Yours

Brian

Frank and I have just been introduced to the one and only Len. He seems a very nice fellow, quiet, not too talkative. We spoke to him for quite a while about cricket and who we had played for.

*　　*　　*

As he indicates to John before signing off his previous letter, Brian and his family have by now moved home from Rawdon to 48 Hawthorn Avenue, Yeadon. He returns there after the Somerset match and writes to John on the second evening of the game against Worcestershire at Bramall Lane, May 23. He is being driven to and from Sheffield by Yorkshire wicket-keeper Don Brennan. There are complications with the postmarks as the letter is redirected from the RAF Padgate mailroom to RAF West Kirby with the Padgate mailroom stamping the re-directed letter with the date, 6 May 1948! The back of the letter is postmarked Warrington 26 May 1949. Brian is particularly keen to tell how well he is getting on with young female admirers.

Dear John,

I was so glad when I received your letter this morning, now I can tell you something of what's happened since the last letter. By your letter you seem as though you like it out there and sorry for not being sorry in the last letter. I was so surprised and astonished I didn't know what to say. I suppose I put a jumble of meaningless words together.

Anyway, I'm glad you've got some Yorkshire lads with you, "don't forget [to] spread my fame far and wide".

I got another "quack" today [Yorkshire v Worcestershire at Bramall Lane, c Outschoorn b Jenkins]. I won't bother you with the reason for it but there was [one] of course. I won't tell you the result of the game because you'll have seen it long before you get this.

I went to your house tonight and had quite a nice time joking and talking to your mum and Marjorie [Margery]....

I don't know whether I told you about Wells or not but I'll tell you now. The very first night we were invited to a dance and Ted Lester, Frank and myself saw a party of girls and I went and asked one for a dance (of course, the best of the lot) and after brought her over to Ted and Frank and introduced her. They soon followed suit and we got fixed up smashing.

Anyway, we spent our stay in Wells in luxury. I've had letters and telegrams from loads of people. This morning I had a letter from a girl in Sheffield saying how much she admired me and congratulating me, aged seventeen, still goes to a high school, she has loads of horses and dogs, adores cricket and came specially to watch me, and sealed it with Your Ardent Admirer x x x etc. Joan M. Winter.

She sounds as though she's rich, anyway I made it in my way to find what she looked like and found she's a bit of alright, she was trying to take my photograph all the day. I shall have to get to know her. She says in her letter she would like a reply. She's got a phone No. and special notepaper. Lives at Glaisedale House, Chapeltown, Sheffield, sounds like a palace, doesn't it!

I had a telegram from Margaret wishing me the best of luck and congratulations. She probably wants to come back.

I had a visitation at Sheffield today, Marjorie Ellis who is at Sheffield Training College. She brought about three other girls from the College with her. I spoke to her a bit but I had to hurry up because I was going in Don Brennan's car home. Anyway, she says that she'll see me in Chesterfield if I am playing next week. I shall soon have all Yorkshire to pick from. Anyway, I shall have to close now as I want some sleep tonight. I don't want a 3rd 0.

(Best of Luck)

Yours

Brian

I hope I shall soon be hearing from you. Keep away from the women in Warrington.

Yours

Brian

*　　*　　*

Although the next letter to John is enclosed in an envelope with The Station Hotel, Chesterfield, printed on it, it is actually written at the Queen's Hotel, Birmingham, and postmarked 2 June 1949, the second day of the North v South Test Trial in which Brian has been selected to play at Edgbaston. Already, he is on England's radar less than a month after making his Yorkshire debut.

Dear John,

I was sorry to hear that you hadn't received my last letter while you were at Padgate. It probably landed the morning you left, anyway sorry again.

Thanks for your telegram congratulating me today, there was no-one more shocked than me when I heard my name on the wireless last Sunday [Included in the North v South Test Trial].

I had a marvellous time in the Essex match as you probably noticed and at Chesterfield I didn't do so badly. I got 22 and 17 not out and managed one or two wickets for a few runs.....[1-13 and 2-28].

....anyway, get back to cricket. We managed to win against Derbyshire handsomely and arrived at Birmingham a little after six. We went straight to the Queen's Hotel in which we are staying and plonked our bags and went straight out for a walk round the shops with Frank [Lowson]. After about half-an-hour we came on a posh restaurant and we went in and had a real first-class meal for 8/- (it ought to be for that price). Roast chicken and loads of it, boiled ham as well, chips, peas and cabbage plus soup and sweet of course. Sorry if I make your mouth water!

The expense doesn't matter, seeing we get £30 for the match, 1st Class railway fare to and from Birmingham and 10/- a day incidental expenses, not bad eh!

When we came in after the walk Brian Sellers [England selector] came to speak to us and told us to stick into the buggars (is that how they spell it, not having seen it in writing I wouldn't know). He said that they are no better than we are. Anyway we went upstairs to change and came down and Sellers had gone for a drink and Tom Pearce the Essex skipper [England selector] saw us and introduced us to Mann [George], Edrich [Bill] and Co. We managed to get on talking but we both wished the earth would swallow us both up. What a relief when they asked us to go in and have a drink, we said 'Sorry, but we think we'll go to bed' or words to that effect.

Mann seems a very decent chap from what I had formed an opinion. He's a very nice chap.

If you are coming home I might see you Saturday night because we are coming home from Manchester [Roses match, no Sunday play of course]. Anyway I'll come down when I get home from Manchester if it's reasonable time. If not, see you Sunday.

Anyway I shall have to close now as its getting late. I don't think there is anything else to say, anyway if there is I'll make up for it next weekend.

Cheerio and Good Luck
Brian

*   *   *

Brian reveals that he has now changed his mind about going into the RAF but has just informed them of his preference for the Army in the nick of time. Annoyed at agreeing to play for Yeadon in front of a record gate and not getting a penny or a word of thanks for his considerable efforts. The letter shows his home address but was written in Worcester and postmarked 20 June 1949 St John's Wood! On the back of the envelope he apologises for its lateness and says he forgot to post it!

Dear John,

I left from writing the letter until I could get to Worcester and have something to write about. Anyway, thanks for the letter.

You seem to be having a nice time cleaning the tables and washing up, I wonder what your mum and Margery would say, probably faint.

I specialise in being batting when they are broadcasting, but that time I wasn't out. We beat Northants, I haven't half worked for my money, what with being the only fast bowler included in the side, they didn't half sweat it out of me.

No, I haven't had my calling up papers yet and last week I wrote to the RAF headquarters in Leeds to say that since my medical I had changed my mind about going into the RAF and wanted to go into the Army (12th R Lancers in Barnard Castle).

Anyway, last Saturday I got a reply saying I had to go and interview an RAF officer at my own convenience. On Monday I went and the Sergeant said 'Just in time, another week and you'd have had it'. He took me into the office to see the chap, I was wracking my brain thinking up excuses for changing my mind. Anyway, it all turned out nice and he said the Army authorities would contact me shortly.

On Saturday the County allowed me to play for Yeadon [probably a charity or benefit match]. Bill Bowes had got Frank and myself, funny enough we were playing each other. I managed to get 44 and four wickets for 30 and we won. I threw away a £20 collection with a daft shot, the ball I got was a foot outside the leg stick and should have been hit right over Billy Mugs's chimney. Anyway, I got Frank out.

The thing that got my goat was that the game attracted a record gate £60 for Yeadon, probably only because Frank and myself were playing, and they never even said thank-you to me nor gave me anything for the trouble. I batted all afternoon and bowled the first four out before he took me off. Surely they could have given me a fiver for it because I could have easily told them I wanted the rest and not played. Frank does get something from BOL [Bowling Old Lane] because he was engaged as a professional for them, I didn't get a sausage.

There was a match on Sunday at Yeadon but after Saturday I gave back word and went to Hanging Heaton to play against Cec Pepper's XI. I got 114 out of 145 and took eight wickets for 30-odd. I had a nice collection of £4 10s. 0d besides getting £2 for playing there and taxi there and back. I didn't half enjoy myself, guzzling pop by the bucketful and eating chicken and boiled ham. On the way back we stopped at a pub and had lemonades, orange squashes and egg flips etc.

On Monday I went down to your house and just as I got off the bus I saw your mum and Margery across the road at the bus stop, they were evidently going to Ilkley. They persuaded me to go and we spent a very pleasant afternoon looking round the shops and then had tea in a cafe, same one as the one we went to last time, remember!....

.....Today against Worcester I didn't do so bad. I got 26 not out, going down a bit [No 8], No 11 next I suppose. It's because I'm supposed to be a fast bowler this match, 'nowt else'. I think we have a good chance having got four of them out for 64. Anyway, we'll wait and see.

We seem to have got into decent lodgings, loads of grub, eggs, bacon, in fact almost anything we ask for.......

.....Anyway, I shall have to finish as it's getting on for 12.

Yorkshire team group v Worcestershire at New Road. Brian is standing third from left

Cheerio and Good Luck,

Yours

Brian

*　　*　　*

A letter from Lord's Cricket Ground on 15 sheets of MCC notepaper! It is postmarked St John's Wood, 7.15pm, 20 June 1949, the second day of the match against Middlesex and was written at mid-day. His previous letter, also posted at Lord's earlier the same day, had a 12.45pm postmark. Brian apologises for the lateness of his letter but acquires autographs etc for John and talks of Hutton's innings. He describes in detail his walking tour of London with Lowson. A new world is continuing to open up to him.

Dear John,

Thanks for the letter I got this morning with the autograph book.

TELEGRAMS
LORD'S GROUND LONDON
TELEPHONE NOS.
CUNNINGHAM 2241 (PAVILION)
CUNNINGHAM 1838 (TENNIS COURT)
CUNNINGHAM 3386 (HOTEL)

Lord's Cricket Ground.
London. N.W.8.

Monday 12·0 a.m.

Dear John,

"Thanks for the"
letter I got this morning with
the autograph B. D. V M not
their ow——
time too
mine dow——
I am very
writing ——
my faul——
in my ——
before I ——
saying to ——
post it ——
onto the ——
on Friday ——
it to the Umpire."

Envelope:

ST JOHN'S WOOD
7 15 PM
20 JUN
1949
N.W.8

POSTAGE

2432689 AC/2 ANDERSON
C 27. 15 R. FLT. C SQDN.
R.A.F. WEST KIRBY
LARTON,
WIRRAL,
CHESHIRE

I'll get their autographs at lunchtime today when I get mine done.

I am very sorry about this writing business. It was my fault, I had a letter in my pocket almost three days before I posted it. I kept saying to myself I must post it, in fact I took it on to the field at Worcester on Friday and had to give it to the umpire. Anyway, I posted it at Lord's on Saturday, so forgive me.

We managed to win at Worcester as you said but they certainly gave us a run for our money. As I write this Len [Hutton] is just in the making of a huge score, he is now 22 not out, just notice how many he ends up with [113]. I think it's Frank's turn for some as well [43], he's had a bit of bad luck the last few innings.

We are going to the Society of Yorkshiremen's dinner tonight (Monday) at the Cafe Royal at Regent's Park. No more about my cap yet. Did the rifle feel heavy?

Yesterday, Frank and I looked round London, honest we saw as much of London as anyone could see in a day. We set off from the Gt Western Hotel at about 11 o'clock without breakfast (we got up too late). We got the tube to Aldgate and started our walk round with Petticoat Lane. Whew! You wouldn't have thought it was Sunday by the row there was. There is thousands of stalls going down the Lane and the side streets off it, crowds of people, you had to walk sideways to get through, everything in the world nearly to buy, barrow boys.... and loads of other kinds of chaps shouting their heads off trying to out-shout the next one.

We walked slowly into the tangle and after ten minutes or so had well and truly got lost and had just to follow the traffic of the people and hope to get out that way. Anyway, we managed to get out of the centre again and walked to the nearest tube and got one to Charing Cross. From Charing Cross we walked all over the place – Trafalgar Square, the Strand, Leicester Square, Piccadilly Circus, Oxford Circus, Fleet Street, St. James' Park and Palace, Regent's Park and Street, Hyde Park and Corner, Buckingham Palace, Westminster Abbey where there was a service going on, Houses of Parliament, in fact all over the place and, of course, Mayfair and Park Lane, Admiralty Arch, 10 Downing Street, all over the place.

Frank was on his knees long before four o'clock but I kept dragging him on and finally about six o'clock we came back to the Strand where we had had a smashing lunch, and had the same for tea – a mixed grill which included mushrooms, eggs, potatoes (mashed and chipped), meat pie, cauliflower, tomatoes, meat and sausages. After that, fruit salad (bananas, peaches, orange, plums, cherries, strawberries, rhubarb and gooseberries all mixed up in cream) and after that finished up with strawberries and cream. What a meal. It took Frank over half an hour to put that away.

At Worcester where we were staying there were two very nice girls, we didn't do so bad after all, we got them up into my bedroom bringing me milk and biscuits and of course enjoyed ourselves immensely. All the time we were in the hotel we were in the kitchen helping ourselves to the hotel's food store.

On the Thursday night we got a taxi to a place about three miles outside Worcester where they were holding the Three Counties Agricultural Show and saw a grass track speedway competition and a motor cycle stunt show. It wasn't half good. One of the chaps ran amok in the crowd when he broke loose through the ropes, you ought to have seen the crowd scampering away. The ambulance came and carted him away on a stretcher plus half a dozen others. It was like the finish of a battle.

Gosh these London women are lovely and gorgeous but somehow we can't exactly get talking to any of them.

Frank and I have just had our blazers sent down, they are smashing and look lovely. You'll excuse the letter going on further because I have so much to say, making up for lost time (Len's just got his 50, now for 100).

Freddie Trueman is a b-----, he's gone and bought three magazines with short stories, they don't half set your blood tickling and pounding, unfortunately they get to a climax and then cut off abruptly leaving you in 'mid air'.

I shall be able to tuck in at lunch because we are batting today, and tomorrow I suppose you've to make your own mistake on this wicket. I'll lay odds on the Test being drawn with each side batting about once in the three days unless there's some rain. Hooray! Lunch. Len not out 56.

......You ought to be here at Lord's, it's a marvellous ground and the pavilion simply gorgeous – rubberised floor, when you are walking on it with your spiked boots its just like walking on a carpet. It's all over the place, up the stairs, bathrooms, dressing and dining rooms and even in the hall. Pictures are hung up over every inch of the wall, a big indicator in the hall gives the scores of the other county matches all over the country. It's marvellous. The practice ground wickets are as good as any you'll find on a good

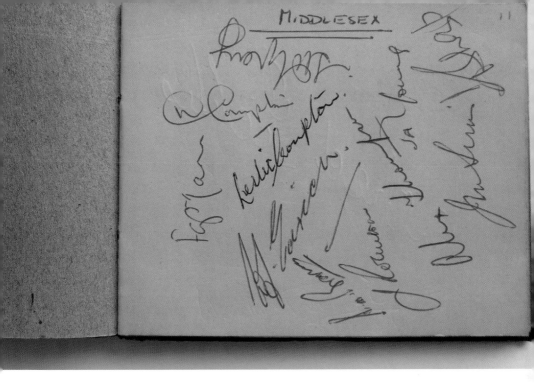

County ground. What a place.

I think after Tuesday I should know London like the back of my hand, well enough to get me round to the important places. If you're ever without a guide when you're in London, just find me, I'll do the job.

I hope you are enjoying yourself at West Kirby lifting your rifle over your shoulder. I shall soon be in the Army but instead of a rifle I'll have a cricket bat.

I've just had to go for reinforcements in writing paper. I have just been introduced to E.W. Swanton, the broadcaster and reporter. He was just remarking that I've done a good morning's work with the pen and asked me jokingly to write a line or two for him.

I've been promoted to No 7 again after my knocks at Worcester. I didn't half enjoy myself there batting, and then I threw my wicket away by hesitating to a ball which should have gone over the sight board like the others, but anyway I shall have to be content with 47. It'll help my average along a bit after those two singles against Northants. Len not out 62. Frank retired hurt 21 (hit on the knee). [Willie] Watson 0. [Ted] Lester not out 30, Total 113-1. I don't think I shall get in until tea time tomorrow (if we bat so long).

....Have you fixed up a decent female yet, or aren't there any about? You want to get the first train down here and come to Lord's. You see a load when you are fielding, some real sights, gaping at you, inviting you nearly. It's really very difficult to keep your attention on cricket when you see such things. Now I see why Maurice Leyland once said there's nothing like a county cricketer's life. I think I am inclined to agree with him at the moment. I think I shall have to finish as I might not be able to get all the paper in a letter.

Anyway, Cheerio and Good Luck,

Yours

Brian

PS: I've got their autographs so Rest in Peace.

Cheerio

Brian

CHAPTER FOUR

JUNE 23 – AUG 21, 1949

ENGLAND CAP

The momentous summer of 1949, Part Two: Brian replies to Mrs Anderson and tells John of Hutton's century in each innings – Another deferment of National Service – On the Radio in Sportsmen's Corner – Smashes Jim Laker around v Surrey – Letters and telegrams galore on being selected to play for England – Thoughts turn to soccer and National Service

It's now the last week in June and on the 23rd Brian writes from Brighton, where Yorkshire are playing Sussex, to Mrs. Anderson. He is replying to her letter of the previous week and the correspondence between the pair indicates just how close to the family Brian is. Upon his return home and during the game with Nottinghamshire at Sheffield, he fills John in on the recent fixtures and describes the punishment Yorkshire are obliged to soak up at Bramall Lane. He also says that Yorkshire secretary, John Nash, has helped get his National Service put back to September.

Dear Mrs. Anderson,

Thanks very much for your letter which I got while at Worcester and I am very sorry I have not written before as I have been waiting for the photographs to be sent to me. Anyway, they landed to me yesterday so I'm enclosing them. Have a good look at them, they look like George Mann, the England skipper, or that's what the lads say....

I enjoyed myself very much at Ilkley, it was a very nice change for me.

I've had a marvellous time in London. After all the travelling about London in the four days we were there, I feel as though I've lived in the place for a few years. We went all over the place on the tubes, visiting practically every important place in town. I'll tell you more about it when I get home. I'll be home on Saturday night, so I'll be coming down on Sunday.

About Len's book, I didn't bring it with me but I [will] get it autographed at Sheffield and bring it later. I have just had a letter from John today. He seems to be getting on alright. He tells me he has been playing some cricket there and bowling them out.

Well I shall have to close now as it's getting near lunch time. Cheerio and Good Luck.

Yours

Brian

PS: I'll come down some time Sunday.

48 Hawthorn Avenue
Yeadon
Leeds
Tuesday [June 28]

Dear John,

Thanks for your letter which I received last Friday. I thought I would leave from writing back until I had something to tell you of the Notts game. If you would like to know about the Northants match [Bradford June 8-10] I got 1, bowled neck and crop by [Robert] Clarke. After the Middlesex match we arrived at Brighton about 8 o'clock and had a nice dinner at the hotel and then four of us went to a dance on the pier. The four of us were Willie, Ted, Frank and myself....

....In the Sussex match it was bl.... hot fielding, the only part I enjoyed was when I was batting. Len batted marvellously in both innings [165 and 100] and just threw his wicket away in the second as soon as he got 100 and left me and Vic to knock off 40 in 30 minutes. Anyway, we got cracking and knocked them off in 15. I had 20-odd not out [24]. In the first innings I hit a four off my back.

I ran down the wicket to J. [John] Oakes and my boots slipped and left me on my back. Anyway, as the ball was passing over my head I swept my bat and hit it for four to square leg, it only bounced a yard or two from the boundary.

After the Sussex match we travelled up to Sheffield by train and arrived at the hotel at 1.30 in morning. We all had breakfast in bed at 9.30 and managed to get up to the ground in time. No wonder we were all out for 250 [252 v Nottinghamshire]. [Francis] Woodhead had six wickets. I think it's the first time he has had over three wickets in a match, so you can tell how they all batted. I managed to get 40-odd [41] runs and then threw my wicket away. I had picked my spot to hit Winrow [Harry] (slow L.A.) and I took a step forward and hit the ground. This made me push through harder with the bottom hand and as a result the bottom of the bat came up and I was c and b.

On Monday when we were bowling them they just did as they wanted. They were playing defensive shots which were going for two runs. Whew! What a day. I hope I never have one like it. By tea I could hardly stand, in fact I was out on my feet and just managing to keep going by keeping my feet moving little by little. If I had stopped I don't think I should have ever started again. The last four overs I bowled before tea I just bowled them straight slow ones, I didn't dare to spin any of them for fear they wouldn't land. Anyway, it's best forgotten [Notts scored 492-5 dec., Walter Keeton 210, Joe Hardstaff 162*, Close bowled 32 overs for 82 runs and no wickets].

Last night I got cramp in my legs. It made me scream nearly. It's a damn good job they declared this morning, but I don't think they'll get anywhere with it. Wally Keeton says it's a better wicket than Trent Bridge. Anyway, just wait and see how many they get out. By the way it's going I think we shall get a result about Christmas. I've just been hearing rain is coming, the sooner the better, a right good ---- down [match drawn at 6.0pm, Yorkshire 197-5].

This morning I heard I had to go and have another medical for the Army, this time next Friday at 9.0am. Mr. [John] Nash [Yorkshire secretary] has told me he has applied for my deferment until September and has had a satisfactory reply and he says he is going to get me in the Signals at Catterick where he knows the CO.

Leeds United are trying to get me to Barnard Castle. I shall probably end up in the Guards or somewhere if they don't watch out.

....Last Sunday morning I went down to 61 [John's home]. They evidently were getting ready to go up to Yeadon to watch me play but unfortunately the County had told me I hadn't to play. They came up and I saw to it they got some tea and I think they saw a good match.

....Anyway, I guess I shall have to close now, I don't want it to be as long as the last one. Cheerio and Good Luck.

Yours

Brian

PS: I forgot to tell you I was going on the wireless this week in Sportsmen's Corner. I have to make a recording in Leeds one morning this week. Alan Clarke and Eddie Waring are in charge I think. I don't know when it is.

*   *   *

Written from home the day after the game ended on July 5, Brian refers in detail to the Surrey match at Bradford in which his 66 and overall figures of 9-148 help to bring victory. Bill Bowes hints before any announcement is made that Brian will play for England v New Zealand and on the morning he writes his letter a photographer arrives at his home.

Dear John,

Sorry I didn't write to you earlier but give me a chance. I was waiting until today to write back so I could tell all about the Surrey match [at Bradford]. Well, thanks for your letter I got this morning.

The Surrey match as you probably have seen was won by us by six wickets. On Monday morning they carried our score up to within about 40 of theirs and then in the first over after lunch Gerald Smithson was out and I had to go in and face [Stuart] Surridge for three balls. Well, he bowled [to] me then and at the end of the over I thought 'Well, if that's what the bowling's like I am going to like it'.

I went nice and slowly for about four or five overs, then they put

[Jim] Laker on at the Pavilion End. His first ball, a half volley, went straight back into the pavilion, his second and third went to square leg for fours but, anyway, he steadied himself for the rest of his short spell (three overs). Then [Jack] Parker came on and he sent me a half volley which I hit over his head for a four. He evidently thought it was just a flash in the pan, he laughed when their skipper said 'have we to have a man behind?'. Next ball I blocked and then the third ball I hit him clean into the pavilion or just in front of it. You ought to have seen his face, and then he quickly despatched two of his men to parade in front of the wall.

Well, I thought I had better not do that again so I remained quiet for a while until I got to the other end against [Eric] Bedser. I got my 50 with a hook off him and then I hit him for a six over by the football offices and dressing rooms. That completed my knock because I somehow hit one into someone's hands [Michael Barton's] and unfortunately this someone wasn't in the crowd.

They went in to bat with about an hour left before tea and I jokingly remarked they would be out before 7pm and Vic [Wilson] wanted to bet but I declined saying I didn't want to take his money away from him. Anyway, we got stuck in and four overs after the start he fetched me on to bowl at the bottom end. Well, my fourth ball bowled [David] Fletcher all ends up and [Stan] Squires came in. The last ball of the over I threw it right up in the air and Squires took a swing and nearly put it into Skipper's hands. He'd have been caught if he had troubled to dive for it but evidently he wanted to preserve the cleanliness of his 'lily white' pants.

After two overs he took me off and changed ends. Alan [Mason] came on at the bottom end and I went on at the top. Nothing further happened before tea. After tea [Laurie] Fishlock hit me for six under the pavilion and I said "What's tha trying to do, bust it?" Anyway, he got 50 odd [57] and then Alan Mason bowled him beautifully. Parker came in and he bowled him round his legs and then he had Squires caught behind. "Three quite useful wickets," Skipper said.

Anyway, then Barton (Dick) and [Geoffrey] Whittaker got cracking and sent the score up by ones until Norman said 'Send a loose one or two to get their shoulders going'. I responded with two full tosses outside their legs which rightfully went for sixes but as soon as I started bowling right again they went back into their shell again.

Well, after much changing from round to over, over to round, and back again, I managed to bowl Dick, sorry Barton, a faster one pitched short and he tried to hit it for four but missed it. [Arthur] McIntyre came in and I bowled him second ball, then Whittaker in the next over tried to do the same as Barton and was bowled. Then we had more or less got them out. Laker was soon out, Surridge was caught and we were left with five minutes in which we had to bowl wide for fear of getting them out and having to go in ourselves for five minutes. Anyway, as soon as it reached 10 to 7, Coxon had [Peter] Westerman out lbw and we packed up needing 161 to win.

In the morning we easily got the runs, Frank batted well for 57 and then threw his wicket away having a go instead of getting his head down and getting another 50. Ted Lester got 44 and Gerald Smithson 27 not.

In the afternoon Bill Bowes came and fetched me to Salts CC ground and asked me if I would bowl Gerry Smithson for half an hour while Bill told him what he had been doing wrong. On the way back home Bill was saying to me 'Do you think you can bowl New Zealand out? Would you like to play for England?' I don't know what I said but anyway he said 'You'll probably be in the Gents v Players match and it depends on that'.

....This morning a photographer came to our house from the Post, he took me in a cricket shirt and sweater, then he said 'Let's have a picture of you gardening' so if you see me bending over a plant (don't know what kind) don't laugh. Then he took me back into Leeds in his car and I got your mother some flowers (carnations). This afternoon I was catching up for lost time cutting all the cuttings and photographs out.

I had a letter this morning with yours asking me if I would write an article with the Greatest Thrill of My Cricket Career for a Youth Club in Huddersfield. Any ideas? By the way, thanks for the telegram of congratulations which I received this afternoon. Thanks.

Anyway, I think I will have to close now as it's getting late. Cheerio and Good Luck.

Yours

Brian

PS: We play Middlesex on Saturday at Sheffield so if you write back address it to my home – that is until next Monday.

PPS: I am sending you one of those passport photographs, I have no other ones of myself. I shall have to get some more of these photographs as they are in very great demand. I gave Margaret one, your mother and yourself. I am

Letter from Bradford Central MP, Maurice Webb, confirming Brian's postponement of National Service

House of Commons,

London, S.W.1

Monday July 18th.1949.

Dear Brian Close,

        This is just to confirm my telegram of yesterday in which I told you that I had been able to secure a postponement of your call-up until October. I will let you have a copy of the Minister's letter when it reaches me. I only got the message yesterday by telephone.

I congratulate you on this development which,I trust,will enable you to complete the season with the record of a 1000 runs and 100 wickets.

May I also warmly congratulate you on being selected for the Test Match next week. This great distinction will be welcomed throughout Yorkshire.

I should explain that I came to take up this question of postponing your call-up at the request of many of your admirers in Bradford. I spoke to my friend,Mr Ernest Houldsworth,the Chairman of the County Club, about it,who told me that it was the wish of the Committee that I should go ahead.

I saw both the Minister of Labour and the Secretary of State for War and they have now both agreed to give you this extra time to enable you to complete the cricket season before going into the services.

I am very happy to have been able to help you and shall look forward to hearing of still greater successes in the next few weeks.

Yours sincerely,

Maurie Webb.

M.P. Bradford Central.

getting played he-- with by my mother for not saving her one. I said to her "I thought you'd have enough with me without a f------ -- (flipping) photograph."

got you there

Bill Bowes' 'hint' is absolutely spot on and Brian is duly picked for the third Test against New Zealand, starting at Old Trafford on July 23, and immediately he is pictured in a newspaper watching a game at Yeadon with his seven-year-old brother, Alan, sat on his knee.

A few days before the Test, Brian writes to John from Hull, the letter started at the Broadway Hotel and postmarked July 20, the day that Yorkshire begin a two-day match against The Army at Anlaby Park. He details his marathon bowling performance against Middlesex at Sheffield and takes great delight in telling how at the end of the game he and others travelled to Lord's for the Gentlemen v Players match and Hutton missed a train! Brian's opinion of Denis Compton undergoes a change after the pair chat together about cricket and soccer. Among 'thousands' of congratulatory telegrams and letters upon his Test selection is one from John.

Dear John,

Thanks for your letter which I got yesterday at Notts. I am very sorry I haven't written for a week or so but I haven't had much time to myself, honest. I haven't even written home, or to Margaret or anywhere.

I have just had breakfast and before we go along to the ground [Yorkshire v The Army] I'll see if I can get this started and I'll finish it at the ground.

Against Middlesex at Sheffield I had my best bowling performance, 2-125 in 60-odd overs. The first 55 overs I had 20 maidens and two wickets for 74 and then they passed our total and I got a walloping, [62-20-125-2] Jack Young straight driving thro' slips for four. If we had had our chances caught we should have easily had first innings lead. Even when at lunch on the third day they came off exactly level with us with eight wickets down. Well, in the first over after lunch Jack Young was missed by Coxon off Wardle in the slips, a simple catch, and then in the next over which

Batting for Players v Gentlemen at Lord's

I bowled [John] Warr was missed by Coxon, an even simpler catch, straight into his hands and out again. This went for a run so then they had got first innings lead, but if we had caught them both we should have got two points at least.

When we were travelling down to Lord's that night [for Gentlemen v Players match] with Denis, George, Bill, Jack, Norman and Len we didn't half have some fun when Len missed the train. You ought to have seen his face when a copper stopped him getting on.

We all went out for a drink but Len was the last to get served and while he was drinking his, we raced back and got on to the train. Anyway, there was a slower train a quarter-of-an-hour behind us. I had to go around London in Len's hat, raincoat – and mine.

I had a good talk with Denis often about cricket and football in general and what I had done at school etc. Forget everything I said about him, he's smashing and after his captaincy at Lord's [he was invited to lead the Players in his benefit year] he's quite a cheerful chap and quite nice to get on with. He's always coming over and talking to you, you know just friendly, and during the Gents v Players match I got quite pally with him. Mind you, I still don't alter my opinion that Len's the better batsman.

I had the honour of sticking in with him when we looked as though they were going through us in the dusk on the first day. I had the time of my life batting my own way for once and enjoyed myself thoroughly. Well, we are going to the ground [Hull] now so I'll finish it later.

On the Wednesday night, Tom Graveney from Gloucester and myself went into the restaurant on the Strand and had a marvellous time eating a lovely meal. Afterwards, we walked thro' Leicester Square and I noticed a picture at the Ritz, 'The Three Musketeers'. When I tell you who was in the film you'll see why we went. Lana Turner, she was marvellous. If you get chance to see this film, go. It's one of the best of its type. There's some marvellous sword fighting in the film and it's so exciting. Well, we stayed in to see it again.

The following night Tom and I went to see the final of the Crown [Real] Tennis tournament at Lord's. It's a funny game, played with smaller racquets than ordinary tennis and the players hit the ball over a net and by the aid of slicing and cutting the ball they make it come off the walls at different angles. It's really too involved to describe it but it's certainly much more difficult than ordinary tennis.

The last day we finished early, just after lunch, so we got packed and said goodbye to the players and Len and I caught the 3.20 train to Nottingham. We arrived at our hotel about 7.0pm and had a real tuck-in down in the grill room. We had so much that Len left more than he ate, trust me not to. By the way, I got your autograph books done.

This morning when I got to the ground I got my cheque for the G v P match (£17/16/-).

Bill Bowes said I shall be getting my cap some time this week as he said they were forced to give me my County cap before my England. Anyway, there is a committee meeting today and from what I gather I believe that is the subject of it.

Last Sunday I managed to get home from Nottingham and I was going to go down to 61 at night but after about 4.0pm I didn't have much time to myself, what with posing for photographs and answering questions. I don't think there was a minute when there wasn't a newspaper chap in our house until the last one left just after ten. Talk about cars, there were Buicks, Chryslers, Packards, queuing up to get in. Anyway, I survived it all, only to start all over again the following morning. Thanks for your telegram congratulating me, I haven't played yet.

....I have had letters and telegrams galore, more than Len, thousands of them from all over the country. I have had an invitation from the Lord Mayor of Manchester to dine with him, an invitation to appear in a sportsmen's service at a church in Wakefield and to read a passage of scripture along with a few others....

Yours

Brian

PS: I think I shall be having an easy time in this match, as Len, Norman and Don have been rested and I suppose they have kept me in to keep interest in it (so Frank said). Alec Coxon's going in before me and I don't think I shall bowl much so I shall just be alright for Saturday if they need me.

By the way, if you can get to Manchester on Monday or Tuesday drop me a telegram as I have two tickets for each day. My mum and dad will be coming on the Saturday but if you can get off for

Monday or Tuesday drop me a telegram as soon as possible and I'll leave one at the gate (main) if you can. Anyway, Cheerio.

Yours

Brian

With the Test match over and also Yorkshire's games with the New Zealanders at Sheffield and the Roses encounter at Headingley, both of which involved Brian, he is given something of a rest by being made 12th man against Leicestershire at Grace Road. Or that was the intention! He gets his first chance in a while to write to John when Yorkshire move on to Wellingborough and makes up for the gap of a couple of weeks or more by sending him two letters addressed from the Angel Hotel. The first is postmarked 6 August, the first day of the match with Northamptonshire, and the second two days later. Brian mulls over the possibility of him going on to complete the double before the season is out.

Dear John,

Thanks for your letter which I received this morning at the hotel.

Well, you know I was 12th man at the last match [v Leicestershire at Grace Road]. What a job, hundreds of autograph books were brought in and I had to get them all signed. Any that weren't finished I had to forge them. I nearly used a whole refill for my pen with them.

I hope you'll forgive me for not writing before but I had such a lot to do the first two days trying to get the books done and have the third day off more or less as Johnny Whitehead had to go and do something so I had to field all day. We only just managed to beat them with 10 minutes to spare, first winning bonus for ages.

On the first day I was the only one in the dressing room as the others were fielding....

....I thought it was a waste of three days for me coming as 12th man but I got paid £18...

I'll see if I can get down on Tuesday night if I can get leave but they might make me go straight on to Hull but anyway I'll try. Willie Watson played marvellously [119], I'm glad he's got going.

Johnny Wardle played smashing, he was the only one who spotted Jack Walsh's googlies and Chinaman. You know he bowls about three different kinds of googlies but Johnny saw through every one of them and hooked, cut and drove him all over the place.

I doubt if I shall get a rest again this season as they are all Championship matches and to stand a chance we'll have to win every game to stand a chance to win, but I don't think we've got a Championship side yet.

At the moment I need 17 wickets and 240 runs for the double. I think I can just manage a hundred in this match and about 12 wickets or so. [He made 17 and took three wickets, Hutton hit 269.] Anyway we'll have to wait and see.

I'm sorry you've got your sore throat again, you won't be able to go around (the girls) while you're at home. Anyway I suppose I shall have to close now... I suppose you'll listen to the news on Sunday, I'll bet anyone I aren't in the side. Anyway, Cheerio and Good Luck.

Yours

Brian

PS: You ought to see the mail I've been having this week, some queer things. I'll tell you about them later. I'll write again on Sunday after I've been golfing. Cheerio
Brian

*   *   *

This second letter from Wellingborough is started in his hotel on the Sunday and completed at the ground the following day. He describes how his bowling eventually came good on a difficult first day and relates how he spotted some of the Yorkshire party more than a bit tipsy after a party that same evening.

Dear John,

Just a few lines while I am waiting for lunch. Yesterday we got a bit of a hiding but we couldn't help it as the ground is so small and the wicket's not a bad one. The only thing wrong was my bowling and Don's stumping. Up to tea I had nought for about 50 and then something happened and I just managed to hit a length and I finished the day off with three for 60-odd.

Freddie Brown batted well and one six off Coxon's first ball when he got the new ball was a marvellous affair, straight over extra cover's head. Anyway it looks like a four points do unless something happens on the last day. By the way I have been enquiring, I shall not be able to come home from Northants on Tuesday night unless we finish the match in two days which seems very unlikely at the present moment unless they bowl us out twice on Monday, so I doubt if I shall see you until your next leave.

I hope you've had a nice time at home what with going to the pictures and playing cricket in the park. You make me envy you, I've been doing the same thing and I feel bored stiff.

I haven't seen 'The Blue Lag.' but I have seen 'The Secret Life of Walter Mitty', I bet you enjoyed that one. It's quite a while since I went to the pictures, I believe the last time I went was to a matinee at Yeadon (don't laugh, it's true).

Last night Don was giving a party, you know, loads of liquor and wine and gambling. I went to it for an hour or so, drank a few glasses of orange squash and won a few bob on a horse race at cards, and then Johnny Wardle and myself went out and called at a dance. Even though we didn't dance we enjoyed ourselves at their expense as the doorman recognised us and we traded our autographs for a free passage.

....When we came back to the hotel last night from the dance we found Bright [Heyhirst, masseur] and Herbert [Walker, scorer] were still at the party at the other hotel so the landlord gave us the key to take to them so he could go to bed. Well, I ran down and just caught them leaving the hotel, absolutely drunk, shouting and singing their heads off and as we were walking up the road all the other lads and Pressmen were hanging out of the window laughing their insides out watching them rolling from one side of the street to the other. Herbert Walker, the scorer, walked across the road and nearly broke a shop window as he crashed into it. Gosh it was so funny, you'd have thought it was a Three Stooges picture.

Well, I suppose I shall finish now as I don't think I can say any more, so Cheerio and Good Luck.

Yours

Brian

PS: Tell your mother I'll come down some night or else at the weekend if I can to show her the photographs. Don't forget to write back soon. At the moment I'm anxiously waiting the team.

Cheerio

Brian

* * *

The last letter of the 1949 season (or the last to survive) was sent from Folkestone where Yorkshire were staying at the Queen's Hotel during their match with Kent at Dover. It was written on the Sunday, August 21, on Queen's Hotel notepaper and enclosed in an envelope with an impression of the imposing Queen's Hotel on it. John by now was stationed at RAF Credenhill, Hereford, and he had requested Brian to fill him in with details of Hutton's magnificent innings at Wellingborough which Brian equates to his double century in The Oval Test. Brian was not at The Oval, so his account is either hearsay or he has read about it in the newspapers. Brian also looks ahead to his Army service and the arrival of the football season.

Dear John,

Thanks for your letter which I got before I left for Scarborough [v Warwickshire, previous match]. How are you going on at your new station, sounds all right with apple trees in it.

Well, we're on the way to the football season now. I see Leeds only managed to draw at home and then only from a penalty.

You wanted to know about Len's innings [269 at Wellingborough, Yorkshire v Northamptonshire], it was marvellous. His first 100 was steady but after that, gosh it's hard to believe, he hit cover drives off his back and front foot and sweeps round the leg side to the slow bowlers, chopping and cutting as though his life depended on it and he'd have been still there now if we hadn't declared. Never the slightest chance.

Similar was his Test innings [206 v New Zealand at The Oval]. He started slowly, then caught [Reg] Simpson up at 40-odd, took a long time to get 50 and went on to take his score into the 90s. Here he took an hour to get from 92-100 and then got his 100 with a snick between his legs. All the critics and reporters were playing ---- with him and every one of them swore they would give him a ---- of a write up in the Sunday papers about wasting an hour on eight runs when England were trying to win a Test in three days.

But as soon as he got his 100 [at Wellingborough] he started hitting every bowler all over the place. He never lifted a ball in all his innings, every one was straight through the fielders without giving them the slightest chance.

We seem to have pulled round a lot just lately, winning four of the last five matches. Middlesex had better watch out, if they slip once they have had it [the sides shared the Championship title with 192 points each].

Against Derbyshire at Bradford we were set 186 to get in 90 minutes against an all-fast attack and we went for them neck or nothing and just got them with five minutes to spare. It was a marvellous feat because all they needed to do was bowl just short of a length and outside the off stump but we did 'em.

In the match v Warwickshire, Ted Lester and Willie Watson batted marvellously in getting a ton each. I got set and was run out again like Len ran me out at Old Trafford [early June] and against Northants [Wellingborough].

I am afraid I shall not be at home around the beginning of September as I shall be at the Scarborough Festival in the matches Yorkshire v MCC and North v South but if you can get to Scarborough on either the Saturday or the Sunday write and let me know and we'll spend the day together. I could come home Saturday night on the 8.30 which gets into Leeds around 10.30 but the job is getting back, there isn't a train early enough on the Monday morning so I should have to leave Leeds round about four o'clock on Sunday afternoon. Anyway write back soon and let me know if you can get to Scarborough for the day. Our matches before then are Gloucester at Huddersfield and Glamorgan at Newport.

We had to travel from Scarborough all Friday night. We left Scarborough on the 4.30 to York and came down to London. We

Brian, centre, and Frank Lowson, receive their Yorkshire caps from skipper, Norman Yardley, in August, 1949

arrived in London round about midnight and seeing I was bagman for the trip I had to dash across London to catch a connection with a load of 30-odd bags and two taxis. I got there and found it was a goods train we were catching so I got the bags away and boarded the train in the only carriage for passengers on the train and it was crowded to the doors so we had to stand up in the tightly packed corridors while the train called at nearly every station on the way to Folkestone where we are staying.

Well, we arrived around 4.0am feeling pretty well shagged and found we had to walk a couple of miles to get to the hotel with our personal luggage as there were no taxis at that time in the morning.

John's autograph book of teams Brian played against during the 1949 season, together with scoring card and local rules folder for Crosland Heath Golf Club signed by the great Yorkshire and England all-rounder Wilfred Rhodes

Trouble was I had to get up at 8.0 on Saturday to take the bags down to the ground.

We made a nice start, so they said I was flat out on one of the tables in the dressing room. I went in round about 3.30 and got 30 batting nice and quiet and then they got Coxon and Wardle out and in came Don Brennan. Well, I thought, I better try to push the score on a bit and was bowled. We went back on for an hour at the end of the day and did a nice bit of work in getting three of them out for 40.

.....How are the Waafs going on at your camp, have they broken down the barrier yet? Another month and a bit and I shall be all dressed up in khaki out of Buckley's way [Major Frank Buckley, Leeds United manager]. I suppose he'll start training me like hell on earth when I finish cricket.

It was Margaret's birthday last week and I got her some nylons for a present from a person who is well acquainted with the stocking trade.

Well, I think I'll close now as I can't think of anything else to tell you, so Cheerio and Good Luck.

Yours

Brian

CHAPTER FIVE

OCTOBER 10, 1949 – JANUARY 23, 1950

SIGNALMAN CLOSE

October, 1949, and now it's No 22185787 Signalman Close DB, 20 Troop, 4 Squadron 7SR, Catterick Camp – 'Smashing' start as relieved of fatigues because of ankle injury – Visits John in Catterick Military Hospital – Assures John's mother of her son's well-being – Describes vividly his boxing prowess – Back training with Leeds United – In Military Hospital himself – May become brigadier's driver

The cricket season is over and so, at the moment, is 'Civvy' life, with Thursday, October 6, 1949, being Brian's first day of National Service. He seems to adapt smoothly to the regime of it and from the start he is obviously aware that a sportsman can have a good life in the Army if he keeps on the right side of the right people. By a twist of fate he quickly discovers that John, in the RAF, has been moved to the Military Hospital at Catterick because of illness and within a few days Brian is visiting him and reporting back to Mrs. Anderson. Ironically, come the New Year and Brian himself is in the hospital and being visited in his ward by John!

Monday [October 10, 1949]

Dear Mrs. Anderson,

Just a few lines to let you know I'm going on alright. Up to now I haven't been able to get away from our 'lines', but I asked the captain if I could go down to the Military Hospital and he said I could go one night this week so I'll be seeing him [John] then, and then I'll write and tell you how he's going on.

I've had a smashing time up till now, I've got off of all my fatigues

etc. When I reported at the lines I was introduced to loads of officers and sergeant-majors. I landed there hours later than the others and I said to the officers that I had had no dinner as we had set off from Leeds about 11.45 and so they took me off to the kitchen and I enjoyed a very nice meal.

After I went back and while the rest of the lads were queuing to see all the officials etc (loads of 'em) they rushed me thro' and I was finished inside half-an-hour with all my kit and uniform and I had the barrack room to myself for an hour or two. I made my bed, laid my kit out and settled down for a lovely sleep. Since I came here I've spent more time lying on my bed and the sergeant-major's bed too than anywhere else.

Well, the first night went alright, the bed is just a wee bit hard compared with the nice spring mattresses I've been used to, but I suppose we would fall asleep on anything the state we're in now.

In the morning [Friday, October 7] I had to report sick with my ankle and wasted a morning getting my ankle strapped and the doctor excused me wearing boots. Our troop had to do some kind of tests that morning and while I was doing the same in the afternoon they went and took some more tests which I managed to miss completely. We had lectures on what and what not to do and by the time we were free we had to turn the lights out.

Saturday morning came and found us all queuing up for inoculations, you ought to have seen them popping off, it was just as though someone had turned a machine gun on them. I was one of the lucky ones, my arm was swollen and useless until Monday morning.

On Saturday I had a nightmare, so I was told. Every time I turned over on my arm I let out a scream and wakened the whole troop up.

Sunday was a hard day, all I did was lie on my bed writing letters or visiting the Naafi which was usually crowded.

We're getting quite disciplined now, we can even halt and, something even better, we can get up within half-an-hour of reveille (anyway in time for breakfast). We had our first lesson in rifle drill today and a bit of marching. I missed the morning work because I had to report sick again to have my ankle strapped.

In the night I went to the gym for some extra boxing training and had a real good time. Well I'll have to close for tonight as it's lights out.

Tuesday [October 11].

Well I've got some good news, I went to see John tonight. I had a little bother getting in but I finally persuaded one of the orderlies to take me to the ward. John seemed to be feeling alright and was walking about the ward when I went in. He was very cheerful and I asked him what developments had been done and he told me almost everything. He said that the condition of his blood is improving immensely and at the present time he hasn't much, if any, pain from his legs.

He says he is almost always grumbling about food every meal but from what I saw while I was there he doesn't do so bad. He has the orderlies running about for him and he also has some nice lads in the ward with him (not meaning the s-majors). Anyway, I left him in high spirits and I'm going down again before the weekend. Anyway, I hope I've consoled your mind and left it at rest because you've nothing to worry about. So Cheerio and Good Luck

Yours

Brian

PS: Hope everything's alright at 61. 'Keep your pecker up.' Polish up your cards while I'm away.

I'm getting quite a regular fan mail from the girls at Ripon G. School and Newcastle etc., some real funny addressed to Brian Close, Cricketer, Catterick.

*   *   *

Thursday [Possibly October 20]

Dear Mrs. Anderson,

Thank you very much for your letter which I received last week. I'm sorry I've not replied before but we've been awfully busy in this gloomy place. Our troop were put on 'Fire Picket' duty a week last Tuesday and each night after we have finished working we have to parade round the grounds of our Regiment and last week with the General I/Co coming round we had to do fatigues every night and nearly every day we didn't finish until somewhere round ten-o-clock each night. Mind, don't think I worked hard because every job I was on I always found someone to talk to such as an officer or a sergeant etc.

You know when you wrote and said you were coming, well I couldn't see you because I got a 48 hour pass to play football while the other lads were confined to barracks. Since then I think 'The Major' [Buckley] has had a talk with our c/o and has agreed not to ask for me off until my first month is over.

Well, last week I had to console myself with having to stay in the camp. I thought I'd die, Saturday went awfully slowly after the parade and Sunday we used to catch up on the sleep we had missed during the week. We still have to get up at that unearthly hour 5.45am. After breakfast we came back to bed until dinner time. Later I remembered that I had been given an address in Richmond so I got ready and went. It was quite nice especially at teatime. It was just like home sitting in front of the fire. There was a daughter aged about 19, so trust me to enjoy myself.

I believe I told you I had started to box a bit. Well, last night we had the inter squadron boxing championships, we won the cup and I had the pleasure of going and receiving the cup from Colonel Ponsonby our c-o, plus a medal and a Naafi chit. My fight was the last one and after the first few I thought to myself after seeing the faces of the other lads who had fought that I was going to look after my facial characteristics so instead of going straight in I boxed nice and quietly and came out without a scratch. The other lad who weighed about a stone more had all his face swollen and bleeding (blood thirsty devil).

After the fight we went to the (excuse the blots, please) dining hall where we all ate as much as we possibly [could] (considering the state of the lads' jaws, teeth and mouths). Well, at the feed we got set into some ham, eggs and chips and afterwards we wallowed up the stairs and finally turned the lights out about midnight.

Next morning we had to be up at 5.30 because we were going to the open range about 20 miles away and had to be away for 7 o'clock. We were half asleep when we climbed into the lorry, one lad could hardly see due to the previous night, but anyway after a few minutes ride in the lorry we were soon wide awake. There was about 20 of us crowded in and the flipping thing was swaying and bucking like a mad horse. Well, we got organised and first we had to fire our rifles from 100 yards. I had a washout, the trouble was I fired three out of my five shots at the next lad's target.

We had quite an eventful day firing rifles and Bren guns and then our troop had to stay and mark for the Regimental shooting team, we didn't half have some fun signalling bulls for outers and outers for bulls and flagging them wide and everything. We were laughing ourselves hoarse.

Tonight I went to see John at the hospital, he seems to be getting much better. We had a game of cards with his bed mate and as usual I won every time, those cards must be lucky for me but it wasn't for money. Anyway, I left him quite cheerful and now that we have finished nearly all our 'Bulling' I shall be able to go and see him quite regularly.

How's everyone at 61, how's Jill, yourself and Margery etc! Are you finding Sunday night quite lonely these days? We'll soon have finished here and then I'll start having every weekend off to play football so I'll be seeing you soon, happen on the weekend after this.

Well, I'll have to be finishing now as it's nearly 'lights out' so I'll be saying Cheerio and Good Luck.

Yours

Brian

PS: Write back soon please, I'm sorry this has been rather late but now we'll have more time to ourselves. Cheerio

Yours

Brian

Either Brian or John or both seem to be in the Military Hospital at Catterick around this time and in mid-December, 1949, Brian is living the life of Riley back home, having been given permission to have treatment and train with Leeds United. Brian is in high spirits when he writes to John, still in hospital, in a letter postmarked December 16, but later that month or early in the New Year Brian is back in hospital and writing to Mrs. Anderson!

His letter to John from home reads:

Dear John,

I'm sorry to be such a long time in writing to you but anyway I've got on the job now.

I suppose your mother told you about why I came home etc. Well, I'm having a smashing time at home, up 'early' in the morning at 8.45, wander down to Leeds for 10.30 for treatment, dinner every day in Leeds, back to the ground in the afternoon and home for tea. It reminds me of the Army!

Buckley seems to be in a good mood these days. He even has a joke or two with us and he doesn't swear any more (not 'alf). One remark he said this morning, he said my Regiment has disbanded until I get back and Oh! the way he said it made us all scream; of course we get a few back at him, you know.

Wonders never cease. I haven't been out at nights at all this week. I've been busy finishing 'My Life Story' for a book. I finished it rough in about 2,500 words but in the real one I've just got into the Test in about 2,300 words so Bill Bowes is going to have a bit of cutting out to do. [This is very probably the handwritten manuscript titled "How It Happened by Brian Close. Yorkshire and England." The 13 page article appeared in "Young Cricketer 1949-50."

Your mother tells me you're improving and able to get up now. I hope you get home for Xmas. I shall probably be up there for it, since I think I shall be coming back some time next week, but even if I don't get a leave pass in I shall probably get a 48 hour to play football if I'm fit.

.....This holiday's costing me something, you know I don't get paid unless I play and I haven't played for four weeks and Bob said it's a long way to go yet.

Well, I can't think of anything else just now as I haven't done

How It all Happened

The Youngest player to be selected for England! I can
see the headlines in the newspaper and can
[...] the excitement in my native
[...] my own little village of Rawdon.
[...] an 18 yr old been asked to
[...] hotel. It was a singular
[...] that, but I also knew how
[...] It was a compliment in-
[...] it was one which thrill
[...] It was only 8 months
[...] had left school, and now, after
[...] of months playing for my county
[...] to play for England. Would
[...] own? What if I dropped a
[...] make a "duck" and get no wickets for
[...]
[...] my name read out over th[e]
[...] slept a wink. Excitement
[...] doubts made sleep out of th[e]
[...] required the quiet words of
[...] next morning to put me
[...] played Brian" he said "Just do
[...] ou'll do fine". Oh! if only
I could produce my best, I thought, everything

Article printed
in the "Young
Cricketer" 1949-50

much while I've been home.

....Anyway, I'll close now, so Cheerio and Good Luck.

Yours

Brian

PS: If I don't see you on Tuesday you'll know I haven't come back, but if I do happen to come back I'll see you then. Cheerio

Brian

*   *   *

On either Wednesday, December 28, 1949, or the following Wednesday, Brian writes to Mrs. Anderson from Ward 5 at Catterick Military Hospital, informing her that John is now visiting him. Returning to Camp after his trip home, Brian reports sick with a knee injury and following X-Rays he is detained in hospital. He gets a visit from mum and brother Peter, a letter from Bill Bowes – and takes up reading philosophy while at the same time eyeing up the possibility of becoming a driver for the brigadier.

Dear Mrs. Anderson,

Just a few lines to let you know I'm going on alright, what a lovely life?

When I left last Thursday night I caught the last bus down to Leeds [from home] and got settled into a nice chair in the tearoom at the station and had a very welcome rest until 1.0am when there was a bit of a rush for the train. It was a special train so I got a double seat to myself and didn't stir until an officer came poking at me with a stick at Richmond. I nearly swore at him 'you silly b-----' but I don't think he heard me! Anyway it was quite a good journey compared with others.

The following morning I reported sick and found a different MO than usual. I told him what had happened etc. and he gave me a note to take to the hospital for an X-Ray. Anyway, before I went down I managed to wangle a 48 off the sergeant and got packed up ready to come home, thinking I would go straight home after the X-Ray.

Anyway, the film showed two large ossifications of bone under my muscles, just above the knee and the hospital MO decided to detain me.

I asked him all kinds of questions and he was quite reasonable, and now I've got to rest in bed for a month at least, poor me! Up to now it's been alright. I have a bit of fun with our sister and the lads in our ward are quite a rum lot. We play 'solo', draughts and all kinds of things. I've managed to head on top except for a s-m at draughts, he's done me every time I've played him.

I get on quite well with the specialist (colonel) and from what I hear Leeds are going to try to get me transferred to the Infirmary for treatment by their specialist, he's going to see what he can do.

John's been in to see me quite regularly, in fact each night, we either discuss the Utd and the Major or play cards of some sort.

In my spare time I've been re-writing my income tax claim out and writing copies of that article I made [probably the one he wrote for "Young Cricketer 1949-50"]. I'll let you have a look at it sometime, I don't think you've seen the finished job.

This afternoon I had a few photographers and reporters asking 'What happened'? and 'What's matter'? etc. A few of the lads joined in to make some photographs.

....It's a bit funny, the first weekend I have to stay in the Army and it turns out to be New Year. Anyway, I don't think I know much more so I'll close.

Best wishes for the New Year.

Yours

Brian

PS: Tell Margery 'Sorry I forgot the New Year's Card', I can't remember everything can I! Looks after yourselves.

Yours

Brian

Dear Mrs. Anderson,

Thanks very much for your letter which I received yesterday.

Quite a bit has happened since I wrote last, mother and Peter came on Saturday laden with fruit and cakes etc., it was lovely. You know I always said I wished I could get into a hospital, well I'm here. Many a true word spoken in jest. Never mind, after my first week everything seems to be okay.

John's got up again and came to see me last night. We talked for a long time and he told me you'd got fibrositis in your shoulder and was having quite a bit of pain from it. I hope it soon gets better. You ought to be in my place, I get no pain at all from it now and I can almost bend it to its full extent. I think they must have planned this convalescence with Yorkshire so that I'll be fresh for the start of the season.

By the way, I'll send you a copy of the article when I finish writing it. I copy a little at a time and should have it done inside a few days.

I had a letter from the brigadier last week and he said he'd come and see me sometime this week and discuss about getting off. He's going to arrange it so that I can get off one day a week for practising, starting February, that is if I'm not still here.

I had an ever such a funny letter from Bill Bowes telling me all about the two Chinese footballers Leeds have signed and a few scenes etc. down at the ground about it. What do you think of them after Saturday's show? [Saturday, January 7, FA Cup 3rd Round, Carlisle United 2, Leeds United 5.] I'll bet the Major is doing a war dance. I wonder if they'll manage to beat Tottenham on Saturday, he'll go mad if they do. [Leeds United 3, Tottenham Hotspur 0 (Division 2)].

We have a smashing night orderly on our ward, he's a scream. The other day some of the lads were discussing something – yes 'women' – and the sister said 'Surely, there's other things in this world besides women' and then the orderly came out 'If God made anything else better, he kept it for himself'. We all laughed ourselves hoarse.

Yesterday I got a boxful of sweets sent by a girl somewhere in Yorks, you know it pays to be well-known doesn't it! They must feel sorry for me being caged up here.

That s-major who used to beat me at draughts has gone now so I'm champion for a while until we get a 'new intake' who can play, because I'm sure I can't.

I picked up a book the other day called 'Philosophy'. I don't know what it's going to be like but, who knows, I might be a budding philosopher!

How's everyone at 61? Has Margery recovered from her late nights at the parties yet, she will have started school again now. Tell her to send some of her homework up, we'll see if we can do some for her! Some nice easy arithmetic or something like.

At the moment I'm about half way up the ward. I was at the bottom when I came. I've only six months more to do and I shall be promoted to the top.

I don't think I shall be in the hospital as long as they say (3 m.) because my leg is improving wonderfully well and has nearly lost all its hardness. If I aren't playing football inside a month I'll eat my hat! I wonder.

Ask Margery if she would like to drop me a few lines some time, they will be very welcome and will be a great help for me to pass the time away writing and reading.

The meals seem to be improving with every meal here and of course I manage to get a little extra with a few persuasive words.

They've stopped me lying on top of the bed and made me get into it now. They say I'm always out at the wrong moments, when the matron or colonel comes round.

This morning two of our officers at 3TR came to see me and get a statement of how I came to be here (three big sheets long). It was something to do with a 'court of inquiry'. Anyway, I had a good 'call' with them.

I have had to leave it for a while as the brigadier came in. He was ever so nice and said he'd bring me some fruit and food etc. and asked if he could get me any books.

He said that with me being here for a while we'll have to scrap the idea of going on a PT course as I'll still be on it when April comes and we talked on it for a while. And then he said that his driver was being demobbed in February and he said he was looking for a driver who could play golf and said I could learn [to drive]. Anyway, he's going to study it and see what to do. So if I get a driver's job and play golf as well I shall not have done so bad after all.

Anyway, I'll have to close now, its supper time. I hope it isn't too boring, you see I start writing and then can't finish. Cheerio and Good Luck.

Love

Brian

*   *   *

John's back home when Brian writes to him from Catterick hospital in a letter postmarked January 23, 1950, and although he complains that life's been dull he still finds plenty to talk about – a motor cycle casualty brought into the ward, games of shove ha'penny and trying to listen to Leeds United on the radio while his mother and a friend visit him.

Dear John,

Well you'll probably be enjoying yourself and settling down nicely at home, lucky devil! Life's been quite dull since you went home on Friday, except of course Saturday afternoon and the times when we have the sister on!

Leeds did well didn't they? Did you go to see the match? It sounded like a thriller on the wireless. Mum came up [to Catterick] with a friend of hers on Saturday and I had to keep silencing them so that we could hear the commentary. I had to hold my breath many a time but when Williams scored I nearly jumped out of bed. I won a bob off a sergeant across the ward. I gave him the draw, needless to say they never seem to pay up voluntarily and of course I shan't ask him for it.

On Saturday morning they brought a civilian into our ward, the result of a motor cycle crash not far away. He had a compound fracture of one leg and his other leg broke, one arm broke and a broken nose besides cuts and scratches all over the place. He was in a sorry state [with] blood flying all over the place but Capt Slaney and the 'civvy' specialist got stuck into him and at the moment he's as right as rain. It was marvellous, the sister said he had lost round about 10 or 11 pints of blood and you know there's only nine in the body, the rest came from what they had fed into him before his operation.

Mum came and stocked my larder again and brought me a conc. bottle of orange squash, it's lovely and sweet. The lady who came up with her was one of my fans – a retired teacher who lives at Guiseley. She also brought me some 'eats'.

She also brought up a small bottle of blackcurrant wine with whisky mixed in and asked me if I would like it. I had one taste of it and nearly poisoned myself.

Jack, the night orderly, kept us awake till round about 12 last night telling us about his escapades in the Army, he had us roaring with laughter.

I can't concentrate for toffee tonight. Peter Sellers and his dummy has just been on and Donald Houston is on at the moment; this with all the lads laughing like ----, the ward's just like bedlam.

How's everything at home? Have you been to see any good pictures? I had a game of 'Shove Ha'penny' last night, a young Scots lad thought he could play so I took him on, on one of these long tables and beat him 6-3, 6-3, by which time he had changed his mind.

I'm hoping the brigadier comes down sometime this week, he said he was going over to BAOR for a few days next weekend so I hope he drops in before he goes.

Sister Boyle had a look at the letter I got with the present and wouldn't believe it was from a middle aged lady, or at least didn't want to believe it. She's even threatened to take my pyjamas off me to stop me getting up and even got them as far as my ankles.

Well John, I suppose I shall have to close now because I've just about exhausted myself competing against the radio, so Cheerio and All the Best.

Yours

Brian

PS: How do you like it, Australia all out for 80 odd. I hope S. Africa beat them, it will do them good. Cheerio

Brian

22185727 Sgt. Close
A Company
Hut B 1/2
114 M.C.D.
Bradbury Lines
Hereford

Dear John,
Just a few lines to let
you know I'm going on alright
down here.

The M.O. up at Catterick suddenly

HEREFORD
6 30 PM
26 FEB
1950

~~ ~ ~ Anderson,
61, Victoria Crescent
Horsforth,
Leeds,
York

CHAPTER 6

FEBRUARY 20 – MARCH 30, 1950

SOCCER INJURY AND CONVALESCENCE

Feeling stronger and fitter – Prepares to have some teeth out – Talks about Leeds United – Transfers to convalescent unit in Hereford – Bumps into Stanley Matthews on journey South – Watches Hereford United – Pulls thigh muscle while training – Returns to Catterick

Brian's letters continue to reveal a zest for life which remains undiminished despite spells in hospital and a convalescent unit. He has this knack of hitting it off with the right set of people, like when he gets invited into the directors' stand at Hereford United.

Ward 6
Military Hospital
Catterick Camp
Monday [Postmarked February 20, 1950]

Dear John,

Thanks very much for your letter which I received just now. You'll have probably got my last letter by the time you get this.

I've no need to ask you whether you're enjoying yourself – the letter betrays you. Anyway you lucky (B.) I wish I was you!!

I've been having a busy time these days what with writing letters, attending a lecture and 'doing a bit of work' – I don't know what I will be doing next.

I've been up all day long for the past few days and at the moment can 'run like he--' and kick with no pain at all, in fact I'm almost as good as new. I shall be playing football again inside a month (touch wood). Except for feeling a little weak in my left knee, I'm as right as rain and I told Mr. Kerr so when I put in a 48 next week-end, so I could be home for my birthday but he says if I'm fit to go home at the weekend he says I'm fit to be RTU'd [Returned to Unit] – well of course I was all for it, but he said he wanted me here a bit longer yet. So it looks as though it will be a while before I'm home.

Sister Boyle has come back but she isn't in our ward. She's in Ward 7, the ward below ours. I had a chat with her and she asked me if I'd had my teeth seen to yet. I said 'No, I'm losing those this afternoon'. So by the time you get this think of me with a 'mouthful of nothing'.

I had an invitation to go to Sandes Home to a lecture last Sunday on 'Miss Sandes' the founder. We had tea and cakes before it and then seeing I had missed my tea at the hospital I had my tea with 'Old John'. He made me promise I'd come and have a special tea with him today. I'm wondering whether I shall be able to eat anything after my 'appointment with fear'.

I've had quite a few letters from old friends just lately – one from an old corporal friend who's in civvies now, an old football friend and another from a sergeant-major – you can bet I'll have some fun writing to them.

I did a daft thing on Saturday morning. I changed my shirt in the laundry and left a ten bob note in my pocket. I called myself everything under the sun when I found out what I'd done.

I hope Leeds keep on like they've been doing, even if they only draw to Arsenal; I'd love to see the match. [FA Cup 6th Round, March 4, 1950, Arsenal 1, Leeds United 0.] I think next week's match at Cardiff will be a hard one but I think they should win if they play their usual (touch wood!). [Division 2, February 25, 1950, Cardiff City 1, Leeds United 0.]

It's smashing now being in Ward 6. We don't have to get up until about 8-o-clock, and breakfast in bed.

We still keep on with our solo games and so far I must be quite a bit up in cash. Next time you play 'solo', when you chuck the cards in after each hand, tell everyone to arrange their cards in the proper order i.e. ace, king, queen, etc., with hearts on the left, then clubs, diamonds and lastly spades. You'll be surprised what hands come out when you deal them. Last night someone had 13 of a suit.

Well, I might be playing golf soon with the Brig. – I think he's going to get me out of here as long as I don't do anything strenuous and go steady. I should think golfing is just the job to get me fit.

Well, I'll close now so Cheerio and Good Luck.

Yours

Brian

Bradbury Lines
Hereford
[Postmarked February 26]

Dear John,

Just a few lines to let you know I'm going on alright down here.

The MO up at Catterick suddenly decided to send me down here instead of sending me back to the unit. I spent the last two days in Sandes Home playing snooker, billiards and table tennis and at night 'John' invited me to have tea with him on Wednesday and Thursday. I had two lovely meals, eggs, sausage and chips, toast and cakes. Then at the end he gave me lots of sweets and chocolates to come down with.

Well, we (three of us) set off at about 8.0am and caught a bus to Darlington. Here we had time to have a snack as we had come away from the hospital without any breakfast, then we bought some periodicals to read on the train and calmly waited for the train 'thinking a good time was ahead of us'.

We caught the train and first stop was Ripon where a 'draught' of Royal Signals going to Malaya got on. A few times during the journey their NCO's came into our compartment thinking I was one of them. They must have been looking for 'deserters' trying to hide themselves away in the train.

We passed through Leeds (City) station and I almost felt like getting off and going home. It's a good job the train didn't stay too long.

We arrived at Manchester (Exchange) and found we had to change stations and as the train didn't leave for another two hours we tried to find somewhere for dinner.

As we were walking through the streets, who do you think we saw? Two chaps passed us and I thought one looked rather familiar – it was Stanley Matthews – he was chatting about horses.

We came to the YMCA just before the station and we popped in for dinner. We had quite a nice meal of soup, fish, peas and chips, and jam roll to finish with. We walked into the games room and there I saw Harry Gibson, do you remember him at school? He was with a party of about 30 RAF lads – every one of them playing table tennis nearby. He said they did nothing else but play TT all day, lucky beggars.

We left just before 3.0pm to catch the train and after a long and tiring journey we landed at Hereford just after 6.0pm. Here a taxi came and met us – this gave us another wrong impression of the place – we thought it must be a posh place to send a taxi to meet us.

Well, after a short run we arrived here and reported to the guard house. We had to fetch our bedding right from the other side of the camp and got put in to a mangy little spider hut. Here we heard tales from the other lads of what they had to do – fatigues, jobs, route marches and all kinds of things – we thought then we had come to a concentration camp instead of a convalescing depot.

They said that the MPs and the RPs are very strict here and put you on a charge for the slightest thing you do wrong, hence the big number on 'jankers'.

I don't know how we managed to get to sleep on those beds that night – we must have been dog-tired, they're awful. On Saturday morning we went across to the "intake office" to report and then to the MOs. The MO Jock Brown is quite a sportsman himself and we had a nice chat as he went over me. He said I'm almost fit and said I just had to get a bit of muscle back etc. Then I asked him how long I would be down here as I would like to get away as soon as possible so that I could do some practising in April. Well, he said when I felt like going I had to tell him and he'd see to it.

Meantime, he has put me on a job in the physiotherapists' place where I can do exercises and training all day – besides, of course, drink tea.

On the Saturday afternoon I went into town to see if Hereford United were playing at home. Unfortunately, their reserves were playing at home. Anyway, I found out that Leslie Hennessy was playing so I went and called on him. He took me into the dressing room and introduced me to the directors etc. It was fun, they got me loads of cups of tea and biscuits at half time and full, and they let me sit in the directors' stand.

After the match which they won 4-2 – Les scored two and played well – I went into town with Les and had tea, then he went back to Leeds by train and I went to the pictures to see 'The Spider and the Fly' at the Odeon. It was a pity he was going back to Leeds. Both he and Brian Woodward who are playing down here are still living in Leeds. Ellis Corbett lives about 13 miles out and up to now I haven't seen him. I should have enjoyed myself down here had they all been lodging in the town, but anyway they'll be down here for Wednesday or Thursday as they have a game on Thursday against WBA.

By the way John, I think I shall be coming home next weekend on a 48. I'm putting in for one tomorrow so I'll be seeing you if you're still at home (touch wood).

How's everyone at home? What have you been doing while on leave? Another thing I'm told, it's easy to get compassionate leave from this place so I told mum that when she goes into hospital she has to send me a letter so that I can get some compassionate leave, perhaps four or five days or so.

What do you think of Leeds, the silly b-----s losing to Cardiff, but anyway it had to come so why not now. Sheffield Utd gained a bit and are going to be hard to overtake. Do you know their manager at the beginning of the season said they would go down into the 3rd Div. if they didn't get some new men.

Well, I guess I've written too much as it is so I'll close. Cheerio and Good Luck.

Yours

Brian

*　　*　　*

Brian's clearly enjoying life at Hereford although he's irked at getting 'scalped' by his hairdresser. John moves on to RAF hospital at Halton, near Aylesbury but the time is coming closer to when he is invalided out of the Service and returning to Civvy Street.

[Physiotherapy Dept, Hereford]
Wednesday

Dear John,

Thanks very much for your letter and also thanks very much for the book which you sent me for my birthday. I haven't read it before and from what I've gathered by just glancing thro' it this morning I'm going to enjoy it. Now I shall know what records to break next season!!

I am definitely coming home this week-end, that is if someone doesn't put me on a 'fizzer'. I see you are having a nice time at home by the sound of your letter. I too have had rather an exciting time down here, lot better than I thought I would. I've made friends with the men that count except perhaps for the RSM who's a right devil. I've kept out of his way so far, for it's odds on if he speaks to you it's to put you on a charge!!

I've got one pal in the MI room, besides Jock Brown the MO and one in the QM's office and one in the CSM's office, not to mention the RP staff.

Well, everything's turning out alright. My pals are seeing I don't get put on fire picquet [a small group to deal with fires on camp] or similar duties and so I've had lots of time in the evenings.

I went out for a walk with my pals on Sunday afternoon, we stayed in town for tea and then went to see 'Mutiny on the Bounty' at the Ritz at night. They all say there are lots of nice women in Hereford (but I can't see any) so we went empty-handed. It was a good picture and we thoroughly enjoyed it.

On Monday night three of us went to the County Repertoire Theatre to see a play, it was quite funny, about a married couple, the woman being in love with another man. Anyway, the lovers planned to do away with the husband but unfortunately he found out and played with them. We laughed our heads off.

Last night I left everyone 'bulling up' for the CO's parade this morning and went to the football ground where they were doing some training. I didn't do any as I'd been doing a lot of it in the morning but I did have a lovely hot bath. I came home in time to press my BD but that's as far as I got. The parade went alright, apart from 'my boots' nearly killing me.

The job I'm doing is smashing. I have practically all the time I want to do crosswords, write letters and do the training I want. It's just the job. I'm getting off tomorrow afternoon, touch wood, to see Hereford play WBA and meet Brian, Ellis and Les. Tonight I intend to go to the Ritz to see Elizabeth Taylor in 'Little Women'. Have you seen it? From the trailer it seems quite funny.

I had a haircut yesterday and I told him 'short back and sides and a little off the top'. Well, he got 'stuck in' and damn near scalped me. I called him every name under the sun when I got out, and for 'a bob' as well.

Well, I'll close now, so Cheerio and Good Luck, see you Friday.

Yours

Brian

PS: I'm getting off early, thanks to my pals and the MO so with a bit of luck I might make Leeds for 7.0pm. Anyway, if I can't get down Friday I'll come down Saturday. We'll go to E. [Elland] Road because I've got to see about something.

*　　*　　*

To John at RAF Hospital, Halford. Brian is getting on so well with Hereford United that the Club are wining and dining him now. He can't play football himself, however, because of his injury and he's missing the action.

[Hereford Physiotherapy Unit]
Friday [Postmarked March 10]

Dear John,

Thanks very much for your letter which I received yesterday. I'm glad you've got settled down and will soon be out and I won't drop any hints when you'll be getting out to your mum.

Yes, I got back quite easily, if a bit tired. At Leeds I caught the train (8.5) quite easily. By the way I did catch that bus up to Yeadon, but I wasn't half puffed when I got to the top.

I got in a carriage with another RAF lad and a chap and we talked about all kinds of things. I had my particular piece to say on the Army of course. This helped to pass the time on and we got to Manchester sooner than we expected. We said goodbye and as I had a couple of hours to waste I went into the YMCA and had a cup of coffee and read the Sunday papers that were kicking around the lounge.

Just after 11.0 I thought I'd walk along to the station and who do you think I ran into – my two pals who I came up with, so together we went and boarded the train. It was a rather tiring journey and arrived at Hereford at about 3.45am. The other two lads couldn't run so they told me to dash out and grab a taxi and hold it until they came.

Well, we were near the end of the train and as it slowed down I leapt off it and sped along the platform to the bridge. I swerved round a lot of them (knocked a few who got in the way out of it), up and over the bridge three steps at a time and was first out of the station, so I managed to get a taxi.

All Monday I didn't half feel tired, I couldn't stop yawning, but it soon got to night when I went to the County Theatre with my two pals. It was called 'The Middle Watch' and I almost fell out of my seat with laughing.

On Monday afternoon I thought I'd try some training so I got cracking round the track. Just when I thought it was doing lovely I went and pulled a muscle in my same thigh. It was probably a bit weak to start with so now I've got to rest it and have some heat treatment. As if I haven't enough trouble with my other injury!!

On Tuesday I got a free pass to the Kemble Theatre second house, so after I had been down to the football club I went. It was quite a decent show and made me laugh. I can't describe the show to you because it would take a long time to write but it was quite a good one.

....On Thursday, Hereford had a Southern League match against Lovell's Athletic so I got a pass from the MO to go into town in the afternoon. I got down to the ground and found the k.o. to be 4.30pm but anyway I saw Ellis Corbett and we went for a cup of coffee in town. After we went back to the ground I massaged his leg for him where he had bruised it.

The game proved to be a real thriller and ended in a 1-1 draw, although Hereford were unlucky not to win by about five goals. I've never seen a goal escape as many times as Lovell's did yesterday. Their crossbar was hit three or four times and the full backs stopped the ball on the goal-line many times without counting how many good saves their goalkeeper made.

After the game, Brian, Les and myself went along to the Imperial Hotel for dinner and had a lovely meal, all at Hereford's expense. Then we hurried to the Odeon to see 'The File on Thelma Jordon' starring Barbara Stanwyck. It was quite interesting but unfortunately I had to leave five minutes from the end just when the trial was coming to a climax. Anyway, I shall have to enquire what happened when I see Brian and Les on Saturday. I wish I could play as well, it's awful sitting and watching the others.

I probably shan't be seeing you for another two weeks yet as the MO (Jock Brown) said he couldn't let me away while I had a pulled muscle (worse luck).

I had a nice letter from the brigadier last Monday to say he was going out this week. He's left everything OK for me when I get back to Catterick.

I hope this letter gets to you before you do get out or it might be kicking around for a few days.

Oh! I forgot to tell you, I was invited out to tea tonight by one of the directors of HUFC who is manager of the Queen's Hotel and then afterwards we are going to the Kemble Theatre. Well, I'll close now so Cheerio and Good Luck.

Yours

Brian
(All the best in Civvy St.).

PS: I've had a letter from the BBC asking me to make a broadcast with Len Hutton on Saturday April 1st. I don't know whether I shall accept it or not.

*　　*　　*

John is home now and Brian is back at Catterick and writing to his friend in a letter postmarked March 30, 1950. Brian is immediately pressed into playing football and his team loses 5-0. He says he is returning home at the week-end, perhaps for good.

Wednesday

Dear John,

Just a few lines to let you know I'm going on alright.

I got back to camp quite early on Sunday and John had a cup of tea and some toast already for me when I arrived at Sandes. Anyway, I settled down to a good night's rest and felt quite fresh in the morning when John woke me up with a cup of tea.

My posting has come through at long last – I'd begun to think it had got lost. It came through this morning and I was in a bit of a hurry to pack my stuff up and get my bedding in the stores by half-past-eight but I managed it – I wasn't going to stay at that place longer than I was forced. [He's obviously had a change of mind about Hereford!]

Since Monday I've been doing nothing more than lie on my bed reading a book – Oh! and perhaps getting out of the NCO's way (I didn't want to pass the time with a scrubbing brush in my hand).

On Monday afternoon I went to see the brigade major to enquire into my posting which should have come last Wednesday. He phoned up and made them push it through or I'd have probably been still at 3TR and we had a chat (of course on cricket).

I've been staying at Sandes all week again and no-one's said anything yet and now I'm at 7SR. I saw the SM and he says he'll see there's no enquiry into it. I've reason to do it at 7SR because it's overcrowded and the stores haven't even a mattress or enough blankets let alone a bed.

When I arrived here this morning I called in to see the adjutant straight away as I'd been told but he said I couldn't see the CO as he was out today but said he would arrange it for tomorrow morning, so I'm keeping my fingers crossed. I think everything should work out alright as the brigadier major has had a talk with him before but I'm still hoping.

When I came out of the adj.'s office, Captain Gillet grabbed hold of me and told me I was playing football this afternoon. They didn't even give me chance to settle down a bit. Anyway he went on saying how good a football side they were and building them up into world beaters (probably to impress me). Guess what! We lost 5-0. I don't think I'd have backed them to beat the Blind School. I thought I didn't play so badly (when I hadn't the ball) but I was doing it on my own with no-one to help me.

Afterwards I got changed and went down to Sandes and had tea and then a bath afterwards. I feel lovely now. I had a lovely supper just now, egg, sausages, peas and chips, and tea and cakes to finish off with. It was smashing.

I shall probably be home Friday night even if it's only for a 48 but I hope it's for good (touch wood) so I'll be seeing you Saturday morning, all being well [was Brian fleetingly hoping to be invalided out of the Army in much the same way that John was with the RAF?]. We'll go to the dance on Saturday night, that is if I'm still in one piece after the match.

Anyway, I'll close now so Cheerio and Good Luck.
Yours always

Brian

PS: See you Saturday.

CHAPTER SEVEN

APRIL 5 – SEPTEMBER 6, 1950

ASHES CALL-UP

The 1950 cricket season approaches – Permission to have from Easter to April 26 off to practice with Yorkshire – Plays League cricket and picked for Combined Services and the Army – Enjoys his luxury 'guest' room at Magdalene College for University match – Gives his opinion on West Indies Tourists, including Sonny Ramadhin – Chats to Sheppard and May and thinks they are 'nice lads' – Brian picked for the forthcoming Ashes tour, but Confined to Barracks on a charge when he hears the news – Preparing for Australia

It's spring and Brian's attentions turn to cricket although he is forced to have treatment for a muscle strain. This doesn't seem to worry him too much as it enables him to have a 'big skive' when not actually having daily heat treatment. He writes to John from Catterick in a letter postmarked April 5 and again on May 4 when he reports playing in a football match while unfit rather than dropping out with the risk of being barred from cricket. Although Brian hopes to be with Yorkshire during the summer, for various reasons, including injury, he only turns out for them once – in the Roses match at Bramall Lane in late May. His other three first-class games that season are for Combined Services and his aggregate in all four matches is 202 runs and 20 wickets. He is not on the winning side in any of the games. The first letter reads:

Dear John,

Just a few lines to let you know I'm going on alright and not in hospital as I thought I would be. I had quite a decent journey back to Camp and before going to Sandes I went up to 'my' Regt. and gave my pass in and caught the same bus back.

John had a nice supper waiting for me, toast and poached eggs and a lovely drink of tea. I soon made short work of that and off I went for a good night's sleep.

On Monday I reported sick and the MO sent me down to the hospital to see Capn. Slaney. The MO who did see me first sent me for an X-ray and then told me to come back at 2.0pm to see Slaney.

I went and had a game or two of snooker and billiards to pass away the time and back I went. Still Slaney wasn't available but another MO saw to me and pointed out there was nothing on the X-ray at the place I thought there was, to show that it was calcifying and said it was probably muscle strain or something. Anyway he put me on heat treatment each day down at the hospital so from now on while I'm here it will be one 'big skive' (not that it wasn't before) for one quarter of an hour's heat treatment. I didn't bother going to the Regt. that day so I went back to Sandes (billiard tables in short).

I had a nice tea, then after a rest I got a lovely hot bath. Meanwhile John was preparing my supper and I dashed out of the bath and tried to dry myself and quickly got 'stuck in' to my supper. It was lovely but I caught a cold into the bargain with not drying myself properly.

This morning I went to see the RSM about the CO's interview. He was quite nice (very unusual for RSMs) and arranged for me to see him at 12.0. Time flew quickly and very soon afterwards I was being marched (much to my annoyance) in. It didn't take long to finish our talk and it was very satisfactory. He did most of the talking and asking me questions which I did my best to answer and then he dismissed me and told me to see the Adj. at 2.0pm for the results of our talk.

After lunch at Sandes I came back and learned my fate. I can have from Easter to April 26th off to practice and then I come back and see the Adj. and he'll have it all fixed for me to go on the Southern tour of three matches. Then I go back once again for a few days. It's alright but I shan't know whether I'm standing on my head or my heels. I'll tell you more about it later when I come home. I'll call down and see you Friday morning....

Well I suppose I've said enough so Cheerio and Good Luck.

Yours

Brian

[May 4, 1950].

Dear John,

Just a few lines to let you know I'm going on alright (but only just). I'll tell you about it at the weekend but I've been in a 'spot of bother'. I arrived back quite safely (worse luck) on Sunday night and found a lovely meal waiting for me, then straight off to bed I went.

On Monday I found I was picked to play football against the 8RTR (supposed to be the crack team). Well I couldn't exactly refuse because the Officer would have stopped me getting the weekends off for cricket just out of spite, so I thought I'd play but I wouldn't run after the ball (I think I made it too obvious). Mind you every time I got the ball I beat one or two men and passed the ball, but only at walking pace. Anyway we won 3-2 so everything was alright. (If we'd lost I'd have probably been shot or something.)

By the way I've been picked for the Combined Services XI to play next Wednesday, Thursday and Friday at Worcester so I shall be coming home this weekend to play at Barnsley, going back for Monday morning and off again Monday night for home again. On Tuesday I will be travelling down to Worcester and coming back Friday night to play for Leeds on the Saturday and going back Monday morning.

I've also been selected for the Army side to play Cambridge University the following week so I'll be off again. Not too bad after all, is it?

There's quite a lot been happening this week but I'll tell you about it at the weekend because I can't say it fully in a letter. It's ever so thrilling!! I don't think.

We're playing at Barnsley at the weekend and I shall have to leave home about 12.0, so I shan't have much chance of seeing you on Saturday morning, but when I get home Friday night I'll try to come straight down (this time it'll be with a pass). Anyway I'll ring you round about 7.0pm (all being well).

How's your legs?...I hope you're alright again, and then we'll go to Broadway or somewhere on Saturday when I get back from Barnsley. I'm going to Darlington tomorrow afternoon; I shall probably end up in the Odeon or some picture house with a nice looking female (not on your life).

Well I'd better close, it's getting rather late so Cheerio and Good Luck.

Yours always

Brian

*   *   *

In Worcester for the Combined Services match, Brian first gets the chance to run his eye over the West Indies, describing the Tourists as 'a formidable side in the field'. He concludes his letter, postmarked May 11, by commenting on the Tourist's next game, against Yorkshire, and notes with some surprise that Ken Smales has claimed five wickets.

Dear John,

Just a few lines to let you know I'm going on OK. I'm having a smashing time down here.

I got down here round about 2.30 and I immediately dumped my bags at the hotel and went on to the West Indies match. Worcester were batting worse luck!! I met the Worcester lads and we had a lovely chat, talking over old times in between watching the game.

The Tourists look quite a formidable side in the field. They look quite smart with their red caps and sweaters and dark faces but I didn't get chance to look at their fast bowlers because the Skipper thought it was too slippery to risk them.

Ramhadin (I don't know how they spell it) [Sonny Ramadhin] isn't a bad bowler, he cuts the ball both ways with almost the same action and few can spot him. Mind you he only 'cuts' the ball so that reduces his effectiveness.

After a lovely dinner at the hotel, I went to the pictures to see Donald O'Connor and a talking mule in 'Francis'. It was quite amusing. [Francis the Talking Mule.]

Yesterday we were out at 10.0am practising and fielding. I must say it did them some good because we fielded quite brilliantly. I managed to scrape 92 together [unbeaten] but no-one managed to stay in with me. [That was his best score of the season and he hit 60 in the second innings.] With my bowling I thought I didn't do too badly at all. My first ten overs produced two runs but then I must have got slightly tired and threw in one bad one every over. It wouldn't have been too bad but they got four off it practically every time and I finished with

0-40 in 30-odd overs. I didn't have the best luck but it goes that way for everyone. [He took 3-54 in the second innings.]

About when I get home I doubt if I shall be home early enough on Friday and we're off to Hickleton at 11.0am so it looks as though I shall not see you till Saturday night when I get back from Hickleton. It might be rather late but we'll be going to Broadway!! so I'll go straight to the dance. It may be 10 or after so it isn't any use coming down to your house as the dance will probably be ending by the time we get up there so I'll see you inside Broadway round about 10......

We're having some lovely meals at the hotel here, I shall be rather sorry when we leave.

Yorkshire aren't doing so well are they? [v. West Indies, Bradford, May 10-12.] Fancy Ken [Smales] getting five wickets including [Frank] Worrell and [Everton] Weekes. The wicket must have been doing 'sommat'. Let's hope he keeps it up then I can just bat and forget bowling (too much like work). Don't tell Margery!! [Smales seven wickets in match, Yorkshire lose by three wickets.]

Well, I'll close now so Cheerio and Good Luck.

Yours

Brian

*　　*　　*

In Cambridge for the Army's game against the University, Brian is accommodated in a guest room at Magdalene College where, he says, he wouldn't mind staying for a few weeks. He considers May a better batsman than Sheppard. His letter is postmarked May 22, 1950.

Dear John,

Just a few lines before I pop off to sleep. I'm a little tired so excuse any mistakes I might make!! Well John I've had a wonderful time so far down here. Everything's been grand.

It took a 'hell of a lot' of getting here but I finally arrived just about 5.0pm. The West Indians had finished (worse luck) but just seeing their 'sickly' looking total on the board gave me a headache, and a few others besides me.

I met the chaps who had already arrived and the Cambridge lads as well. Then, when everyone had arrived we all found out where we were staying. I myself was going with Tony Rimell [born August 29, 1928, Kasauli, India, two matches for Hampshire (1946-50), Cambridge University (1949-50, Blue both years)] to Magdalene College (pronounced Mordelene) and I was told it was one of the best and it's certainly not a lie.

I found myself put in the guest room just above the river. It was lovely, there was a bedroom and a sitting room both nicely decorated, fires in both rooms, bedside lamp, armchairs and a couch. I wouldn't mind staying here for a few weeks.

After I had had a wash Tony and I went down to dinner. Tony is quite a nice lad and he showed me round the place and told me where everything was. He doesn't live in the college but out in 'digs' and we went up to his rooms and had supper (tea, cakes and biscuits) and just after 10.0 I left and went into college.

The porter showed me to my rooms in case I'd lose my way and then we ran into a lad called Dick Crawford, his brother Michael is skipper of the 'Council' side at Leeds. We talked for a bit and then he asked me up for a cup of tea (his rooms are just above mine) and I couldn't refuse so off we went. He introduced me to his room mate and to friends and we got talking (of course cricket was the subject). Well round about 12.30am with almost everyone just about asleep we thought we had better turn in...

Next morning I awoke with a lovely hot steaming breakfast at my bedside. It was smashing, porridge, then egg, sausage, tomato, bacon and mushrooms with lots of toast and butter and a teapot of lovely tea. I almost ate it in a daze and it was no fluke, this morning was the same with a slight variation of the constituents (boiled ham).

We lost the toss and of course we found ourselves fielding. The wicket turned out to be the usual one so we settled down to a nice long day in the field. This Sheppard's a good batsman, really strong on the off side and he played a lovely innings (if a bit slow). Peter May is a good batsman too. In my opinion better than David but he didn't stay long (good job too). I've been talking to both of them quite a lot during the two days here and 'like all cricketers' they're nice lads!!

On the Saturday night David and I went to dinner at some place then we went to the pictures to see 'Stromboli'. You've seen it haven't you? Well I thought she acted quite well but it certainly wouldn't be a film that I'd enjoy. In fact I thought the story was hopeless. Ingrid Bergman must be daft to fall in love with this 'director' or whatever he calls himself. The only thing I can say is that I hope she doesn't have a 'seizure' each morning when she wakes up and finds 'what's' been sleeping with her.

Today, four of us went out golfing on a course just outside town and we had a lovely day out. I did quite well seeing they were borrowed clubs.

Tonight I went back to college for dinner, then I went to the pictures again to see a picture with Jack Carson, Dennis Morgan and Doris Day in, I forget what it is called [It's a Great Feeling] but it was ever so funny, and after I came back and had supper with some of the lads in the porter's lodge.

Well I suppose it's time to go to sleep, though I doubt if I shall be needed tomorrow so Cheerio and Good Luck.

Yours

Brian

On Tuesday unless we are rained off I shall not be able to get back in time John and even if I'm lucky enough to catch the 4.5 train to Peterborough I can't get into town until after ten. So unless it rains I shan't be able to see you till you get back off holiday. Anyway, have a good holiday. Cheerio

Brian

*   *   *

Although Brian writes to John from home on June 5, the letter is postmarked Cardiff four days later and it is sent to John c/o Dr Hibbert at an address near Hilltown in County Down where he is possibly recuperating from illness. Brian refers to the Roses defeat at Bramall Lane and his 'nightmare' performance for Leeds against Ossett when he's dismissed by a dreadful delivery and drops three slip catches in as many overs! His bad luck continues in Cardiff where he is run out for 10, batting for Combined Services v Glamorgan and then scores one in the second innings.

Dear John,

Just a few lines to let you know I'm going on alright. How are you? Let's see. It's almost a fortnight now, or rather just over two weeks....

You've probably read about 'the inquest' on the Roses match [Bramall Lane, May 27, 29, 30, Yorkshire lost by 14 runs] so I won't say anything about it because it would take too long. Actually I didn't know I was playing until dinner time on the day before the match and it nearly got into a mess.

By the way when are you coming back or aren't you? I wouldn't if I were you by what your mum's been telling me. Anyway there's lots to tell you when you do.

....After the Roses match Len gave me a lift right into Leeds and I just had about half-an-hour to go and 'bust myself with grub' at Jaconelli's and then I caught the 7.30 train back to Darlington.

'Old John' had a lovely supper ready for me and then I went off to a very welcome night's sleep. The rest of that week passed uneventful. On the Wednesday I was thinking of vanishing into Darlington but I thought better of it and just lounged about the gym all day. Then on the Thursday I was off for the whole day playing with Catterick District against Sedbergh PS. We had a smashing day and I was rather disappointed about being given out lbw with my leg 'nearer the square leg umpire than the wickets'. But I ought to have known it was their umpire (teacher) and he probably wanted his wee pupil to have something to talk about.

We had some lovely meals and afterwards in the bus going home we started playing pontoon with two of the officers with us. When we arrived in Catterick they had between them both exactly 5½d. It was ever so funny.

On the Friday I got away and was lucky enough to run across someone I know coming down from Darlington in the car. He only lived at Horsforth so he dropped me at the fountain, not bad!!

On the Saturday we were playing Ossett away, but I had to get up early (9.0am) so I could have a haircut. I needed one because it was practically trailing at my heels and the sergeant major had said something about [it] during the week. I took Alan along with me (to get him out of the way of mum who was going to watch the County match at Bradford) [Yorkshire v Derbyshire, Yorkshire lost by 79 runs] and we went into Leeds to meet Jackie and together we all had lunch at the Lonsdale Cafe. Alan had evidently eaten too much breakfast for he couldn't face all that the waiter put in front of him (not like him).

After lunch Jackie went on to Yeadon and Alan and I went to meet the bus to go to Ossett. The match turned out to be quite a funny match (even though we lost). The wicket was terrible but the bowling was likewise so I thought we hadn't much to worry about. The other lads however got themselves out and it came to my turn. At the time a slow left-arm bowler was bowling. He started by throwing the first five down the legside and spinning (trying to) them further away so I was content to sweep him round and collected 16 runs (2x6s). Then came the last ball and the batsman at the other end hadn't been faring well so I thought I'd get a one and pinch the bowling.

Anyway up came his last ball and it was the worst one he'd sent down, about three feet wide on the legside and well pitched up, just asking to be hit for six. But instead I ran out to it and tried to push it for one, mistimed it and the ball hit the back of my bat and bounced

The Miss Broadway competition. Brian is fifth from left, standing

on to the wickets. To make a good job of it they went in and in the first three overs I missed three catches in the slips, all off the same bowler (much to his annoyance) and got no wickets for about 20 runs. What a match. I believe some of the spectators didn't think I was trying. I couldn't have cared less to quote an Army expression.

At night Margery and I went to Broadway and had quite a decent time. Old Harry Paver grabbed hold of me and persuaded me to go and present the prizes in the Miss Broadway competition next Saturday night (what have I let myself in for!!). At least I shall have one consolation in 'kissing' the winners!!

On Sunday I went to Rawdon to play golf and saw your father playing. He topped the only shot I saw him play and it only went just down the hill – he was probably trying to hit it out of sight to 'impress' me.

That night I went back to camp (only to collect my pass) and I was off again the next morning just after 10.0. On Monday night I called down at your house and found out you'd written at last. They were wondering what had happened to you and were thinking of phoning through to Ireland.

Next morning I was up early to pack up and catch the 10.0 train to Cardiff. It was a horribly slow journey and I was glad when we finally arrived in Cardiff just after 6.0. I got a taxi to the hotel and went straight to the bathroom to clean myself up a little. It's quite a nice hotel and we have had some really marvellous meals.

We all crowded into the lounge to listen to the 'Big' fight and to hear my 2/6 go down the drain (your Pa'll gloat over the half crown, he'll probably frame it).

Well my luck seems to be carrying on (run out for 10). I've never heard the last of the run out v. Lancs., Brian Sellers 'had me on the carpet'.

Well I don't know anything else I can write about so I'll close now, Cheerio and Good Luck.

Yours

Brian

PS: 'Enjoy yourself, Enjoy yourself' that's the song Lee Savold [heavyweight boxer] had played while he was training!! See you soon.

*   *   *

A variety of topics in Brian's letter to John from Catterick and postmarked July 13, 1950. He nips into Sutcliffe's sports shop in Leeds to collect his repaired bats and also get a short sleeve sweater and enjoys nights out with Richmond cricketers. There is a recurrence of sight problems and a headache. He meets the winning jockey in the 1948 Grand National and gains kudos at Catterick for cracking on and leading the way in PT trek.

Catterick
Thursday

Dear John,

Just a few lines to let you know I am going on alright as 'I promised'! Well, it has been rather a wasted week for me up here. I've done hardly anything except answer the phone a few times and arrange for 'some' leave.

How did your 'work' go down Monday, in fact all the week? Have you thought of getting your ticket? I've been thinking of getting mine but they won't give me it!!

On Monday I went shopping into Leeds. I called in at Sutcliffe's and got one of my 'bust' bats back. I also got a short sleeve pullover (Yorkshire) there as well. It'll do fine when its too hot for a sweater and yet I have to wear something to stop me from catching cold after bowling. After that I called up to Headingley to get a postcard to take to the OC to get me off this weekend. Incidentally, it has.

I got back that night and 'Old John' had a lovely supper waiting for me and after eating it I went straight to my room for a good night's rest.

Tuesday was ever so dull except for the time when I went to the SM to get some more leave. He nearly went 'up in the air'. It wasn't half funny! His eyes nearly popped out and he nearly swallowed his teeth. Pity he didn't.

That night someone (a friend) called for me in a car and took me down to The Talbot hotel where we spent the night. It was lovely. I met a lot of the Richmond cricket players and we had a 'real round the table' conference, lots of orange squash and then after nine we had a fish and chip supper in their dining room, and after the supper the chap drove me back again. Before we left they invited me to go again yesterday night to see a cricket match and have a 'bit of a do' afterwards so of course I accepted.

Next night the same chap called for me at six and we went down to the ground to watch the match. I enjoyed it immensely. I laughed my head off at some of their antics and comments (I hope they weren't annoyed) and I met a few of the jockeys from the Middleham stable who are regular visitors in Richmond. Among them was Arthur Thompson who rode Sheila's Cottage when she won the National [1948, 66-1]. He was a grand chap to talk to. I also got invited to a 21st party in the town on the 27th – if I'm here at that time.

Anyway that night we went to The Talbot again and got swamped in fish and chips and orange squash, enough that my eyesight started going blurred and my head ached like 'hell'. Don't jump to conclusions, I only had orange. I think it must have been the smoky atmosphere!

Today, all our squadron has been on the range and left me 'all alone'. The QMSI [Quartermaster Sergeant Instructor] saw me and asked me if I wanted some exercise so I told him 'yes if it didn't mean work' (I don't think). Anyway he set me and another lad taking 2 Squadron on their PE test of five miles in one hour. Well of course we started all in step, us at the back, and after about two miles we were straggling all over the place. Sergeants, corporals and 'the lot' (no recruits, just permanent staff) – we were still at the back. Anyway I thought it was about time we got cracking so we lengthened our stride a bit.

At the end I finished first, about quarter of a mile in front of my friend and the rest just strolling in. It's the first time I've done any 'work' since I came here, and the other PTIs used to pull my leg about it but since I did it in record time (58) it's knocked their smiles to the other side of their faces. 'He who laughs last, laughs longest!!'

Anyway I shall have to close now so I can catch the post (touch wood). So Cheerio and Good Luck.

Yours

Brian

See you Friday.

Throughout his long career, Brian and controversy were invariably close companions and so it was in late summer when he first heard the news of his selection for the MCC's winter tour of Australia. He was on a charge at Catterick through not having played in a weekend cricket match – he claims he was given permission not to play – and he then further disobeyed orders not to leave Camp by going to Sandes Home for lunch and tea. It was while there that the CO at Catterick rang the guard room instructing Brian to be sent to meet an officer working for the Catterick Express who had news of his selection. The sequence of events is Brian's own version as described to John at the time. He says he won't go to Australia unless it is agreed his time there is part of his National Service.

Dear John,

Thanks very much for your telegram which I received yesterday morning. It's been quite an active few days, at least since Monday, what with CB charges and interviews. I haven't known whether I've been stood on my ---- or my ---- .

When I got to Camp on Monday I found I was on a charge for not playing in the cricket match the week-end before the one that had just gone. I had a good explanation and proof that I'd been told I needn't play but he didn't take any notice of me and gave me seven days CB [Confined to Barracks]. I had to report to the guard room to hear what was the programme for it and then I went back to the gymnasium feeling sick. It was an awful sensation to feel that I couldn't leave camp until next Sunday night.

Anyway, I broke that rule at the dinner time to go down to Sandes Home and have lunch. That was all right but when I went down for tea I ran into more trouble because while I was away from 4.30 to 5.30 the CO rang to the guard room to tell them to get me to the guard room by 5.30 to meet a certain officer who works for the Catterick Express.

Anyway, they found I was down at Sandes Home and so I'd dropped another 'clanger'. Nothing was said when I got back and when I'd donned my FSMO [Full Service Marching Order is the equipment carried by an infantryman] (It wasn't half a weight) I went down for the first parade at 6 o'clock. This was the time when I first heard the news when I met Mr. Child. I was terrifically pleased and he told me to dump my kit somewhere and come with him to his house where he had to make loads of phone calls to all the newspapers.

We did this and then went down to the NAAFI club to have a few photographs taken and also, of course, to have a drink or two. We finished all this quite early and Mr. Child said 'Go and enjoy yourself now, I've got you off CB until tomorrow night', so off I went down to Richmond to see my friends. I had a lovely time and we finished off with a very appetising supper – fish and chips. Afterwards they drove me up to Sandes where I had decided to stay the night because I hadn't to go on the 6.15am parade. That night I tasted my last (for a while at least) of a nice spring bed. These Army beds don't half feel hard compared to it.

The next day, Tuesday, I found myself on CO's orders but it wasn't much – just to tell me that as I was on CB my cricket at Ampleforth etc had been cancelled. I came straight out and the adjutant called me in to talk with him about this tour business and also about this CB. He asked me how I got on it and I told him everything about the 'case' to which he was very sympathetic but said he couldn't do anything about it so he advised me just to do my CB and have done with it, then he would organise my leave as soon as anything is done.

We chatted about it in general and I told him that I certainly wouldn't accept the invitation if the time off wasn't going to count as service. I've been considering it all and I think it far more valuable for me not to miss another season with Yorkshire than go to Australia and have six months service added on. .... Another thing, if they don't think it more important for me to go to Australia with the English team than to stay here in the gym doing nothing, well that's their fault and probably the newspapers will give them such a 'hiding'.

And besides I shall be doing more for England out there than I ever will do here. After I had been into the adjutant I was told I was on another charge, this one for being down at Sandes Home at 5.0pm on Monday when the CO rang for me.

I just felt like doing away with myself there and then but it wasn't needed. I had quite a reasonable excuse which he accepted and he admonished. Straight afterwards he asked the SM to send me in for a private talk and this time he seemed quite human (for once). He congratulated me and then urged me to go steady from now onwards. He told me that he couldn't help but give me the CB because it had been authorised by the brigade major at STC Headquarters and then told me to come and see him the moment I came off CB to get leave to get myself ready for the tour (if I go).

Well, so much for that. My CB is going on 'damn' well. I get off of all the work and the worst is having to sleep in the Camp so that I can report in FSMO at 6.15am at the guard room. I'm well in with all the RP staff now and after 10 o'clock at night I go down to Sandes for supper – my only meal. I don't eat anything other than that – at least till Sunday night when I come off. It's just about done my Bank Holiday in for me but I'm hoping to come home Monday, all being well.

How are you going on at home? I haven't heard anything from home and I don't know which ward my mother is in so I can't write to her. She will have to wait until I get home.

Well, I don't think I can say anything else for the time being but I'm going to see the adjutant this morning to find out the position about it.

So Cheerio and Good Luck. See you soon.

Yours

Brian

PS: I was right when I selected my team for Australia at your house wasn't I? Ask your father if I have to work my passage now!!

*   *   *

This is Brian's last letter of the summer, addressed to John, on holiday at the Waverley Hotel, Skegness, and postmarked September 6, 1950. Unfortunately it is incomplete and the first page to have survived is detailing the match at Lord's on August 30-31 in which Brian was playing for the Army against the RAF. There was no play on the second day because of rain. It goes on to say that he has visited Slazengers at Horbury to get fixed up with cricket gear for the tour and has been promised a set of golf clubs to pick up in Australia. Also in his diary before leaving for Australia is an appointment with Rugby League's Eddie Waring. His letter reads:

.....and batted very well but was rather fortunate in being missed a few times, once on the first ball. I went in and got 25, never lifted the ball once and just as I was getting settled (I'd been in an hour) he sent me a long hop which I tried to hook and got caught right on the boundary. What luck!

At the other end, Sid [Smith, 151 not out] was lifting every other ball but they either fell short or at the side of the fielders and then when I did lift one I would have to hit it down someone's throat. The anguishing part about it was the short boundary and if I had got hold of it, it would have probably gone over 'Father Time'.

Anyway, we didn't have to bowl much [Close 12-5-14-0] as it was raining most of the second day and Jackie Wainwright, who had been playing for the RAF, and myself got away and caught the 5.0pm Pullman up to Leeds.

The following day (Friday) I had to be back at Camp to see the adjutant to see what was going to happen to my kit. He said I had to hand in all my kit and get a fresh lot when I come back, but I told him that all my kit was at home and finally, after a little persuasion, he let me keep everything. Mind you, that meant take it all home, so I packed all my stuff up and trailed down to Sandes. Here I had tea and then called down to Richmond to fix things up for the 10th and to say goodbye to a few friends. George, one of my friends, offered to take me and my kit down to Catterick village where I catch the bus – and as my luggage was a little too heavy for me to think of carrying it about, I didn't refuse.

No sooner had we got out of the car at Catterick than a friend of mine from Pudsey passed in a car and told me to 'bung' my stuff in the back with 'all the rest of the stuff' (two girls) and he took me right home.

On Saturday, we managed to win a match for once – against Castleford. I managed to get four wickets for two runs in eight overs, so I didn't do so badly. They kept pulling my leg about 'It was a pity it was the last match as I'd only just started'. At night I went to Broadway, probably for the last time before going to Australia, because this Saturday I shan't be coming home until late from [unreadable].

Sunday, I spent all day answering letters and correspondence regarding the tour as our match at Roundhay was cancelled.

Brian with his mother – reading of his selection for the Ashes Tour – and saying farewell to happy neighbours before leaving for Australia

On Monday, I had a lovely day. In the morning I went shopping in Leeds and got quite a few things, then in the afternoon I made a trip out to Wakefield and then to Horbury to have a look round Slazengers factory. It's a wonderful place, well planned out, lots of room and exceptionally clean.

Mr. McNab, the sales manager, took me round every department and told me if I saw anything I wanted I'd to get it or ask for it. We went through the cricket, football, tennis, golf and ball departments. I watched people make golf clubs, tennis and all kinds of racquets. If I'd have had enough cheek I'd have got one of everything and set up a sports shop but I'd only come to get fixed up for the tour, not for 'life'. I did get a smashing pair of pads, five bats and two pairs of batting gloves and numerous small items but the best thing of the lot – he is arranging for me to get a matched set of golf clubs (Bobby Locke's) from their factory in Sydney to save me the bother of taking mine out.

Before I left, we had tea and he gave me a letter of introduction to the factory salesman in Sydney and then said that when I get home they would be very glad if I would call in for a whole day and he would be able to go over the factory more fully.

Well, I enjoyed myself immensely, some of the methods of producing and testing were really marvellous, especially the one testing bowls for crown and flat greens. It was really ingenious.

All my stuff has come from Brown Muff's [A Bradford store] now so I can get cracking with all my other stuff, but there's still a few things to come from Simpsons etc.

About Monday night, I don't think I shall be able to see you as I have an appointment with Eddie Waring, the chap who has been managing the Rugby League tour in Australia. It's about something to do with the Radio out in Australia (he did quite a lot of commentating for the two wavelengths out there) and also he's going to let me have the gen on Australia, give me a few addresses and places to get things from, including several wealthy people 'with lovely daughters' so I shall be all right!

On Tuesday, I shall probably be working all day – I've got to have my jabs on Tuesday afternoon – so when you can, come up to Yeadon and call in, then if I have enough time perhaps we'll make a trip down to your house. Mum's going down to London on Tuesday morning and I shall meet her on the Thursday morning at the station.

Well, I can't tell you how much I'm looking forward to next Thursday – it doesn't seem real – I only hope it doesn't pass quickly.

One of the things I've got to do before I go out is to just make sure of my driving as the Australians are very fond of loaning out their cars while we're staying in their district, so I'm told. Practically everyone in the Rugby League team had one loaned to them while they were over there. Another thing, we have been offered 200 cigarettes a week by a firm over there, so I shan't do so bad selling them will I!!

Well, I suppose I've said enough and I want to get some work done, so I'd better close soon.

Are you having a nice holiday? How's the weather down there? It's been pretty lousy up here so unless yours has been different I can't picture you all coming back 'a different colour'.

Anyway, Cheerio and Good Luck, See you Tuesday

Yours,

Brian

CHAPTER EIGHT

OCTOBER 4 – OCTOBER 15, 1950

AUSTRALIA BOUND

Australia-bound on the Stratheden – Having a 'smashing time' and enjoying the journey – Autograph-signing sessions, swimming and running – Shuns alcohol, apart from Champagne – Cocktail parties – Sailing the Suez Canal – Souvenirs in Aden – Cricket in Colombo – Slip machine practice – Escorts a 'charming and intelligent' New Zealander – Prizes on the dance floor – Wins at 'horse racing' – Arrives in Fremantle to welcoming crowds – Civic reception – First real practice – A letter from Norman Yardley

Barely a week after writing his previous letter to John in Skegness, Brian was leaving Tilbury on September 14, 1950, on his way to Australia after a summer of very little meaningful cricket.

The party that sailed on the Stratheden was comprised of:
F.R. Brown (Northants, captain),
D.C.S. Compton (Middlesex),
R.T. Simpson (Nottinghamshire),
T. E. Bailey (Essex),
J.G. Dewes (Middlesex),
D.S. Sheppard (Sussex),
J.J. Warr (Middlesex),
L. Hutton (Yorkshire),
D.B. Close (Yorkshire),
A.V. Bedser (Surrey),
W.E. Hollies (Warwickshire),

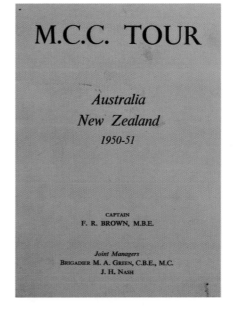

M.C.C. TOUR

Australia
New Zealand
1950-51

CAPTAIN
F. R. BROWN, M.B.E.

Joint Managers
BRIGADIER M. A. GREEN, C.B.E., M.C.
J. H. NASH

Official tour itinerary produced by MCC for Tourists and Management staff

D.V.P. Wright (Kent),
A.J.W. McIntyre (Surrey),
T.G. Evans (Kent),
R. Berry (Lancashire)
W.G.A. Parkhouse (Glamorgan).
Brigadier M.A. Green and Yorkshire secretary, John Nash, were joint managers.
C. Washbrook (Lancashire) flew out to join the team later.

History shows that as far as the cricket was concerned, Close had a wretched time of it, playing in only one Test after making an early century and then being plagued by a serious groin injury. Close himself would often write or refer to his miserable time Down Under but for the first time it can now be revealed, through his letters to John, that this was certainly not the case off the field. England's youngest Test player had a whale of a time socially and no wonder. Here was a teenager, feted and dined, who was experiencing a new and wonderful world after his austere upbringing in the years following the end of the war.

Brian's first letter to John was begun on October 4 and postmarked Perth, October 9.

Dear John,

Well I guess it's about time I wrote to you before we arrive in Australia. I've only written one letter so far and that was to my mum and dad just before we arrived in Colombo last Saturday.

Well John, I've been having a smashing time so far and everything points to an even better one when we land. We've met some very nice people while we've been on the boat and although many of us are getting slightly bored with the long journey, myself I wish it could go on for another few weeks.

We're on the go almost every minute of the day and have hardly a second to rest, even at night. Usually our day is filled up like this. First we get up at about 8.0am and go for a swim before breakfast to work up an appetite. Then at 9.0am we go down to the dining room for breakfast. The meals are absolutely smashing, as much as you want and lots of things to choose from. It's nothing to have four eggs or more for breakfast, two or three steaks for lunch and

One of the countless items of memorabilia signed by the Tourists during their daily "Autograph Hour" sessions on board Stratheden.

then at dinner we usually go "right through" the menu.

After breakfast, all the team have to assemble in the children's dining room every day for the "Autograph Hour". We have to do hundreds a day and pity the poor chap who misses a day. The next time he comes he has a very neat pile of post cards etc. waiting for him in the corner. After this we go to our cabins to change into shorts or swimming trunks and go up onto the sports deck where we either have a swim or play a game or two. The water is lovely and cool and after a game of deck tennis which is very strenuous

we are so hot and covered in sweat we just have to go and have a
dip. Occasionally we go down to C deck for a run and I've managed
to pull my time for the mile well below five minutes (the mile is
seven times around the deck house).

We have lunch at 1.30pm and then after coffee in the lounge we
go (or at least I do) on to the sports deck again. The others go down
for a snooze to their cabins to make up for what they have missed
the night before! Tea is at 4.15pm but I never go down for it – I'm
too busy.

We play games or swim until about 6.0pm when the sun goes
down terrifically quickly and leaves everything almost pitch black.
It's funny watching the sun go down. From the time the sun
touches the horizon to when it disappears completely it only takes
two or three minutes but in that time the colour of the sky is most
wonderful. It changes from a lovely shade of blue to yellow, then to
orange and finally to a deep red. It's beautiful to watch and if there
are any clouds around they reflect the sun to you long after the sun
has gone down.

After the sun has gone down we usually sit up on the deck and
talk or go down to the lounge for a drink.

We have dinner at 8.0pm at the second sitting and this meal is the best of the day. We each take it in turns to buy wine, but I don't drink the b- stuff except when we have champagne. We had some last night and it was lovely. The gas in it seems to make it more refreshing and a much better taste.

After dinner, in the way of entertainment we have dances three times a week, which are very popular!! And on the other nights we arrange all kinds of games.

One night we had a horse race meeting. A great circular track around the dance floor with squares all round it and the six horses move around it with the throw of a dice. Well Godfrey [Evans] and Denis [Compton] started out as bookmakers and were in such a mess after the first race that I came and helped them out with the book and the odds on the gee gees, we had some marvellous fun. We started off with about £20 and at the end of the night were about £10 in hand!! Some fun!

We have been to lots of cocktail parties, almost one every other night to which we have been invited, and we have another one

Brian, right, and team-mates practice catching on the cradle

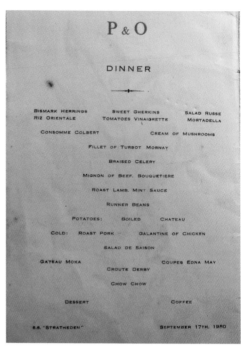

The front and middle of the dinner menu on board ship for September 17, 1950, and the back of the menu which is signed by every member of the MCC team and the joint managers

tomorrow evening before dinner. The only thing I have against them is that you all stand up to talk and drink. The players gave their cocktail party the other night, and we all had to turn out in evening dress with our blazers substituted for our dinner jackets. We looked wonderful (!!!). But we had fun.

When we stopped at Port Said we had a lovely time. We had to go to a cocktail party at 10.0am and I met up with three or four extremely nice girls. They had been educated in England and had come out to live with their parents. After the party they escorted Denis and I round the town and then we went back to the ship for lunch, in time for the ship to leave. They were rather sorry they couldn't come on board, in fact we were, but we said goodbye in the usual fashion! From the side of the ship we carried out some business with the [men] in the boats and got some real bargains. We passed down the Suez and out into the Red Sea and it began to get warmer and warmer until the only place where it was cool was the swimming bath and that was almost boiling – well about 90 degrees.

Passing down the Suez was a marvellous experience. The sight of a convoy of about a dozen ships passing within 100 feet of land was simply wonderful. Cars and trains caught us up and passed us on the road and railway at the side of the canal because our speed was limited to a few knots owing to the wash we made which would soon fetch the banks down. There were some marvellous sights on the way down and we were all very sorry when darkness came down.

Next stop was at Aden where we arrived at the dreadful hour of 1.0am. Even so, almost everyone was still up, ready to go ashore and there was such a rush we didn't get our feet on ground until 3.30am. Aden at this time was lit only by moonlight and the lights of an occasional shop which was open but it was a cloudless night and there was no case of it being too dark. Again, as at Port Said, we bought lots of things for souvenirs. It was a funny sight down the wide main street leading from the docks where loads of the latest American-designed taxis were parked and at the side of them their drivers and families and other people were curled up in the gutter fast asleep with a rag or something round them. Fancy, they owned a £1,500 car and couldn't even afford somewhere to live.

We left Aden before breakfast but hardly any of us turned in as we were too busy telling each other where we have been and what we had got.

After Aden we came to Colombo where we have to play a game. In the morning we all went round on a tour of the town by car and then at 10.30am we assembled at The Oval. It was a lovely ground with a marvellous wicket and we all enjoyed ourselves, even though the match was a draw. After the match we all went to the Grand Oriental Hotel where a cocktail party was being given for us. We were a tired lot so we didn't stay long but before we left we were presented with quite a few things, including a Ceylon tie to add to our collection and also most of us promised that if we called here on the way back we would look some of our friends up and they would show us the island. This was definitely the best place to which we had called and most of us were rather disappointed that we hadn't seen more of the island.

Well, I guess I can't think of much more to say or is it the other way round? I have lots more to say but it would almost fill a book so I'd better stop where I can.

How's everyone at home? Tell me all the news that I've missed won't you? I see Arsenal are second at the moment and Leeds down in the dumps again.

I might have something to tell you soon about -- yes we'll leave it at that for the time being but 'she' is ever so charming and intelligent!!

Well I must close now after giving such information away so Cheerio and Good Luck.

Yours

Brian

*　　*　　*

Just 11 days later, Brian is writing to John again, this time from the imposing Palace Hotel in Perth where the Tourists are staying.

Dear John,

Thank you very much for your letter which I received yesterday.

I'm glad that you're going on so well. You didn't mention anything about your work. How's that going on?

Well, since I wrote to you last, which was I believe just before arriving in Colombo, a terrific lot has happened to us.

At Colombo we had a marvellous time. First in the morning we were taken by cars on a circular tour around the town, being pointed out the landmarks and places of interest as we passed them, among them being the famous Galle Face Hotel where we stopped for a drink. It's a marvellous hotel with almost a mile of lawns and gardens exhibiting the most luxurious flowers between the hotel and the sandy beach.

Unfortunately we couldn't stay there long as we had to go on to the cricket ground in time for the game. I won't tell you anything of the game because the reports in the papers would have said far more than what I would say, except that it was good to be able to move about and throw a ball about once more. After the game we all went to the Grand Oriental Hotel where a cocktail party was given for us and at which we were presented with a few things, among which was a Ceylon tie to add to my collection of County ties.

Well, even though we had had such a good time there, I went away a little disappointed not having been able to make the trip up through the lovely tea and timber plantations to Mount Lavinia. Everyone who had been there during the day said it was a marvellous trip. Actually it is about 60 or 70 miles away from the port and anyone who went there had to have a full day at their disposal. After leaving Colombo things began to move quickly, we had a lot of practice on the slip machine in readiness for the tour, to harden our hands and get them used to the hard ball again.

On one of the nights I saw the picture 'The Third Man'. It was good and had me spellbound, enough so that I couldn't pay any attention to the person sat next to me!! The first half hour was a little difficult to understand owing to there being a fault in the soundtrack.

I believe I said I would tell you more about the girl I met on the boat. Well, her name is Gaye Castle and she comes from New Zealand. I didn't get to know her until after Port Said when, after I had "laid my plans", I accidentally made her acquaintance. She is a very charming and intelligent girl and even though she wears glasses she is extremely pretty. We spent hours and hours together and I can say with honesty that I never did anything to her that I wouldn't tell my mother or for that matter anyone else. She is a sports mistress in a grammar school at Wellington where she was a pupil for quite some time. We went to all the dances and other things together and I had become rather attached to her by the time we arrived in Fremantle. She is a wonderful tennis player from the reports of her friends and can dance beautifully. I just wish you could meet her. I am sure you would like her. But then maybe you might some day!!

Towards the end of the voyage we had a grand dance at which the prizes for the various competitions were presented by the MP, Mr Harvey Watts, who was on board. Almost all the men's prizes were won by the team's members and then we started on the statue and elimination dances. We had lots of fun and won three of the four novelty dances which was rather an achievement since Godfrey [Evans] and Trevor Bailey were the judges and were trying like hell to get us out.

The Saturday before arriving in Fremantle the sports committee arranged a race meeting. Each male per person could enter a horse, make up a funny name with a pedigree and nominate a lady or a girl to ride the horse for him. The owners had to pay 12s 6d each to run in the races which were performed by the rider standing just over the winning post turning the handle of a wheel and pulling the horse along by means of a length of string. There were six of these machines, all identical, and so we had six heats with six riders each heat and then a final for the winners of the heats to decide the winner of the Stratheden Cup. The ship's stewards also run a tote and we had a bet on races almost as though we were at a real meeting. Gaye was riding my horse "Vanish" by "Scram" out of "Sight" and we managed to win our heat. We went into the final and with great speculation I put all the money I had won already on Gaye and she literally walked away from the rest of the field and won easily. Our total winnings for the night came to about £15 since before the last race I had already backed four out of the six heat winners. I think my study of form for that night was exceptional.

Later we invited all our friends down to our cabins and gave a bit of a party and by the time we had finished we had had just about enough excitement anyone could stand in a day. I think everyone on the ship had enjoyed themselves more that night than on any other night of the voyage, even the fancy dress ball.

We arrived in Fremantle and the first thing we had to do was to pose on the deck for photographs and other items for the Press.

There was a tremendous crowd to welcome us there and after breakfast we all pushed our way through it to the waiting taxis which took us into Perth to our hotel.

First we had to meet the Press representatives and get to know them. This meeting had been planned by the skipper so that it would create a friendly atmosphere between the Press and the team. Everyone thought it was a swell idea.

After the meeting I had arranged to take Gaye off her parents' hands for a while so that I could get her a present for her share in our winning during the racing. They had come into Perth for a few hours whilst the ship was in dock and called at our hotel. Her mother and father stayed in the hotel whilst we had a look round the shops. We hadn't much time but we managed to make a choice out of the many things there were and she was very pleased.

We came back to the hotel where I said Goodbye in the 'usual manner' and as they took their taxi back to Fremantle, about 12 miles away, I dashed into the dining room for dinner. I was very sorry that the voyage had come to an end for it seemed strange to be in a new land. I had enjoyed every minute of the last three weeks or so and I'm sure I behaved myself better on those three weeks then at any time in my life. I don't know, something must be getting at me, because of all the girls I've ever been out with I've been absolutely bored stiff unless I've been 'doing something' but with Gaye it's been entirely different. Now I've got to wait until March before we get to Wellington. Then everything is being laid on for me and also a few other members of the team who were acquainted. Listen, not a murmur of this to anyone!!

The day after we arrived here, three of us went across to the Slazenger agents in Perth and were given the choice of all the golf clubs they had in stock. I chose a new matched set of L.G. von Lida irons and also a matched set of four woods, also his design. They're lovely clubs. Also we were given a sand iron, golf bag and lots of new balls.

We arrived on the Monday morning in Perth and owing to the softness of the wickets due to rain that had fallen before we had arrived the skipper wouldn't allow us to do any real practice so we have to content ourselves with a bit of catching and throwing practice. This of course couldn't go on all day, so we were given the afternoon off which most of us used to polish up our golf. To start with, there were a few frayed tempers walking around, probably due to the rolling of the ship, but after we had had a few rounds we got used to having our feet on firm ground once more. We were given a civic reception at the Town Hall on Tuesday but it was so boring I paid little attention to the speeches which were made. The Australians seemed to have a flair for "lengthy meaningless speeches"!! While we are in Perth we have been invited to go to any of the cinemas or theatres in town and a lot of us have taken advantage of the offer! I've been to the cinema once and to the theatre to see the Ice Follies. The latter was really marvellous and sported some of the best ice skaters in the world.

I've also been to an informal dinner given by the officers of the Australian Corps of Signals Regiment here. I enjoyed myself very much but the conditions for the Australian Forces are far different from ours and I told them so as well.

On the Thursday the skipper declared the wicket fast enough and we had our first real practice of the Tour. The wickets are simply marvellous and batting on them is a treat. Bowling on them isn't so good, though!

Today we were all invited out for the day to a golf club a few miles out of town [Lake Karrinyup Golf (Country) Club]. We had a smashing time, especially when it came to drive over the lake at the 8th hole!

Well I guess I shall have to put an end to the letter somewhere or else I shall never get to sleep.

Write as often as you can won't you and I'll write as often as I can because it's grand to hear what's going on back there. We don't get any news at all of England and the papers, which are about six or seven times as thick as our Sunday papers, are useless. They are full of advertisements. Don't forget, save me all the cuttings to look at when I get back home (if I don't stay in New Zealand)!! It'll be funny reading how badly I've bowled and how many ducks I've got.

Already I'm snowed under with photographs I've collected from the Press photographers so I shall have something to show you when I come back – all being well.

Anyway, Cheerio and Good Luck

Yours

Brian

*   *   *

Waiting for Brian when he first arrived at the Palace Hotel in Perth was an Air Mail letter from his Yorkshire captain, Norman Yardley, which wished him good luck and was full of sound advice. It was sent from Wetherby Gardens, London, SW5, and postmarked September 26, 1950.

Dear Brian,

I was sorry not to see you before you left, hence this letter. I just want to wish you the very best of luck for the tour. It is a wonderful opportunity for a young fellow but whatever else happens you will have a magnificent time and it will be a great experience for you.

As one who has been to Australia may I be permitted to give you a little advice. Success on a tour means getting off to a good start. The skipper has only a short time to get his side settled for the first Test Match. So if you want to be in the running you want to do well from the start.

Bowling in particular needs great concentration in Australia. Except on rare occasions you won't turn the ball and you won't get on sticky wickets as the fast bowlers do more damage, therefore your great asset as a bowler is going to be accuracy which means concentrating on every ball. As soon as you start at the nets practice accuracy.

You'll like the wickets for batting on as they are true and fast and easier to play strokes on than ours. Don't be afraid to hit the ball, it's what we need, but don't throw your wicket away by making silly shots. You can get plenty of runs and quickly without being silly.

You'll have plenty of people to advise you so I won't trouble you any more. Just remember the old Yorkshire saying of "Get stuck in" and I know you'll do well.

Once again the very best of luck to you and I hope you knock hell out of the so and so's.

Yours

Norman Yardley

CHAPTER NINE

NOVEMBER 3 – NOVEMBER 14, 1950

TIME OF HIS LIFE

'Marvellous' win over South Australia – Brian acts as runner in big stand – Bradman confounded – Golf on Australian Open course – Arthur Askey invite to show – Sees cine of voyage to Australia – Cashing in at snooker – Prime Minister's speech at Melbourne reception – Meets Woodfull, Ponsford and McCabe – Invited back stage at theatre – Watches Melbourne Cup and picks the winner – On to Sydney and a motor cycle escort – an invitation to go shark fishing

Unless an earlier letter has not been saved, Brian's next correspondence with John is postmarked November 3 and written on Victorian Cricket Association notepaper. It is penned while he is waiting to go out to bat in the first innings against Victoria. There appears to be more pressing things to write about now than Brian's only century of the Tour – 108 not out in the drawn match against Western Australia at Perth which ended on October 24.

Dear John,

Thank you very much for your letter which I received yesterday. I'm very glad to hear you're all going on ok and always glad to read about anything which is happening in dear old England because we hear b..... all out here. The newspapers are about six inches thick but are full of anything but news.

Well, we finished up in Adelaide very well by beating South Australia. It was marvellous to watch. Unfortunately I couldn't as I had to run for Reg [Simpson] when he pulled a groin muscle. I was due in next but I'd nearly run myself "out" running fours and threes, so the skipper called me in when Reg was out and went in himself. But this earlier attack was nothing like the last five minutes when Godfrey [Evans] let loose at everything and scored five fours off successive balls. At the beginning of our last innings Don Bradman told the skipper we shouldn't win when we had to get 185 in 105 minutes on a lousy wicket. Lousy because the ball wouldn't bounce up onto the bat but only kept very low. It was so bad that the scoring rate had never got higher than 45 at any part of the match. Anyway, it was a wonderful performance and the skipper was tremendously pleased about it.

While at Adelaide we played golf at the Kooyonga Golf Course, the course on which the Australian Open was played this year. It was a smashing course and Bobby Locke himself said that it would be one of the most difficult courses in the world if it were a few yards longer. We had a smashing time last Sunday when we went out and Len [Hutton] and I played the professional and another young lad. At lunch time we went to this young lad's house for dinner (yes he's married) and we had a lovely meal. After lunch we went to his father-in-law's for a drink and the house was really marvellous (it ought to be, he's a bookmaker), in fact all the houses in Australia are. With every one, there's always a lovely view both back and front for, unlike in England, space is no object for them and also the gardens are simply marvellous.

One of the nights we were there, we were all invited out by Arthur Askey to see his show 'The Love Racket'. It was marvellous and some of the cracks he made about us nearly had us toppling out of the boxes which he had reserved for us. Whether he turned the heat on for us I don't know, but every one of us came away thinking it was the best show we had ever seen, even better than 'Nights of Madness' which we saw at the Victoria Palace in London before we left. The supporting cast wasn't so good, the chorus were all out of step when they appeared, but there were three leading ladies who weren't so bad!! Arthur said they were especially hand-picked (!!) from the Windmill Theatre. After the show, a few of us went backstage to Arthur's room where we had a drink and (trust him!) he brought the young girls in to meet us. When we finally left for our hotel it must have been nearly midnight but we had thoroughly enjoyed ourselves and were glad in a way (!!) that we hadn't to play cricket the following day.

Another place where we went, which was worth noting, was when a gentleman who had travelled with us on the Stratheden invited four of us to go out to his house for dinner and a night out. Arthur, Bob, Eric and myself went straight after the cricket last Monday and we had a marvellous time. The dinner couldn't have been bettered, then he gave a show of the cine films which he had taken on his trip to England. They were very good and it was a change to see the English countryside once more. He also had a few films which he had taken on the boat journey, including some very fine snaps of myself playing deck tennis and one or two of me sitting writing my diary up with a very studious frown upon my face! Oh! And there was one of me in the swimming bath showing everyone scattering as I came to swim. I used to wage a war with everyone in the water, often with about four or more at once, but I always came off best. I'd have been drowned (!) if I had relaxed for a second while I was swimming. They all used to stand on the edge waiting for me to turn my back on them!! Anyway, getting back to this chap's house. We went into another part of his house, separate from the living part of the house, where he had a big garage for his motor boat (a terrific one) and also a games room in which he had a billiard table, tennis table and places to play loads of games, skittles, quoits etc. It was a marvellous place. We started by playing table tennis but then we had a game of snooker and finally finished up playing American pool. This was very good but not being a snooker fan I won't waste space describing it to you and Mervyn and myself walked the board with it. We each won four and Arthur one. Anyway it was quite a profitable evening, especially as I won the last one when the stakes were high and after a lovely supper he drove us back to our hotel. We had thoroughly enjoyed ourselves.

We left Adelaide at 5.30a.m. last Wednesday (what an hour!) and drove to the Parafield Aerodrome where we boarded the plane for Melbourne. The flight was a good one until we started to descend when we ran into some b.... awful weather. On the way we had a marvellous view of the countryside. It was beautiful but as we neared Melbourne we started to rock about a bit. We kidded old Bob on telling him the wings were dropping off (he is a bad flyer) and by gum we nearly convinced ourselves!!

As soon as we got to our hotel we had our breakfast ready for us – I think we needed it too. Have you ever travelled over 500 miles before breakfast? We bolted our breakfast down and just had time to have a wash before we went into the civic reception which, fortunately for us, was next door to the dining room and not at the

Town Hall as we had been at the previous places.

We had as speakers Mr Menzies, the Prime Minister, and lots of other "notorieties" and the speech which Mr Menzies gave was wonderful. He described himself as the most one-eyed cricket fanatic in the world. Afterwards we met him and chatted with him for a while. He is a very nice chap. We also met various members of the Victorian side.

In the afternoon after lunch – an enormous one at that – I could hardly move so I went to bed. I got up just before 6pm, just in time to get dressed and be down for the taxis which had come to take us to a buffet dinner given by the Sporting Globe. I was just in time for the last taxi, like a few more of us, or else we should have been 'fined' half-a-crown for being late at an official function (one of the many 'rules' of the '1950-51 Club').

It was very enjoyable and Bill Bowes introduced me to most of the old Australian players, Bill Woodfull, [Bill] Ponsford and [Stan] McCabe etc. I got talking to a gentleman who owns the biggest sports goods warehouse and manufacturing business in Melbourne and he invited me to have a look round it the following day so I accepted.

After the buffet dinner had died down a little Bill and I went out to the Comedy Theatre where we saw 'Worm's Eye View'. It was smashing and we nearly died with laughing. During the interval we were told to go across to His Majesty's Theatre for a drink with the managers so off we went round. You know, all the theatres and cinemas have been thrown open to us all the while we're here so the next night I went to His Majesty's to see the musical play 'The Song of Norway'. I don't know whether you've seen this in England or not but it's a really fine play of the life story of Edvard Grieg the Norwegian composer and the show finished up with his piano concerto being played. It was ever so good. At the end of the show I went backstage to thank the manager and I was introduced to Charles Durning, the principal actor in the play. He introduced me to several of the principal actresses and some of the more beautiful chorus girls and I finished up being escorted back to my hotel by two girls at an awful hour (midnight). Unfortunately the skipper saw me slip into the hotel and gave me a nasty look. We were playing Victoria next day or rather today.

Well at the moment we've been rained off and I'm just debating whether to go and play Solo or not. So I will finish the letter off because I haven't much more to write, only that Len [Hutton] and Cyril [Washbrook] are out. Len's lbw, according to everyone, was "nowhere near" but we aren't in a bad position, being 142-2.

Well, I'll close now, so Cheerio and Good Luck. Write soon and tell me all about what's happening won't you?

Yours always

Brian

* * *

By his own admission, Brian wrote letters to many other people as well as John during this early period of his career and sometimes he appears to refer to events that he has already written about in a previous letter. It seems quite likely that Brian thought he had lost the previous letter to John dated November 3 when he had actually posted it because his next letter, dated November 14 and postmarked November 22, starts off with events he has already described. These have been omitted from this correspondence.

Dear John,

I'm just about 'bloody' fed up!! I started writing to you a day or two ago [probably well before that] and I've gone and lost the whole damn lot. Oh! I could murder myself and now I've got the laborious job to do again and write the whole six pages of it.

Well John, excuse me for a while, I'm in a raging mood, but I'll soon work round. It's a unique way of opening a letter don't you think?!! But now we'll get back to some more conventional sort of language for a letter.

Anyway, thank you so much for your two letters, one which I received last week which I was answering, and one which arrived this morning.

.......On the Tuesday we had a day off from cricket and we all were invited to attend the Melbourne Cup, the Australian counterpart to the Derby. All Melbourne is given a holiday for this and by the size of the crowd 'all Australia' were given one. We were given tips for a few races but not one came up. The first race we had been told to back a horse called Promise You but unfortunately it got baulked and it ran second. We won a few shillings on that because we had backed it each way.

We couldn't bet on the next race because we had to have lunch in the committee room with all the rest of the officials. There were champagne, cocktails, oysters and a most wonderful meal (I enjoyed the meal not the liquor). Afterwards we all dashed out to place our bets on 'The Cup'. I had been given a tip for Alister by an owner when I first arrived in Melbourne at the reception. It had won the Melbourne Derby easily in its last race a week ago, so I backed it for a win. It was favourite so I looked for another to back each way and I picked Connie Court who was said to be the best horse in Australia but was carrying top weight in a 'weight for age' race and there was some talk of it not staying two miles as it had never run more that a mile-and-a-half before. Anyway, I had a "small bet" on him at 30-1.

When they paraded before the race started it was a marvellous sight. My two horses, Alister and Connie Court were easily the best two looking horses in the race (good 'form' picker!!) and the way they held themselves took them head and shoulders out of the rest of them.

Alister was a lovely chestnut while C.C. was dark brown and the sun dazzled you as it was reflected off its glistening body. Anyway, the race began with Connie Court pulling away in the first furlong or two, the rest crowding in a bunch just behind. As they came up to the Post for the first time (where we were sat) C.C. had dropped back a little into third place, Alister being in the centre a few lengths behind. This proved to be its downfall because the race was an extremely hard fought race with everyone trying. The horse in front of Alister fell and he ran into him and nearly fell over as well. However, he recovered but had lost so much ground he just couldn't make it.

Anyway, getting back to the race. The horses completed one mile with them all fighting it out, C.C. still about third and if I remember Saxone last (trust a horse with that name to be last). They came to the half mile post and all of a sudden C. Court burst out of the pack, grabbed the lead and going like a thunderbolt charged into the straight. In the straight it just lengthened its stride and away it went, winning by four lengths pulling up to Chiquita.

Alister came fourth.

It was a marvellous thrill and it made my flesh go up in goose pimples as the crowd cheered it past the post and an even bigger cheer when the time was announced – an Australasian record over two miles and at top weight too.

I didn't dash away to rob the bookmaker of my winnings straight away. I stayed and watched it being led into the winners paddock and its owner being presented with the Cup. Oh! I could have given it a lovely big kiss (!!) then – it had won me £20. I went away that night feeling very satisfied with myself.

Later we, or rather a few of us, changed into Evening Dress and went along to the Oriental Hotel (one of the best in Melbourne) where a party was given for us by a girl who had travelled with us on the Stratheden. Her father owns almost 'everything' in Melbourne and he's one of the richest people in Australia and 'there's some mighty rich folk in Australia'.

We had a smashing time, a lovely dinner, dancing, lots of nice girls and I was rather lucky – I chose 'one' who was staying at the hotel for the night and I didn't leave until about 2.30am when everyone in the hotel were fast asleep, including the 'Hosts'.

The next day we finished off the match against Victoria – somewhat jaded no doubt, and at night I went out to this gentleman's house and spent it quietly.

I think that takes us up to Sydney I believe. Oh! Before I forget. On the Sunday we had a day out at the Royal Melbourne Golf Club and it was smashing. It was a lovely course and Denis [Compton] and I, who were playing with each other lost our game at the 18th. He didn't have a good day. The following day, Monday, the whole team went out to a cocktail party given by the UK Liaison Staff headed by Major General Castle (the youngest General in the British Army). He was a very nice and likeable fellow and I spent quite a lot of time chatting to him.

Well, we're on our way to Sydney now, to the 'New York of Australia'. I say New York because it all seems so American in its ideas, shops, etc., but in buildings it represents London more than N.Y. (just a matter of a few storeys out!!).

We arrived by plane early last Thursday morning and found cars and even a motor-cycle escort to take us to our hotel. It was really funny sitting back in the cars and watching the police open up the crowded traffic for us as we drove on. In Australia the car ratio to its population is 1 to 7 so you can tell what the streets of Sydney are like. The escort would turn on their sirens and make a hell of a noise as we were approaching all the big crossroads so that the policemen would stop the traffic and let us through. It was very impressive. We found a terrific crowd at the hotel when we arrived and to get in we almost had to fight. However, we soon got settled in.

In Sydney we did all kinds of things, went to nightclubs, out to people's houses, pictures and shows. I can't give them to you in order but I'll try and describe them to you. The nightclub we went to was 'Christies' and it was a lovely place. The manager had invited us all here, everything on the house and we started with a tremendous meal which took us from 7.30pm to 10.0 o'clock to finish. Of course we danced in between the courses – lots of 'champers' or rather champagne and, of course, orange squash. We had a big long table right opposite the dance orchestra and we claimed (for the night) the attention of the girls in the show which was put on, and also the girls who were sat with us making up the party. We didn't half have fun.

One of the turns was a Hollywood Square Dance where the 'girls' came to the dining tables and picked someone out and took them back on to the floor to perform the dance. Trust me, I got bagged but it was fun. Another one was when the girls split up again and got partners and did a 'novelty dance' with a lemon pressed between the partners' foreheads. It was funny dancing quicksteps, foxtrots, waltzes, sambas, and lots of others I'd never heard of, without using our arms too! You just had to keep pressing as hard as you can so the lemon wouldn't slip. My luck was in and my partner and I won for which she was rewarded with a lovely box of chocolates, and poor old me a great big bottle of beer which I let the lads at the table dispose of!! Draw your own conclusions what happened after that!!

I went to see two films, 'Let's Dance', starring Fred Astaire and Betty Hutton and 'Captain Blood'. They were quite good and I enjoyed them very much.

On Sunday, I went out with Bill Bowes to an old Yorkshireman's house (from Halifax). He's almost a millionaire and has three beautiful houses, one in the country, one at Palm Beach (Florida of Australia) and the one in Rose Bay, Sydney Harbour, which we went to. It's a lovely place, right on the shore, with a bathing pool in its garden, a nice little yacht in a shed at the bottom and he even has

The MCC Christmas card which Brian sent to John. It was one of about 60 which he posted

To John,
with All Good Wishes
for
Christmas and the New Year
"Happy Hunting for 1951"
Brian

his own oyster bed in a little creek. I nearly cut myself to ribbons picking them, but at the end I was quite expert with them, and at opening them, too.

Next time we go back to Sydney, this man, Alan Turner, he's going to organise a trip out to Palm Beach, about 40 miles away, and go shark fishing on his big yacht. It's supposed to be one of the biggest and best yachts in Australia. Anyway, we're assured of a marvellous day out even if we don't catch any sharks. Oh! if only these waters weren't infested with sharks, they would be smashing, but now when you go in there's always that thought in your mind that a shark is going to sneak up from behind and grab a leg – how delightful!

Well, I guess that's about all I can tell you for the present. If I did tell you all what we do and who we meet it would fill a book nearly and I'm sure nine or ten pages is long enough for a letter.

By the way, I've just sent off the Xmas cards (about 60 in all) and a few food parcels. Tell your mother to accept hers as a Xmas present to you all and I hope you enjoy it. It should be arriving a few days after this letter reaches you but don't say a word until it arrives.

By the way, would you thank Margery for her letter for me and tell her I will drop her a line shortly when we have a 'rainy day' and at the moment we're having quite a bit of that too. (The rainfall is supposed to be a record for Australia this year and there's over a month to go yet – they have had over 90 inches so far.) But you know we still get a 'little peep' at the sun now and then!! My little turned-up nose is almost burned off!!

You asked about Gaye. Well, it is short for Gabrielle and for your information my intentions are strictly honourable, in fact very honourable. I've heard from her two or three times since we last saw each other in Perth and we're both looking forward to our stay in New Zealand.

Well, John, it's about time I closed the 'shop' up so 'Au Revoir' and best wishes until next time.

Yours

Brian

I see Leslie Compton finally got 'capped' – none too soon either!! Write soon and tell us all the 'gen'.

CHAPTER TEN

DECEMBER 3, 1950

FUN AND GAMES

Great golf with John Dewes – Bumpy roads in Lismore – Eight in a Chevrolet – Swimming 'scrap' with Bill Bowes – Girls galore at dance – Coach ride through spectacular scenery to a wet Brisbane – Hutton 'set up' at Governor of Queensland's cocktail party – First taste of surfing – 'Skipper's' launch in fishing trip thunderstorm – Detailed description of First Test defeat – Bedser criticised – Hutton's brilliance

MCC are in Brisbane now and there has been plenty of action since Brian's last letter from Newcastle where they played New South Wales Country Team. This was a two-day game as was the match against NSW Northern Districts which followed at Lismore before the party flew on to Brisbane where they played out a rain-hit draw with Queensland. Brian picks up his pen again on December 3, the rest day in the First Test, and over the next few days compiles one of the longest of his letters to John. It is written on Lennons Hotel notepaper and he begins by berating his friend for complaining that he is not writing more often but he is soon his amiable self again as he covers a wide range of topics.

Dear John,

Just a few lines to let you know I'm going on all right. Thanks for your last letter which I received a few days ago, but <u>please</u> don't keep harping on about not writing. I try my best and write as often as I can but I've so much to write about, it takes about three or four days to write a letter and when you are writing to lots of people it takes quite a while before I get round to you again.

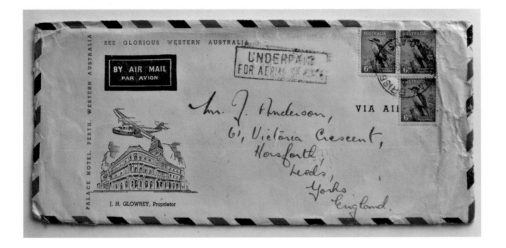

Well, I'll get back to where I left off the last letter at Newcastle.

We had a bit of a grim time there, what with losing on the first innings to a 'Country' side, thanks to a couple of 'extra' men they employed 'behind the stumps'.

After rain had stopped play on the first day, four of us went along to the local golf course and had a lovely game. John Dewes and myself played Gilbert Parkhouse and the professional. We finished after nine holes with us 'five up' and later John and I went out to play another nine against each other. We had a lovely game, first he would win a hole, then I'd draw level and then go in front for him to catch me up again. We went right the way round until the last hole when I was left with a 20ft putt to win the game. Well, my nerves cracked and I missed the b- thing and we finished up all square.

At night a lot of us went along to the cinema to see John Mills in 'Morning Departure'. It was quite a good film but 'not in my line'. The following night, after the match, we went to another cinema to see Humphrey Bogart in 'In a Lonely Place'. It was a really marvellous film, in fact one of the best I've seen for a long time. If you haven't already seen the film, I specially recommend a visit to see it if it comes round your way. It's really touching!

We were thankful to leave Newcastle which was a 'dirty little town' with old, rusty, derelict barges and ships rotting on the sides of the river and dirty buildings all over the place – a typical mining town. We left on the Sunday morning by air for Lismore, another country town. It was a lovely trip, following up the coastline and the pilot flew quite low (a few hundred feet) so that we could see the beaches and the scenery along the coast. We flew to about 30 miles short of Lismore then we cut inland to a place called 'Evans Head' where we landed. Here a motor coach came to collect us to take us the other 30 miles (evidently Lismore hadn't got an airport). On the way, we passed through some of the country that had been flooded with the torrential rains they've been having here. All the countryside was lovely and green instead of 'reddish brown' as we'd been led to expect at this time of the year in Queensland. However, to offset the lovely colours, the roads were terrible with holes all over the place and chunks taken away by the floods. They gave us a terrible jolting as we came and by the time we arrived in Lismore my backside was aching like h-.

We got settled down in the hotel, had an early lunch and then most of us went out to the Lismore Golf Club for the afternoon. Oh! We had some fun. The skipper and I were playing two chaps who were members of the Club and managed to hold them to a draw, but one of the chaps had a very peculiar swing and every time he played a shot we nearly laughed ourselves hoarse. He would lift his club miles away from his body, then swing it round behind his head, give it a little 'twiddle' and down it would come. Honest, you would have never thought he'd have 'knocked' the ball off the tee with a swing like that but he hit the ball miles. After the game we had one or two drinks in the bar and then the other man who we'd been playing with took me round the town in his car, showing me the different places of interest. It is a very nice little town, population about 16,000 and its main source of trade lies in its dairy and agricultural farming done round about. It is only 20 miles from the coast where there is one of the best surfing beaches in Australia (so they say). The town is very clean and modern and places of amusement and entertainment are very nice and well organised.

That night after the golf the whole team were invited out to a private dance organised by the cricket association and all the girls who wanted to come had to pass a 'test' by going in front of a Board composed of men from the local cricket council. There were some -- girls there and we had the time of our life. When the band were getting a bit lazy and tired, and our lads who were playing the following day thought a little about the morrow we set off back to our hotel. We piled in a big Chevrolet (about eight of us, four each sex) and someone tried to steer with one hand on the wheel and the other on – well someone's knee!

The following night we had our official dinner at our hotel and we had a marvellous dinner. Your eyes would have popped out at the things we ate, and you'd have probably dropped dead if you'd have seen the menu, indeed, almost any menu at the hotels here. After the dinner, the most we could do was to 'roll' into the lounge, drink and talk. We were absolutely done – we had an early night.

The next morning, after breakfast, Bill Bowes and I went along to the swimming pool for a swim. It's a lovely open air bath with some smashing diving boards and the water was nice and warm. I enjoyed the swim very much and then Bill and I had a ducking fight in which, I'm glad to say, I came off best.

After the game had finished in a draw we all went to a dance at the Town Hall given in our honour – I've never seen as many females in my life (!) – and there were some 'smashers', in fact we had difficulty in choosing who to dance with. As soon as you had 'picked' one girl out as 'decent' enough to dance with another one popped up and so on until our heads were in a whirl. In the end I found myself dancing with the nearest approach to Lana Turner I've ever seen and didn't I have a nice time and finished up by having a cup of coffee in her home at about three o'clock in the morning.

After grabbing a few hours sleep on top of the bed we got up 'early' to pack our things, have breakfast and we were ready for the road. We were given a great send off and then we settled down to a nice long journey by coach to Brisbane. It was quite an interesting ride through the lovely countryside, over the hills and then as we dropped down on to the coast we saw the first signs of sub-tropical Queensland in the pineapple and banana orchards on the side of the hills. We stopped at one or two and got quite a few bunches of bananas and some pineapples. They were lovely and juicy. On our way along the coast we stopped at Coolangatta for a cup of tea, then later at Southport (is called Surfer's Paradise) for lunch. They are beautiful places to spend on holiday with lovely long beaches glistening like gold in the sun and lovely surf to bathe and splash around in.

It took them a long time to round us up to proceed on our journey to Brisbane after we had all split up and gone off in different directions, some on to the beach, some into the shopping centre, but finally we got settled down in the bus and away we went. When we arrived in Brisbane it was tippling down with rain (nothing unusual to us, now) and we almost passed unnoticed except for a few officials who were waiting to welcome us. We were glad of this because until arriving in Brisbane we'd almost had the life pestered out of us. Later that day we had a dinner given by the Queensland Cricket Association with the usual speeches etc.

The hotel we're staying in at the moment is a really marvellous place, the best one we've been to so far. The rooms are really good, clean and well furnished and all are air conditioned and are beautifully cool at night when outside the atmosphere is 'hot and sticky'. The room service is really good too – unlike all the other hotels we've been staying at because they are having all kinds of labour troubles out here with the shortage of men etc. The food is the usual you know – it nearly knocks you over when you get a thick steak or pork chop about an inch thick and leaving no room on your plate for the vegetables. One of our favourite courses here is the mixed grill which contains a thick juicy steak, a lamb cutlet, a pork chop (small), a couple of sausages, an egg and the usual vegetables, chips, tomatoes, peas, etc. It's a sight for sore eyes!

Well, we have been to that many places since we arrived here that I shall have to cut a few and just tell you the outstanding parties. One of the first things we went to was the Governor of Queensland's cocktail party where we met lots of English people. We had a good time and a few of us were talking to the attractive wife of the ADC to the Governor. He was in the Navy and we were telling his wife that Len was a Commander too and saying he was on the Ark Royal in the River Plate fiasco and lots of other sea battles. She was ever so interested and kept trying to go and fetch her husband to introduce him to Len, and Len was getting rather worried! We kept on egging her on and Len kept trying to keep her talking and we got so 'deep into the mire' that we were almost 'hysterical'. It was fun.

The whole team were invited to go and see the opening night of the show 'Oklahoma' which has just started at a theatre here. It was a very good show and the music and singing was really nice to listen to. Have you seen it?

I've been to quite a few cinemas, all thrown open to us, and I've seen the films 'Convicted' starring Broderick Crawford and Glen Ford, 'Love That Brute', 'My Foolish Heart' and 'One Way Street' starring James Mason. They were all good films especially the first and third but 'Love That Brute' was really funny.

The first Sunday we spent here we went out to Surfer's Paradise as guests of an Englishman who has his 'weekend' home there. We had a smashing time on the beach on a lovely sunny day and we had our first taste of surfing. It was good fun only we daren't go out too far as there's quite a few sharks hanging around the district waiting for a tasty meal! Only last week a life saver was swimming about 100 yards off shore when he was attacked by one. He had one hand taken off, part of his buttocks torn away and the other hand mauled. It was awful to read about and he was still conscious when he was brought out of the water. At the moment he has recovered and is doing quite well in hospital but they say that the worst comes after the attack when they are first coming out of the shock. It must have been horrible for him.

Last Sunday, three of us went out fishing in a 35ft launch owned by a certain Mr. Gow who I had met at the Governor's party. We had a smashing time with lots to eat and drink, pretty female company supplied and some lovely sunshine into the bargain. I was allowed to be 'skipper' of the launch and steer it and you ought to have heard the yells and screams of the girls and even our lads when we nearly ran right in front of a fast going coastal steamer coming up the river estuary. I just managed to get her out of the way but we got such a wash from the ship we performed everything bar a somersault! Out in the Bay, the wind was blowing quite strongly and we decided it was too rough to anchor on the sand banks so we had to go into a sheltered cove to fish and we only caught a few fish, mostly whitings. We caught a lot of 'catfish eels' but as they're no good we killed them and then threw them back into the sea. They have three long stings behind each gill and they look awful creatures and from what I'm told they inhabit the river but had been brought down by the heavy rainfall and flood water. Anyway, we had a smashing time and as I 'skippered' the launch up the river a thunderstorm broke out and it was real fun. You could hardly see more than a few yards ahead of us and we nearly ran over a rowing boat which suddenly loomed ahead of us.

As we have finished the Test early and have a couple of days to spare, Mr. Gow is going to take us out again tomorrow so I'd better take a little more care this time but you see it's so hard to keep your attention on what you're doing when the others are 'boozing away and having fun' in the cabin behind you!!

Well, I'd better tell you something of the Test. It was bad luck we lost because in everyone's estimation we did better in every department than the Aussies, but only the fact that they had batted on a plumb wicket the first day and got 228 did they win [Brian was slightly out with the score which has been corrected]. It was a pity because our bowlers had bowled magnificently to get them out for 228 and if Neil Harvey hadn't got 74 they would have been in the cart! We couldn't play on the Saturday because it was raining all the time nearly and we spent our time playing solo and pontoon etc. I was lucky and won a couple of quid but Jack Moroney, whose luck was dead out for the match (he bagged a pair) lost quite heavily. On the Monday after having a wet Sunday which soaked the wicket again, we started at one o'clock. We started quite well even though the wicket was at its worst and the ball was popping up all over the place but fortunately for us neither Miller nor Johnston bowled well. All you have to do on a wicket like this is bowl straight and pitch it well up to the batsmen and they were doing the opposite. Cyril [Washbrook] and Reg [Simpson] let everything on a length and not on the wicket go past, covering up with pads and body and everything they could find. Anything short they lashed out

AUSTRALIA 1950-51

at scoring runs and when occasionally they pitched one up they let everything go at it. It was ever so funny to watch for both Reg and Cyril were made to look like No 10 and 11 batsmen with their antics and wild 'swishes'. They missed every other ball but luckily every one they hit went everywhere but the right place.

I think we got 29-0 before lunch, but afterwards it was a different tale. Don Bradman had had a chat with them and told them what to do during the lunch interval and straight afterwards Cyril was caught at silly mid-off for 19. This began a steady procession and when we had got to 68-7 the skipper decided to declare and see if we could get a few of the Australians out before the wicket got easier. We had had the worst of it but when the Aussies went in they made a shocking mess of it. Morris, Moroney and Loxton all went before a run had been scored, then Johnson almost 'holed out' at fine leg but the ball just cleared John Dewes' outstretched arms. Neil Harvey came in and you could tell straight away that the wicket was easing as instead of every ball popping up or shooting along the ground it was one in three, which wasn't so bad.

However Alec [Bedser] and Trevor [Bailey] (who had cut his pace down) were bowling very accurately and Trevor made one bump at Neil who, trying to protect himself, caught the ball on his fingers and was caught by Denis [Compton] at leg slip. He just started to walk then bethought himself and stood still until Denis and the rest of them realised he was staying there and appealed but the umpire gave him not out. It was a bad mistake, especially as the same umpire had given Denis out when he had been caught off a Bill Johnston bumper in our first innings when the ball hit him half way up his forearm. To prove this was the fact that by the time Denis got back to the pavilion the bruise had started to come out and you could tell plainly where he had been hit.

Anyway, to get back to the story, if Neil had been given out we'd have probably got them out for under 20 but they scraped away getting 32-7 and then Lindsay [Hassett] called them in. This left us with just over an hour to bat and Freddie Brown sent in Reg and Cyril to open again, saving Denis and Len for the following day. Unfortunately, everything went wrong! and Reg was yorked by Lindwall's first ball. John Dewes went in but was soon out, sticking his bat out like a little kid at a ball outside the off-stick. Cyril went and with 10 minutes to go Trevor and Alec were together. Everything looked all right but then Alec, who had been sent in

as nightwatchman, took a swing at one and was caught skying one
– the b..... fool. Then Trevor was out pulling a short one and to
crown everything Arthur McIntyre was run out in the silliest run
I've ever seen. He needs his head examining for such a thing but I
blame the last three wickets entirely on Alec Bedser who, sent in as
the nightwatchman, tried to hit one. Surely he ought to have had
enough sense for a man of his experience not to have a 'blind swipe'
at ten-to-six.

Well, after that exhibition we'd almost lost hope, but were
praying that we would have a fine night so that the wicket would
dry a little and then hoping that Len and Denis would get together
for a while and get the runs.

Next morning, Tuesday, Len and Godfrey [Evans] continued,
but after building our hopes a little, Godfrey tapped one from Bill
Johnston into Sam Loxton's hands at silly mid-on. Denis joined
Len but first ball he did exactly the same thing as Godfrey and got
out for a duck. It was an awful blow and you could have heard a
pin drop for a moment, then, as the crowd got over the shock, they
yelled with delight. Len was now left with the skipper and Doug
Wright to knock off the hundred and odd runs. The skipper helped
him for a while, but looked anything from safe and was edging
them all over the place. It was pitiful.

If only any of them could have played a dead bat. That was all
that was needed to guard the wickets and stay in with Len but no,
he would have to try and hit one and was caught. Doug Wright
joined in with 120 needed for victory and, believe me, the next half
hour was the most interesting cricket of the whole match.

Len was cracking the ball all over the place off everyone who
came on with some magnificent shots, while Doug at the other end
managed quite ably to hold his end up. Whenever the ball was off
his wickets he quite wisely took his bat out of the way and let it past
and when a straight one came along he played it confidently into
the ground. The way these two were playing gave us fresh hope but
I'll bet there were a few short finger nails after the match, especially
in our side. They survived until the last over before lunch when Len
was unable to get a single from the last ball of the previous over to
sneak the bowling as he had been doing so well before. However,
ball after ball came down with Doug playing them very confidently
but then Iverson with the last ball before lunch sent the worst of the
morning down – a downright long hop, and Doug couldn't resist

the temptation and holed out half way to the boundary at fine leg. It was a shame for we had played far better than the Aussies had and certainly deserved a draw if nothing else but we didn't have much luck. So much for that. Now we have to win two to bring back the Ashes and will have a damn good try. We're not coming back empty handed.

Since then we've had a couple of days free in which we've (all those not playing in the Test) had to practice in the mornings but in the afternoon I had a game of golf at the Royal Queensland Golf Club playing with Gilbert [Parkhouse] against Arthur McIntyre and Bob Berry. We beat them and won a few bob into the bargain and had a real time.

This afternoon, Gilbert, John Warr and myself went fishing again on Mr. Gow's launch. We had a wonderful time and John, who had never been fishing before in his life, threw a hand line in and first go he had a real tug o' war and pulled out a fish about a couple of feet long. It was a baby shark, a 'grey nurse'. It was funny to see John's face and we got our cameras out and took a snap of him holding it up. In the whole afternoon we caught 28 whiting so it wasn't a bad day, was it? We had two lovely meals prepared for us and enjoyed ourselves immensely – the right way to spend life!!

Who's this Pat Healey you wrote about? Probably the fool who wanted to take a snap of me on the ground and then rang me up on the phone at our hotel and asked me if I'd mind if she sent some food parcels home. What could I say? There's one born every minute!!

John, I can't send any photographs home to you because the ones I have are large ones and they would only get bent and damaged in the long trip home. I haven't developed any of the films I have taken myself yet, so wait until I get home and I'll let you have a real look at all my souvenirs and photos etc. I've got thousands.

I've been reading you've been having snow just lately. Has it been heavy? You know, we could do with a little at the moment. After the Test match finished the weather completely changed and now we're in a "heat wave" (to us). Well, I shall have to close soon because I've got to get a parcel off to New Zealand!! I can't send you anything home for Xmas – sorry – but, you see, if I do you'll only have to pay loads of duty on it so wait until we return home and we'll see what we can get.

Well I guess I've not much more to tell you for the time being except that we're going to Toowoomba early tomorrow morning for a few days and from what we've been told it's a very nice place and I've already got someone to look after me. Stuart Gow is ringing up his brother there to tell him to look after us.

Did I tell you about the fellow Eddie Waring told me to look up here in Brisbane? Well, Mr. Gow is the chap and I stumbled on him quite accidentally and he's a grand gentleman. He's sending food parcels home for me from his wholesale business (two million pound turnover a year) and says he's going to continue sending them to my mother when we're gone. It's very nice of him but it's typical of lots of people we've met out here. They'll give you anything, even their car.

Before I close I must apologise for scribbling this last page or so in a Biro but I ran out of ink, then borrowed Gilbert's pen, but his ran out too so I finished off using his Biro and it's a shocker!!

Well, Cheerio and All the Best. I'll write again before Xmas. Love to all at 61.

Yours

Brian

CHAPTER ELEVEN

JANUARY 12 – FEBRUARY 24, 1951

FEELING THE STRAIN

Test match tension saps energy – Nerves on edge – Champagne Christmas in Melbourne – Helps beat Lindwall and Miller at golf – Meets world billiards champion at party – Retires early on New Year's Eve – Arrives in Sydney – Enjoys sailing again – Speaks at Speedway Test – Enjoys Sydney Zoo – Watches cine film of first three Tests – Parties with top tennis pros – Takes in the sights of Hobart – On the Murray River – Wonderful Adelaide and Melbourne – Final letter and Final Test

Things have gone badly for Brian as far as cricket is concerned by the time he writes to John in a letter dated January 12, 1951, on notepaper from The Australia Hotel, Sydney, but it is not completed and posted until the Tourists have moved on to Launceston for a match between MCC and Combined XI. By then he has played in the exciting Second Test at Melbourne, which Australia win by 28 runs, but contributes virtually nothing, being dismissed for nought and one and taking just one wicket – that of Sam Loxton – with his medium-pacers. He comes under criticism for his dismissal to a poor delivery in the second innings but he always maintained that he was pressured into playing with a groin injury which got progressively worse. The injury kept him sidelined for quite a while and he looked on as England were crushed by an innings and 13 runs in the Third Test at Sydney. Perhaps not surprisingly, Brian hardly mentions cricket in this letter but although he's having a rough time of it in the environment of the team his spirits remain high when it comes to off-the-field activities.

Dear John,

Thank you for your letters. I'm sorry I haven't written back earlier but I've tried and tried to start writing to you, in fact to everyone, but I can't think clearly and I only succeed in writing a few lines before I scrap the lot. It's impossible to write when there's a Test match on every other week or thereabouts. You're all keyed up during the game and the tenseness of it saps your energy even more so than a day in the field and the only thing you feel like doing after that is flop into a bed – and in between matches you have a kind of a hangover, a 'morning after feeling'. My memory seems to be going so if this letter takes quite a lot of understanding don't blame me. I can hardly think back a couple of days let alone a week or so. My brain seems to be muzzy and keeps wandering into all kinds of thoughts and my nerves are on edge. Oh to hell with it all, I just feel like doing away with myself.

Well I'd better try and tell you what we've been doing this last week or two. We had a nice Christmas in Melbourne. We had a party in which we had about 20 bottles of champagne on the table and we didn't half have fun. My head was swimming by the time we had finished and then I went out to another one at a friend's of mine. The previous night I'd been out to a Christmas Eve party and we didn't finish till about 4.0am. It was a smashing party. There were about 30 of us and we had dancing, games and everything to make it a success. We got down to some real games round about 2 or 3. I spent most of my nights at this friend's home playing billiards etc. They had a beautiful table there and thought they could play until then. Walter Lindrum, the world champion billiard player, is a friend of the family and he was there one night and just showed how easy it was and someone broke off for him and he went on and made a 1,500 break in half-an-hour and picked the balls up, otherwise he would have gone on all night.

One night I went along to a party at the Oriental Hotel with some of the lads. When I got there I met a girl who had been at a previous party there when I was there. There was dancing, we had champagne and then, when the dance closed, we went out to one of the chap's homes for a drink or two and to chat.

....I didn't celebrate the ending of the year and the beginning of the next. Instead I was early to bed – I was needing some sleep by then. We had a very nice time in Melbourne and were very sorry to be leaving it. I'd also been at His Majesty's Theatre to see the show 'Ice Follies'. It was a wonderful show and I thoroughly enjoyed myself especially when they started playing badminton on the ice. It was ever so exciting to watch.

By the way, I forgot to tell you that this friend of mine, Graham Heeney, had a lovely sister, one of the prettiest 'things' I'd seen since arriving in Australia. The only snag was she was engaged. However, that didn't matter much when a friend of hers who was at the party and who is the pianist at a nightclub called The Coffee Lounge invited her to bring me down for a night there. Of course we arranged it and had a marvellous time especially as it was on the house. This pianist friend played quite a few requests for us and at the close he played his own version of the Flight of the Bumblebee. It was lovely.

Well, we arrived in Sydney and before long I had lots of phone calls from friends which I had made on my previous visits there. Do you remember a lad at school called Phillip Morris from Guiseley, he was in Cavendish House and was a reasonable swimmer? Well, he's out here buying wool. He says it's quite a good job and has a car to transport himself around. He looked me up and we had a night out together with two females and we went out to a nightclub. He's picked up quite a nice young girl – daughter of a wealthy Sydney businessman. He's got his head screwed on the right way hasn't he? This girl that I was with was a model by profession and she was very nice.

I had two or three days out with friends playing golf at the different courses – Royal Sydney, The Lakes, where the PGA tournament was played recently, and Manly. All nice courses but not as nice as the Melbourne ones.

I didn't tell you of the time when after the Melbourne Test I went out with Keith Miller and Ray Lindwall for a game at the Riversdale course. Well I was playing with another chap against them and before then they had never been beaten playing as a pair under their normal handicaps as they're quite good. However, both my partner and myself struck a marvellous patch and we whacked them hollow. In the finish we were both giving them strokes at practically every hole possible. I also had a day out with Jack Iverson and Jimmy Burke at Jack's course but I didn't get to bed the previous night until about 5.0am and I didn't hit one all day. Needless to say Jack, who was on my side, pulled us through. He's quite a good golfer. It's a good job he doesn't bat like he drives a golf ball!

At the weekends (Sundays) I went out with some friends on a 44 foot yacht. The first Sunday it was very rough so we didn't go out of Sydney Heads into the sea but were content to stay in the neck of the harbour. It was fun and big as the yacht was we got drenching after drenching. Oh! It's marvellous when you're running across the wind. The boat almost turns over when you've got the full sail up. We had two lovely meals in the yacht and finished them up with beer, rum, Scotch etc (not me, I had squash). Just as we got back into the bay where the yacht is anchored and left a storm broke and talk about rain. I've never seen it rain so fast in my life and we were still in the yacht. The surface of the water was literally turned into foam and Bill Bowes and I were praying it would keep up all night even if it meant being marooned on 'The Lass' all night (there was room for six people in the bunks in the cabin underneath). Unfortunately it didn't rain long enough and next day Australia batted on a plumb wicket, worse luck, but the rain did us one good turn. It washed the top of the yacht and so we hadn't to clean it up.

The next weekend we got fixed up and went out into the open sea and ran a few miles down the coast and pulled into a cove where we anchored and went on to the beach. We lit a fire and set to and grilled some steaks and chops etc. It was fun. I ate three thick juicy steaks, bigger than the size of my outstretched hand and a couple of chops whilst the others ate until they almost burst. After this many of them wanted to walk back but we all boarded the yacht and raced back to Sydney in front of a following wind and she didn't half scoot along (it's already won two races this season). When we got into the smooth harbour I took a few snaps of it gliding through the water. They're smashing.

Whilst I was in Sydney I did all kinds of things. I went to people's homes for dinner and nights out at cinemas and theatres (they're the same out here), the Speedway Test Match between England and Australia and to the zoo at Taronga Park. We were invited to the [speedway] Test match one Friday night and quite a few of us went along because it would be something different and it certainly was. England have a weak side out here because for the star riders there isn't enough money in the game so they don't come. However it was a thrilling fight and although we lost we enjoyed it very much. At the interval we were taken into the middle of the track and introduced over the microphone to the crowd. Oh, it was awful. When it came to my turn to say a few words my heart was in my mouth and up to the very second before I hadn't thought of anything to say and I thought I was going to be left stuttering away into the mic. However, just as I was about to open my mouth a brainwave came to me and I muttered something about 'Thank goodness we've only to face Lindwall and Miller with a small leather ball and not the Aussies on their roaring motorbikes', plus, of course, with a few trimmings, and it produced quite a laugh – what a relief.

We met all the stars who were riding and had a drink with them after the match. I met Eddie Rigg, another Yorkshireman, from Odsal, and we had quite a chat. He knows my brother Peter very well.

The zoo in Sydney was a wonderful place covering almost a square mile on one of the headlands in the harbour. There's almost every type of animal, reptile, bird and fish there and it took me a whole day to look round it and even then I had to miss quite a few things out. The sharks were a horrible sight and sent shivers down your spine even though they were in an aquarium and out of reach from everyone. The way they glide about in the water is almost enough to bring fear to your heart and you get a lump in the throat and you can't swallow. It's an awful sensation. I used a couple of films taking snaps of the animals and views across the harbour and they should turn out quite good I hope.

I saw lots of films whilst I was there, namely 'The Happiest Days of Your Life', 'Rogues of Sherwood Forest', 'Where the Sidewalk Ends', 'A Life Of Her Own' (Lana Turner), 'Outriders' and one or two more that I don't remember. They were all good pictures, particularly as we never had to pay to go in to see them.

The last night I spent at a friend's house who had taken films of the first three Tests with his cine camera in colour. Anyway he had a special building in his garden behind his house which he had equipped as a cinema, complete with a projection room and a marvellously furnished room where his guests sat to see the films. It's the best cinema I have ever been into – three or four settees and couches and a few armchairs to relax into, a drinking cabinet in the corner for the thirsty ones and a wireless in another to provide the music during the interval. It was wonderful and above all he had a very nice young daughter who he'd been hiding away! Anyway, I got sitting next to her 'by some stroke of fortune' and enjoyed the rest of the evening very much.

When he took me back to the hotel he said he would be seeing us again in Melbourne for the last Test so I told him to bring his daughter along for the holiday – hope he heard me!

Whilst we were in Sydney we were staying in the same hotel as were the tennis professionals Donald Budge, Frank Parker, Dinny Pails and Richard [Pancho] Gonzales. We had a bit of a party with them one night and they seemed very decent fellows. On the tour over here Richard Gonzales is winning practically every match he plays in – he's dynamic. In their spare time they are typically American in style – they walk around with collarless shirts in all different colours, gaudy socks and jackets and usually a pair of light fawn trousers but in themselves they're very decent types.

Well, I'm getting to more recent times now. We arrived in Hobart last Friday after a very tiring air journey over the Tasman Sea. Everyone said it was a bumpy journey but I fell asleep so I didn't feel any of them. It's a very nice place is Hobart. It's clean (as are all cities and towns over here) and fresh. The climate is a little more like ours than it is on the mainland and at night we've slept solidly and got up feeling much fresher in the morning, probably because of the much cooler and healthier atmosphere.

I had a couple of days out golfing, one at the Royal Hobart Club and the other at the Kingston Beach Club. First of all we went to a reception at the Town Hall, then the following day we were guests of the Governor at his 'refuge' on the hill overlooking the harbour. The harbour of Hobart is the best natural harbour in the whole world and during the last war both the Queen Mary and the Queen Elizabeth came into it and turned round under their own steam. Across the River Derwent, which is a continuation of the harbour, there is a floating bridge, the only one of its kind in the world, and it stretches across the river in a great arc and is about a quarter of a mile long. It's a marvellous construction and has to be seen to be believed. In the background of the city there's Mount Wellington (lovely name, isn't it?) which, unless on a fine day, is always covered with clouds or snow and the cricket ground is a lovely place with the scenery blending in with the mountains to make it one of the most beautiful in Australia.

The actual town itself is rather quiet, especially at night, and all the social life there goes on in a hotel called Wrest Point which Noel Coward described as the best and most modern in the Southern Hemisphere. Each night you can go to the hotel and into the beautifully decorated lounge and dancing hall, no charge for entering and you only pay for what drinks you get. Each night there is an orchestra playing dance tunes and there's a beautiful dance floor. In fact rather than being a hotel it's more like a nightclub only you don't have to 'pay through the nose'. Each night you'll find practically all the elite of Hobart there (and the females aren't bad either).

Well I guess that's all I can say for now so I'll close. I'll try to write more often but they'll have to be ordinary airmail letters as it takes me about a week to write one of these 'damned things' and I'm so far behind on my correspondence I don't know what to do.

Well, Cheerio and Good Luck.

Yours always

Brian

PS: Good old Arsenal's pulling round again I see and Leeds knocked Middlesbrough out of the Cup. What's the matter? Has Buckley left!

*   *   *

Brian, it seems, is penning so many letters on tour that he continues to repeat himself on occasions, as he does when he writes to John from Adelaide on the first day of the Fourth Test on February 2, 1951, apparently forgetting that he has already described Hobart.

This part of his letter is now omitted. Unsurprisingly, he is not included in the Fourth Test, which England lose by 274 runs, his scores on his return in the three matches leading up to the Test being 4, 5*, 6, 4 and 14. But Brian again claims he was pressured into playing while injured.

Dear John,

Just a few lines to let you know I'm going on all right. We had a very nice time (quiet) in Tasmania – it was more like being in England again. The countryside and scenery were lovely and very green compared with the mainland.

....From Hobart we motored by coach across the island to Launceston where we spent another quiet few days (except for Saturday night). Then we went to a dance at a golf club and had a smashing time finishing up at a doctor's home having supper with three ladies at 2.0am. After this I got up at 7.30am and went out and played the game of my life at golf, so it must have 'done' something to me!!

On the Sunday afternoon a few of us went up for a ride into the hills and I saw the most beautiful sight ever. We came into a valley and all you could see were purple fields surrounding a few farm houses. It was lovely and we went down into the middle of the farm to have a real look at the 'stuff'. It was lavender, field and field of it, and there was a lovely smell (or should I say scent) when we got down into the fields.

Well, we left Tasmania and called at Melbourne for a night before going on to Renmark (SA) the next morning. It's a beautiful place, very clean and has an ultra modern hotel in the centre of the town owned by the Township. About half-a-mile out from the town you come to fields and fields of fruit. Phew! It's simply marvellous – peaches, nectarines, oranges, apples and grapes and apricots, all intermingled in rows. We were lucky, we came just when the fruit was getting ripe and we nearly ate ourselves sick with them. We had crate upon crate delivered to the ground or the hotel and before we left we were nearly playing football with them there were so many.

We had an afternoon trip up the Murray River to Snake Island (an appropriate name) and also a trip round a distillery (Renmark Wines) and were given a few bottles of sherry, brandy etc. The last night we were there the Association had organised a kind of a dance for us and practically every girl in town came. There were some good ones too!!! The dance was in a packing shed, a huge place with a concrete floor (Oh! My poor feet) and at the interval four chaps came on all manner of cycles and had races round the band floor in the centre. It was quite funny, especially when two of them crashed.

At the moment we're in Adelaide, but are staying in the suburbs of Glenelg on the coast. It's a wonderful place. Each morning we get up and before breakfast don a swimming costume and walk across the lawns in front of the hotel on to the beach. The water's lovely and warm and the girls in their costumes simply 'stupefy' you, especially one (a daughter of one of the hotel managers) and she's simply marvellous. She's only 17 and still at school but she certainly knows how to carry herself and what looks, what a figure!! ....

Cheerio and good luck.

Yours

Brian

*   *   *

The final letter from Australia is started on Brian's 20th birthday, February 24, 1951, which is also the second day of the final Test in Melbourne, England ending on a high note with an eight wicket victory. Although not playing, Brian seems to have shaken off all of his depression and as well as continuing to throw himself wholeheartedly into the social life, this remarkably versatile young man is also entranced by ballet and opera. The final Test was the 26th match of the tour and Brian only played in nine of them, scoring 231 runs with one unbeaten century and claiming 13 wickets. Brian is soon on his way home, his injury preventing him going on the New Zealand leg of the tour.

He promises John a further letter before leaving Australia describing his 20th birthday celebrations but it appears he never had time to write it.

Dear John,

Just a few lines to let you know I am going on all right. I'm sorry I didn't write last week, but I was so busy buying things – blankets, sheets, cloth and crockery etc that we hadn't much time to spare. At the moment we're all getting ready for leaving, doing our last minute shopping and planning out what we shall need on our way back so that we can pack most of our stuff up. You know, I started off with one trunk, one suitcase and a cricket bag. Now I've got one trunk, two crates, three suitcases, cricket bag, golf clubs and two small 'holdalls' and then I shall have a 'helluva' job of getting everything in!!

Well, to get on with something more interesting. I've had a wonderful time in Melbourne this stay! I've been to the 'Swan Lake' ballet and it was a smashing show. Later, I went with the manager of the Ballet Company for supper to his flat and the following day we went out to dinner at one of the 'posh' nightclubs in town. The two of us ran up a bill of about £6 – just for dinner. Of course, two bottles of champagne and other wines composed most of that.

Since then I've been to see 'The Barber of Seville', 'Aida' and another light opera. They were all good. Of the films I've seen, 'All About Eve' and 'Toast of New Orleans' were smashing. You don't want to miss the former and the latter was one of the best musical comedies that I have seen for a long time. I laughed myself hoarse. This last week I ran across a fellow I met in Sydney – he's head of a wheat distributing organisation. We went to Menzies, a posh restaurant, for dinner, and he took me to the Athenaeum Club, a very select club, and I proceeded to take a 'quid' off him at snooker.

We've had a few days out playing golf at the Metropolitan Club. It's a lovely course, in fact one of the prettiest I've played on. Yesterday (Sunday) we went out there and I managed to take another quid off him and later we went to his home for dinner. In the back garden he has a beautiful swimming pool and also a lawn tennis court. We went for a dip in the pool to refresh ourselves, then we had dinner.

The first Sunday we were here about half a dozen of us were invited down to a gentleman's house who travelled across on the Stratheden with us. We had to drive about 30 or 40 miles down the coast to a place called Sorrento, but there we had a wonderful time awaiting us. The house was a huge affair, white with a blue-tiled roof. We started off with a drinking party. There were two nine gallon kegs of beer, numerous bottles of gin, Scotch, and of course some squash. Well, after everyone were 'on the way' they brought out the steaks and chops and grilled them on a fire in the garden and with all the other things they brought out, eggs, salad etc, the barbecue was a great success. We were like a lot of hungry savages eating with our hands but that's what a barbecue is. It was wonderful – I ate about half-a-dozen thick juicy steaks and chops and, in all, about a dozen eggs, plus a few other minor things.

Afterwards, I went with three of the people at the party for a game of golf at the Sorrento Golf Club – I was the only one who could hit them straight!! – and then I joined all the rest down on Portsea Pier for a swim. They had had their swim so I found myself going in alone. Well, I had a beautiful swim, then I climbed out on to the pier and had the biggest shock of my life. A huge great black stingray came swimming out from under the pier with a long thin tail. They are horrid things, something like this [Brian sketches one] with its sting at the end of the tail. I've seen big ones in the aquariums but this one was almost 6ft wide.

My birthday was quite fun [February 24] but I haven't much space left so I'll tell you in the next letter before I leave Australia. Thanks very much for your cable.

Yours

Brian

Brian and L N Devereux going out to bat for Combined Services v the South Africans at Portsmouth

CHAPTER TWELVE

SEPTEMBER 19 – NOVEMBER 3, 1951

SIGNALMAN TO GUNNER

*Cricket at Pateley Bridge – Compares his luck to Denis Compton's
– Farewell to Catterick – Hello to Muswell Hill – Gets Arsenal
kit and trains at Hendon – Watches England v France – Plays for
A team – Rigorous training – Fixes up his first driving lessons –
Arsenal Reserves v Southampton – Becomes ice hockey fan – Crazy
Gang with Alex James and family – Chooses a car – 'Branded'
on electric fire after training – Dismay at Tories' election win –
Scores v Spurs Reserves – Plays for Arsenal v Cambridge Univ.
and up against May, Warr, Sheppard and Insole*

Upon returning from Australia it was back to Army life for Brian
and once he had recovered from the injury which had so plagued
him on tour he was able to start to enjoy his cricket again. He played
in a variety of matches for Army and Combined Services teams
among others and he also managed two Championship matches for
Yorkshire during August, 1951.

But it was while playing for Combined Services against the
touring South Africans at Portsmouth in late June that Brian
demonstrated quite clearly that the outstanding form of his
inaugural season with Yorkshire in 1949 had been no flash in the
pan. After the South Africans had made 499 for five declared –
Brian holding three catches – he scored 66 out of 235 and when
his side followed on he came to the rescue with a dashing 135 not
out with 15 fours and three sixes to save the match. It was his first
century on home soil.

A month later, Brian scored another unbeaten century, this time
at Lord's for the Army against the Royal Navy. In the first innings
in the two-day drawn match he took two for 34 in 20 overs before
the Navy declared on 249 for six and he then thrashed 134 not out

in a total of 293 for two declared.

In all, he played in six first-class matches that summer, hitting 384 runs at an average of 34.90.

Brian was demobbed on September 26, 1951, although he returned to Catterick for around a fortnight a year later, and he was immediately into another new and important phase of his life because he had moved on from Leeds United and had been signed by Arsenal where he was soon to rub shoulders with some of soccer's greatest players.

Leeds had given him a free transfer at the end of July, 1950, and he signed professional forms for The Gunners as an inside forward on August 17 but injury prevented him playing any football in the 1950-51 season.

He wrote to John from Catterick on September 19, his last correspondence while in the Army, and he enclosed his letter in an envelope marked on the back Hotel Windsor, Melbourne. His supply of hotel stationery had still not run out, however, because his next letter on October 5, from his Muswell Hill digs in Muswell Road, London, was begun on notepaper from Grosvenor House Hotel, Edgbaston, and concluded on notepaper from the Hotel Canberra, Canberra! He communicated regularly with Brian right through to April 1, 1952, when his days with Arsenal were coming to an end and he was soon back full time with Yorkshire.

It will be noted that after returning from Australia in February, 1951, Brian did not write to John in the summer until his last letter from Catterick in September, 1951, the reason probably being that Brian returned to Leeds fairly regularly to play league cricket and the two friends were frequently able to meet up for a chat.

Catterick Camp
Wednesday 19th Sept

Dear John,

Sorry to be writing this short line but I feel that I had better let you know that I shall not be coming home until Saturday afternoon and so will not be able to go to the dance after all....

The reason I cannot get home is that the OC has let me have a 72 hour pass till Tuesday morning (very unusual for him) so that I can play in this match at Pateley [Bridge] but to compensate the

Squadron for my absence on Monday he's made the pass for AD [?] Saturday. [Pateley Show is the last agricultural show of the year in this area and, over the years, Yorkshire took a team to play a friendly match against the locals.]

Life's been cleaning up these last few days. I've had my medical to go out and after this all you're supposed to do is 'lie on your bed' (how thoughtful of them). You aren't even supposed to do any clerical work or even lift a pen in case you prick your finger with the nib and get blood poisoning(!!). Anyway, I haven't been so lazy – I've managed to write an odd letter with a couple of lines etc and finished a crossword or two. Each afternoon I've been over to the sports field doing a bit of training to 'keep my weight down' you know.

You know I was missed on Saturday morning last but fortunately it was Capt. Hiles who noticed it first and he performed a neat piece of explaining to the OC just in time – they used to call Denis Compton Golden ---- out in Australia because he was the luckiest devil alive. I think I must qualify for Golden ----'s II.

I've spent these last two nights down at Richmond at friends. We've played a few games of cards – I won a few bob at nap last night so I'm feeling in high spirits.

Well John I don't think I can talk about anything else for the time being, so Cheerio and Good Luck.

Yours

Brian

* * *

12 Muswell Rd.,
London N10,
October 5, 1951

Dear John,

Just a short note to let you know I'm going on OK and having a wonderful time down here.

On Monday, I caught the 6.50 bus down and then when I got down to Leeds I was lucky enough to catch the 7.20am train.

I met Kenneth Thornton, who's in the RAMC for a couple of

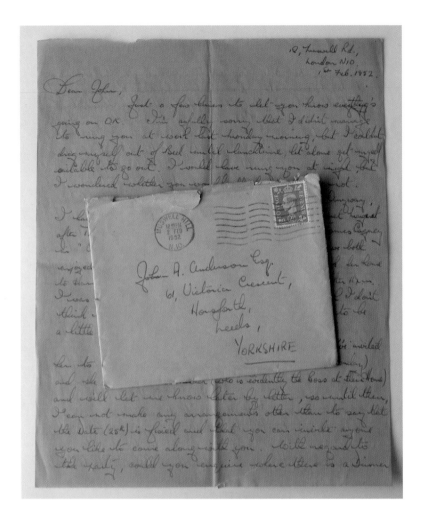

years, going back off his first 48-hour leave. He was reporting to a place somewhere in the Salisbury Plain where he was supposed to be on an exercise before going out to Hamburg in BAOR.

I gave him a little bit of encouragement before we said goodbye in King's Cross Station. I said 'Don't worry Ken, the first two years are the worst' and then we wished each other good luck and away we went.

I caught a taxi to take me and my luggage to Muswell Hill and arrived there just on 12 o'clock; I said 'Hello', shook hands and away I went again, this time to Highbury where I had a huge lunch.

After lunch I called in the office to see Jack Crayston [coaching staff, former player who went on to become manager in 1956] and fixed up all the forms etc and got to know what I have to do. Everything went according to plan and I even fared better than I had hoped – what a Club.

Later I went along to the dressing rooms to get fixed up with training kit, spikes, football boots and baseball boots which we do our light training and ball work with.

From here, I went and paid a call to the tax office to fix up my coding etc, then went home for dinner.

After dinner, Don (the lad who's living with me) and I went along to the Ritz to see the film 'Captain Horatio Hornblower' starring Gregory Peck and Virginia Mayo. It was very good and nice and pleasing to the eye!! Our only regret was that Virginia Mayo wasn't on the screen all the time – she only had a small part.

On Tuesday morning, I spent the day at South Herts Golf Club with a few of the lads. We played a round in the morning, lunch on the Club, and then another round in the afternoon, followed by a few games of snooker in the clubhouse.

.....On Wednesday, I had my first morning's training at Hendon where I shall be for the first few weeks with Arsenal with about a dozen other lads. We have fun, especially as wee Alex James [Arsenal youth coach, former Arsenal player and Scottish international] and George Male are in charge of us.

In the afternoon, after lunch at a posh hotel in Hendon (the manager's got a lovely little daughter, too!!) we all went along to the ground to see the international match [England v France 2-2]. It wasn't a good match but the first half was quite thrilling. Don't believe anything you've read in the newspapers. Looking at them the next day I thought I'd been at a different match than the reporters. Of course, they force the selectors to pick a certain man and so they have to back him up etc, etc. Willis played shockingly, so did Medley but they come from Spurs and according to the writers they couldn't put a foot wrong. Now they're trying to get Bailey in the side. Next it'll be the whole side.

Anyhow, we should have won by at least two goals but in the end were lucky to draw when in the last minute their centre forward grabbed the ball and with only the goalkeeper to beat shot straight at Williams. Now I wish I had gone out for a game of golf instead.

....On Thursday, I slept in until 10.0am – we were playing in the afternoon. We played the Spurs A team which included a first teamer and a couple of reserves in as well.

Anyway, we drew 1-1 but should have whacked them hollow. We had a penalty miss and about four other 'almost goals' and their goal came from a free kick which one of our full backs ducked out of the way thinking the goalkeeper was behind him and it went in (10/- bonus down the drain!!!). I had a good game considering I was out of condition – I felt, to put it mildly, as though I'd slept with

ALEX JAMES

Lana Turner, Ava Gardner or some such beautiful creature!!! Don't show your mother this or I'll be for it next time I come up there.

....This morning I was b----- stiff but Alex James got stuck in to me. He said 'Come on me lad, 10 laps for a start' and then said that if I got myself fit I could get into the first team, so off I went and kept on until I was dropping. Even then, he wouldn't let me stop and made me do some body exercises for quarter of an hour. He's got it in for me (!!!) but it's all for the good so I don't mind.

This afternoon we went down to the ground to pick up a few things, tickets, an Arsenal tie and wages above all else, then

I went into Finsbury to enquire about a school of motoring. I fixed myself up without any bother and I start next Thursday. If all goes well I should have a licence (but no car) by a fortnight's time.

Well, I guess I can't say any more for the moment – I stayed in tonight to press a couple of suits that I've worn this week – so Cheerio and Good Luck until next time.

Give my regards to your mother, dad, Margery and last but not least Jill.

Yours

Brian

*   *   *

For all his intensive training and football activity, Brian continued to find time to write long letters from Muswell Road to John practically every week with unbridled enthusiasm.

To publish every letter in its entirety would consume too much space, so I have run some of them together, omitting much of the youthful tittle-tattle but still concentrating on the sporting achievements of this remarkably versatile man.

Writing on October 12, 1951, Brian says that he got up early on the Saturday morning to slip over to Victoria to collect a provisional driving licence from Middlesex House and he continues:

In the afternoon I had to go down to Highbury to watch the Reserves play Swindon. It wasn't a good match. We were losing 2-0 at one time and then with quarter of an hour to go something seemed to click into place. Swindon had been the better team but after this our passes seemed to find their man and we began to attack for minutes on end. It seemed too late when we got one goal and the Swindon defence seemed to be able to withstand it until the end which was only a few seconds off so I left as I had to meet Peter in town at 6.0 and I hadn't much time left. I went back home for tea and told them we had lost 2-1. Unbeknown to me we had scored from a penalty in the last minute and when they read the result in the papers they began to kid me that I'd been to a different match.

In the evening, Brian had a walk round Piccadilly and Haymarket before moving on to the Wembley Olympic Pool to watch an ice hockey game between Wembley and Streatham. Perhaps not surprisingly he found the sport exhilarating.

It was smashing. In the first period Streatham had practically all their men sent off into the penalty box and finished the period leading 5-1. It was fun. Streatham with three men were crowding their goal while six Wembley players were crashing them in but couldn't pierce the defence. The Streatham players would push, block, shove, kick, dive, in fact do everything to stop Wembley from scoring and then suddenly one would break out and go haring down to the other side chased by two or three others to score. Anyway, in the finish Streatham won 8-4 and now I'm an ice-hockey fan. At the intervals they had several attractions including the Swedish national ice skating champion (she was lovely), and a duet [with] a young boy and a young girl doing different dances. It was a very good night's entertainment.

....On Monday morning Alex got stuck in again and told me I had to do 30 laps. However, just as I'd got my second wind on the 19th lap he stopped and told me to do some exercises on my back. The only exercise I felt like doing on my back was going to sleep (!!) and by gosh I felt like it then.

In the afternoon I had to go along to the dentist to have my teeth checked over. He was quite a reasonable old fellow, very interested in cricket so he was very kind on me – 'he only took four', no sorry, he gave my teeth a polish. ....On Tuesday, I had it pretty easy (day before a match) only doing 10 laps (!!) for a start, followed up by the usual sprints and body work.

....On Wednesday, I slept in until 10.0am – breakfast in bed, then in the afternoon we went to play at Crystal Palace. We lost 3-1 but that was entirely to do with our goalkeeper who was on trial from Liverpool. Alex said after the game 'Someone played a joke on him, sending him for a trial' and we just had to laugh, but he lost us a £1 bonus!! – anyway I had a good game, scored the goal and enjoyed myself. I felt a little bit better after this game than I did the previous one – only as though I'd spent an evening with the ones I referred to in my last letter, not a night!!

After the match, I went with Alex James, his wife and small son, Andrew, to the Victoria Palace to see The Crazy Gang in the show

'Knights of Madness'. I'd seen it before I went to Australia but Alex invited me to come along and meet the family. Anyway, we had a marvellous time, sat on the front row in the centre and had the best view in the Palace. A couple of The Crazy Gang recognised Alex and made a couple of cracks about him and 'the wee devil' nearly fell out of his seat. At the interval Alex and I went behind and met some of them, had a drink and a chat but the show had begun again before I could get the conversation round to the 'girls' (what wretched luck) and we dashed back.

....Well, after the show we had supper and then came home. We're going to play golf on Sunday against two of his influential friends. If I stick with Alex, he'll show me how to get around and who to know which at the moment, as I'm new down here, takes some thinking out. He's a grand old chap but he's a hard task master. The next morning 'he'd forgotten the nice things he'd told me the night before' and there he was sending me round at a cracking pace until my heart was nearly kicking a hole in my chest and my lungs were bursting for breath.

In the afternoon, I went for my driving lesson No 1 in a little Morris Minor. It was quite easy and we toured round the streets of London for an hour before we put her nose back towards Finsbury Park. He said I shouldn't find any difficulty in passing after a little more experience.

....Nothing much has happened today except that it was 'pay day' and I had lesson two in driving. All I do now is to drive around where he tells me to go and leaves the car entirely in my hands for the whole hour. Tomorrow I'm playing for the Reserves at Tottenham. 'Lots of chasing with my tongue out.' Anyway, I'm on the way up and sooner than I expected.

*   *   *

A week later, Brian wrote that a nice week had started on the Saturday when he played for Arsenal Reserves v Tottenham Reserves at White Hart Lane.

In the first few minutes we forced a corner and I got up to it and headed it on to the bar – tough luck! and I thought I'd had my chance. Don Oakes put us one in front with a lob over the goalkeeper as he came running out. Then I had a shot from the edge of the box and the goalkeeper dived to put it round the corner, but I needn't have worried because our right winger crossed one over and I got my 'nut' to it and in it went. Oh! I felt on top of the world and we went on dictating play. If we'd had any luck at all we could easily have been 5-1 in front at half time instead of 3-1.

All this came against everyone's expectations as Tottenham had turned out an almost First Division side – it was fun. The second half failed to bring any more goals so we came off victors by 3-1. I felt........ but it was worth it.

At night we went along to Wembley and saw the Wembley Lions beat the Brighton Tigers 6-5 after being 5-1 up at one time. It was a very near finish and everyone in the end were shouting Brighton on hoping that they would score a sixth and draw level. It was very thrilling.

On Sunday morning, I got a phone call at 8.30 from Alex James telling me our game of golf was on and that I had to be there for 9.15 – I don't know how I got there but I managed it somehow and I went to play a smashing game – I beat him 2 and 1 in a great game (he plays off a nine handicap) and afterwards I was introduced to a few of his friends – influential people at the Club and elsewhere – a bright sign for the future!!

....Monday morning came and back to work again – hard work too. In the afternoon I went and had a driving lesson on the roads round Finsbury Park. It's quite fun and I came home and told Don I'd bust up two cars when I was going round a corner. To add to these words I came in shaking and holding my head. He really believed me and I let him go on for a few minutes 'asking questions' and so forth until I told him I'd been kidding him on – he nearly killed me with his looks!!

....On Tuesday afternoon I went out to South Herts for a game of golf. I played fairly well and came back well satisfied.

....On Wednesday, Don and I had the day off so we slept in until lunch time. In the afternoon we went along to Hendon to watch our A beat Q.P. Rangers 2-0. At night we saw another match – the Glasgow Rangers match in floodlight at Highbury. It was a spectacle – marvellous football throughout and I think we just deserved to win, as we did, by 3-2. One of the goals was scored direct from a throw-in – Cliff Holton picked up the ball near the corner flag and threw it right into the goalmouth where Doug Lishman headed it straight in. It was terrific.

At the match I met Stuart Surridge who was sitting just behind me – we chatted for a while but I could kick myself – I forgot to ask him for some bats when he was in a good humour.

On Thursday, I packed a day's work into the morning so that I could have a game of golf in the afternoon. I just picked up a couple of bob from an 'enthusiastic golfer' who threw out a challenge – I won the first seven holes – it wasn't really fair, was it?!

....Today, I did a couple of laps to loosen myself up and that was that. I think I'll save my energy for tomorrow, I might need it in the second half against Southampton Reserves at Highbury. Incidentally, it will be my first match on our ground so I do want to bring out a good performance. If we win we'll be top of the league as Southampton are the top at the moment. However, we will be hard pressed to do it as we have lost our full backs to the first team whose players are playing in the International. Well, touch wood and hope for the best!!

In the afternoon, Peter and I went along to the Motor Show at Earls Court. It was marvellous and took us hours to walk around studying the different models, huge sedans, saloons, sports models, in fact every type of car. It was fantastic. There were stands for every different make of car, from all the British makes, American and all the foreign types. They had every different kind of gadget possible in a car, gas stove, frying pan – no, that was in the caravans. Oh! I cannot hope to describe the splendour of the show in writing, it would take hours but it was absolutely smashing.

The two cars which drew most attention were the Daimler in 18ct gold, and the little Austin 7, but others were almost as popular. Gosh, didn't I fancy some of them.

....PS: I hope to be able to come soon and see you all – perhaps the first weekend in November. I don't know exactly, I've got to get fit first and it might be a while. I should get my driving licence by then, possibly November 5, and my uncle's already notified me that he's got one or two 'items' he wants me to see. He says they are very good. Also, I've had the offer of a Sunbeam Talbot (7,000 miles) for £400 which I might consider too.

12 Muswell Rd.
London N12
Friday, October 26

Dear John

Thank you very much for your letters which I received last Saturday and Tuesday respectively.

Well, I guess I should start with last Saturday's game v Southampton Res. at Highbury. We drew 1-1 but could possibly have pulled it off if we'd have had any luck. Their goal came from an incident which should have been pulled up for hands. However, we did well as our regular full backs were away with the 1st team and we had the 'A' team's backs playing. Besides this Southampton were the league leaders and had a 'league' team playing for them which included Ernie Jones, the Welsh Int. right winger and George Curtis who is one of the best ball players in the country and is just finding form after an injury.

At night, Don and I went to Harringay where we met Peter and went to see the [ice hockey] match between Harringay Racers and Streatham, the league leaders. Streatham are a 'wonder' side, terrifically fast and powerful but somehow Harringay scored first. After this Streatham piled on the pressure, cutting and thrusting down the wings and up the middle but couldn't get the puck into the net – then, towards the end of the second period, the long expected goal came from a rebound from one of the defenders and after that it was almost slaughter – they beat Harringay 6-1. [Harringay Racers was founded in 1936. A new team named Harringey Racers was founded in 1990.]

On Sunday nothing much happened except that we slept in until lunchtime, read the newspapers and saw a very old film at night over at Barnet. I think I deserved a day's rest as I felt awfully stiff after the match.

On Monday I had my nose to the grindstone once more whilst the other lads had a nice easy day – 'poor' me!! and in the afternoon I went along for my fifth lesson on driving. He said I shouldn't have any difficulty in passing the test when it comes around. It's fun. He puts me in awful 'jams', bad intersections and tells me to back up. . . . no, sorry, I meant narrow lanes.

....On Thursday we spent the morning as usual training – I had 20 laps to do without a rest as an 'imposition' for slacking off in the game the previous day or so they said. I must have been running out of volts!!

....Today Wee Alex didn't turn up so I had a nice easy day, a couple of laps and a few sprints – 'I feel a new man already' and after lunch we came over to Highbury to collect something which 'is very dear to us' (£.s.d.). I had my sixth lesson this afternoon and came out with honours. The only snag is now that it will be quite some time before I can get my test through so I shall not be able to drive for a while yet.

My uncle has written to tell me he has several cars I have to see to choose one, and so I'm coming up home overnight Saturday night after I've got back from playing for the Res. at Watford. He is picking me up on Sunday morning to take me over to Bradford and then I'll be on my way back again. Unfortunately I have to be back for training on Monday morning – I can't get up there for a few days until I'm absolutely fit, so I have to be back for supper on Sunday night and that means setting off back in the afternoon from Bradford. I can't possibly get down for an hour or two – I shall have hardly chance to have lunch at home (or rather breakfast) as my uncle is calling for me at half past ten. From there I shall go to Bradford where I'll be spending my time looking over the cars and taking them out for a run to see which one I like the best.

It won't be long before I shall be coming for a few days, perhaps in a fortnight or three weeks so I hope you will see that it's only a flying visit for a few hours or so, and that I shan't have chance to pop down and see you all down at 61.

Oh! I forgot to tell you – I was branded the other day!! After training one morning (I strip near the electric fire) I was taking my shorts off and as I bent down to take my feet out of them I touched the heating wires with my behind. I let out an awful scream and then when I looked at myself in the mirror and saw a lattice shaped 'brand' like xxxxx. The lads down at Hendon didn't half pull my leg and kept asking me 'which ranch did I belong to, Cross B?' (The B standing for ------!!)

Well John, it's time for some sleep, so Cheerio and Good Luck. Give my best wishes and love to your mother, Margery and Jill.

Yours

Brian

PS: What a calamity!! the Conservatives have won. They'll make a mess of it as they have always done so I can expect to be in khaki again soon (short-lived freedom). 'It's alright for the 'old fellows' voting the Cons. in to power – they've no thought for the young fellows'.

*   *   *

Brian's next letter, postmarked November 3, 1951, gives further accounts of his soccer prowess and some of the big sporting names which he continues to rub shoulders with.

....Well, I'm back with my nose to the grindstone once more, mind you, it hasn't been so bad this week, in fact it's been pretty easy compared with past ones.

....Monday found me lapping the ground at '50' all morning apart from half an hour spent doing exercises on my back making the muscles of my stomach stand out and 'my eyes pop out'. It's hard work but there's always a good lunch to look forward to. In the afternoon Ralph Prouton and I went along to South Herts for a game of golf. He did insist on playing for a bob or two, even though I had a sprained wrist and could hardly swing. However, I managed somehow or other to square the match with him and we returned home for dinner.

....On Tuesday, I went golfing again, this time my wrist felt much better and I played fairly well, going round in under 80 and winning the match plus the £.s.d!! We met Les Compton, Arthur Milton and Reg Lewis [prolific goal-scorer who spent his entire career with Arsenal] up there and had a drink with them afterwards.

....On Wednesday we had a very easy day, a few sprints and exercises in readiness for the morrow's match and then we went off to lunch.

....In the afternoon, I went along to Finsbury Park to find out about my driving test. Unfortunately they couldn't fit me in until November 30 for the test so it looks as though I shan't get up home again until the weekend after the 30th. Mum's doing the preparations for making a garage at home – getting permission to have one built etc, so it might be there by that time.

....On Thursday, Arsenal were sending two teams away to play Oxford and Cambridge Universities at Oxford and Cambridge. I was in the team to go to Cambridge where I met John Warr, David Sheppard, Doug Insole (who was up there for the week) and Peter May who captained their side. We managed to win 3-1 and had a fairly good game into the bargain. They didn't half 'dish' their weight about in their enthusiasm to beat us but we soon had them in hand and in the finish beat them with nine men on the field. Incidentally, three of the goals were scored by cricketers, one by Peter May, Don Bennett and myself for us. Besides this, Big Les (Compton) played a 'blinder' at centre half.

In all, we had quite a fair trip out and when we got back we heard that Oxford hadn't escaped it either and had been beaten.

Nothing much has happened today except that my wrist is badly strained and I'm having treatment for it, but it doesn't stop me doing my training (how unfortunate).

Tomorrow, I'm playing for the Reserves at Highbury against Plymouth Argyle – hope we win, its about time we got some bonus to help us along (!!) and at night we're going to Harringay with Peter to watch the ice hockey match.

Oh! By the way, tell Margery that if she wants a cure for her 'supposedly' Conservatism she should listen to the programme 'Any Questions' each Friday night – I said 'supposedly' because she doesn't know the difference between the parties except that the people of one particular party 'which shall be nameless' usually send their children to private schools etc (!!) and are recognised 'by the fools' as the elite of the community. It's quite a good programme and very funny when you get the questions answered by the different political representatives chosen to answer them. Of course Labour always come out on top as they rightly should when people don't have blinds pulled over their eyes.

....I've never felt fitter for a long time; my legs are strong and getting stronger every week, my wind is almost perfect and I've lost a lot of weight, in fact I haven't felt fitter since I used to run round the sports deck with Gaye and Judith....

Yours

Brian

CHAPTER THIRTEEN

LIFE IN LONDON

Angry at John's demands for more letters – Writing to over 20 people – Plays well against Argyle – Knee injury treatment – Plays 'a blinder' v Swindon – Pleased for Eddie Leadbeater – Golf v Kent Constabulary with soccer injury – Upbeat meeting with Arsenal boss – Uncle Harry delivers new car – Views Aussie Tour cine at Bill Bowes' home – Cricket practice at Mill Hill

Brian remained a prolific letter writer during his time on Arsenal's books and rarely a week went by when he did not communicate at length to John Anderson.

There is no record of John's letters to Brian but there is good reason to believe that Brian received more from his friend than he himself wrote and in early November the pressure of keeping up with the correspondence was beginning to tell on the young sportsman.

"Thank you for your two letters which I received this week," wrote Brian on November 9, 1951. "I'm sorry I couldn't oblige you by writing so that you would get another letter this week, but you see my time has to be planned out [and] during the week I might go out most nights but that is solely to rest my tired mind (!!) and free my concentration. Instead of entertaining myself reading, thinking, sleeping and eating football, I really think I need something to take my mind off the subject at some time during the day and the only way is to go to shows and cinemas etc.

"But when I come in each night, I have to start work all over again, and I write almost a couple of letters a night. You know, I have to write to other people besides you – almost 20 – and I put Friday night away (the only quiet night I have) to write to you.

"....one of your questions in your next letter will probably be 'why didn't you write again during the week? I wrote twice or three times' or whatever it was. You see John, I have other things to do, other people to write to, and when all boils down I might say that my time doesn't belong to me – it belongs to my career and I have obligations to perform to lots of things both on the practical side of the sports, theoretical and also social side. My difficulty is to try to fit everything in without undue friction.

"....The reason why I couldn't come up last weekend is simple – I just can't afford to come up too regular. You seem to forget that I stand upon my own feet and [am] entirely dependent upon my earnings as a professional soccer player, for the moment at least. These are split up between sending something home, paying my lodgings, laundry, entertainment and fares etc, so I don't know where the money is going to come from to go home regularly. I hope after this, that you won't be continually imploring me to come home – there's nothing that I long for more than to get home to see you all up there, but I aren't a millionaire, you know."

In the same letter, Brian describes his side beating Plymouth Argyle Reserves 2-0 and having a fair game himself. "In the second half I was 'on my knees' again as usual – what made me pick inside forward, you're allowed no rest (!!) except for when you can't run no more and your legs are caving in. Then you just have to stop!"

That night Brian and a couple of his friends went to watch Harringay Racers play Earls Court Rangers at ice hockey with Harringay squandering a 5-1 lead as Rangers drew level. It ended 6-6.

Brian and his Arsenal team-mates had a day off on the Monday and went on a Club outing to South Herts where they had a wonderful time playing golf – in teeming rain. "We had a round in the morning which I managed to win with the very last putt. After a lovely warm and very welcome lunch we went out again – after all a drowning's as good as a soaking. This time we found pools on the greens, one on which the hole was in a huge lake where it was impossible to putt it out – needless, it cost me that hole but I managed to win the round by 3&2."

A couple of days later, Brian had the afternoon off to watch the FA play the Army at Highbury and in his writings to John he shows himself to be an astute judge of emerging talent. "It wasn't a good match – probably due to the rain and mud – and the FA were only going at half speed," he observes.

"This Johnny Harmer's terrific. He is a marvellous ball player – everything he does seems innocuous and so very, very simple but he has them all going round in circles. If only he was bigger and stronger he would be a world beater."

Harmer was in his first season with Spurs, the No 8 going on to make 222 appearances, scoring 51 goals, before moving on to Watford in 1960 and then Chelsea where he became youth team coach.

Also during the same week Brian intended to go to Fulham to watch the London mid-week side but before he and his team-mates set off he complained of pain in a group of tendons in his knee, so he stayed back for treatment. It was a build-up of fluid at the back of the knee which was causing friction when he bent his leg but shortwave diathermy brought about a rapid improvement leaving him ready "to play a blinder at Swindon on Saturday (I hope)".

Brian was as good as his word. His next letter confirms that he did, indeed, "play a blinder" against Swindon, scoring Arsenal's first goal and helping to make the next two in the 3-0 victory. His account of the match is: "We started off quite strongly and should have been one up in the first few minutes, but Peter Goring failed to square the ball to me where I was stood in front of the goal. Unfortunately he thought he had been pulled up for off-side – I shouted myself hoarse in that second or so 'imploring' him to give me it but he didn't. Later, I managed to head (yes, another header – I can't hit them with my feet) a cross in to make it 1-0 which was the score when we turned round. Soon after half-time we ran riot and scored another two (both of which I had a hand in) and could almost have scored another five or six. However, we eased up and finished at 'walking pace'. Funny thing though, the same Swindon team had drawn 2-2 at Highbury earlier this season when our side included Leslie Compton, Reg Lewis, Don Roper and a couple of other first teamers, so we didn't do too badly."

The recent optimism shown by Brian after shortwave diathermy on his knee proved to be largely unfounded and he was soon going to Highbury again for further treatment – and admitting to John that although he had been picked for the match against Spurs he may not be able to play. But he added: "I don't feel it until I start sprinting so tomorrow, if it's heavy, I might risk it as the mud will slow everything up to my pace!!" On the day of writing, Brian said he had been to Hendon for some light training but when he started sprinting he felt his knee again so he had to stop.

Brian then turns his thoughts to cricket. "I was awfully disappointed to hear the West Indies lose. The Aussies have the better balanced side but I think Rammy (Ramadhin) and Val (Valentine) will turn the tables later when the WI batsmen get some runs and give them some room to bowl them out. I do hope Clyde Walcott and Frankie Worrell run into form soon. I'd love them to 'murder' some of these bowlers out there.

"I'm glad, too, that Eddie's [leg-spinner Eddie Leadbeater] gone out to India [with MCC]. It's a wonderful chance for him and will probably earn him his cap with Yorkshire [it didn't]. Anyway, I hope he comes off and gets a few wickets.

"Down here, we're always arguing on cricket – usually it's the people who know nothing at all about cricket who argue most, and then we step in and clear the mess up. There's great cricket rivalry in the Club between N and S. The North have a terrific contingent down here and they kid me on that I might get in their Second team!! They have cricket matches down here, and are as much looked forward to as anything."

Now back to football. "I'm glad John Charles has recovered from his cartilage operation, not for Buckley's sake though. Wales look like winning the Championship this year, don't they? John will have a hard job to get into the international team the way Ray's playing. On this year's form, he's just about the best centre half there is. A 'hunch' that I've got on this Austrian game. The right wing will be composed of Arthur Milton and Tom Finney, Tom playing inside right. Arthur's playing remarkably well these days." Brian was right about Milton but Finney was not in the starting line-up. The match, at Wembley, ended 2-2.

*   *   *

Brian has information on a wide variety of topics in his next letter to John which is postmarked November 24, 1951.

Dear John,

Thanks very much for your letter which I received during the week...

We didn't play last Saturday against Spurs as the ground was flooded so, as soon as it was cancelled, a few of us went along with the Spurs' lads in their coach to see the match, Spurs v Chelsea. It was quite a decent match considering the conditions they were playing in, in fact it was quite funny in parts. Occasionally, someone would get the ball and dash for goal as fast as they could. Then, all of a sudden, the ball would stick in the mud and he'd go charging on for a bit before realising the ball 'wasn't with him no more'.

It was a pity Chelsea didn't win after being in front twice but I guess Spurs deserved their win. Bailey was lousy, Nicholson wasn't too good, so God knows why the reporters were pressing their claims for the international team on the Sunday morning.

At night, I met Peter and we went to see the match between Harringay and Nottingham Panthers which Harringay managed to win 6-4. However, they weren't the best side by any means and if they hadn't scored three in the first period when Nottingham had a couple of men off serving penalties, they might never have won. It was a good match though and towards the end Nottingham pulled their goal minder off the ice and put another forward on ice in their efforts to equalise.

Sunday was a very quiet day. I spent the morning down at Highbury having treatment, then the afternoon writing to various people and at night I went along to the Odeon to see the film 'Variety Girl' containing dozens of stars. It was a smashing film and I thoroughly enjoyed it.

On the Monday, I started training as usual, but I felt a pain in my knee again so I cut it short and then, after lunch, I went for some more treatment....On the Tuesday, they sent me out to have a 'bash' at a ball to really decide whether I was fit or not, so off I went. It came through OK, so they told me I could have the following day off to play for the Arsenal against a golf team from the Kent Constabulary.

We play golf matches quite often against various teams and this, played at South Herts., was one.

On the Tuesday night Peter and I went to the Empire to see a show which starred Max Wall and the Radio Revellers. It was a smashing show and we had the time of our life. A couple of the jokes that were told were 'Did you hear of the Eskimo couple who were engaged?' 'The woman broke it off.' The other was 'Did you hear of the cowboy who made a lass-oo with his finger!!' We nearly p----- ourselves with laughter.

On the Wednesday, we got up early to get up to South Herts. for 9.0am but we needn't have hurried because the 'Cops' had got stuck in the 'tunnel' down near Charlton and didn't arrive until well after 10.0. However, we spent the time waiting and drinking coffee. We played nine holes in the morning before lunch which Ralph (Prouton) [Hampshire wicket-keeper/batsman who had a spell on Arsenal's books before moving to Swindon] and I won by 3&2 and after a huge lunch we played a whole round in the afternoon, which we again managed to win quite handsomely. We had a wonderful time though, cracking jokes all day long. Our opponents were awfully 'dry' and we couldn't help laughing at everything they did.

After a few drinks in the bar they offered to bring us back to Muswell Hill in their Police car (a huge Super Snipe) and dropped us off just outside our digs.

When I went in I got

an awful shock!! I was wondering whose the car was outside the house and when I went in I found my Uncle Harry and a friend waiting for me, they'd brought my car down.

After a chat, discussing various things about the car we went out to have a look at it and then we took it along to the garage and arranged to leave it there until I want it. It was in superb condition and looked like a monster from the front – five huge headlamps glaring down the road. Wait till I come up with it a week tomorrow (touch wood). I was very thrilled and before they left I got the gen on the various gadgets and switches on the dashboard etc and on how to change a wheel if need be – although I sincerely hope I don't have to!!

On Thursday, I woke up very early, eager to tell some of the lads about it, I suppose. In my training that morning, I felt my knee again. Oh! I could have cut the damn thing off for two pins. However, I kept on as though nothing had happened in the hope that I could run it off. It was not so, and only got worse so I went and had a hot bath and called it a day.

All through the day it began to stiffen up and I was in a shocking state. I'd caught a dreadful cold and my head was awful and this, with my knee, certainly made me feel like falling off the Empire State Building or something 'equally' as high or that would produce the same effect!!

.....This morning, I did a bit of training then went in and told them I wasn't fit. You ought to have seen their faces!! They didn't know what to do, whether to report it to the Boss (Tom Whittaker) or to try their persuasive powers on me to get me to play with my injury. I'd had enough of that so there was only one thing left to them. So that was that. I was picked to play at Southampton but now I've got to stay and see the doctor and also watch the match against Bolton. It should be a good match and I shall be able to meet my pal Bryan Edwards who plays right half for Bolton and with whom I played a lot of junior football in Leeds and West Riding teams [Edwards later became manager of Bradford City].

However, when I got down to Highbury in the afternoon I went in to see Jack Crayston and afterwards I went up to see the Boss. He wanted to know 'Why, when I went golfing on the Wednesday, wasn't I fit to play tomorrow?' but after I had explained he was alright and we finished up chatting 'nice and friendly'!!

He told me he had received some very good reports on me and

wanted me to keep on playing as often as possible and finished by saying he had great hopes for me both in my football and my cricket. He told me that if I ever had any trouble or bother etc I had to waste no time and come and see him and they would do whatever they could. He's a grand bloke and later we had a chat on my car. He said that he didn't mind me using it so long as I didn't let it 'control' me and not put on any weight with riding around in it. I assured him I wouldn't and that I would only use it for the most important uses. After this we shook hands and away I went feeling very relieved and pleased. Well, that's that.

I'd better close now as it's getting very late, so Cheerio and Good Luck until next.

Yours always

Brian

PS: Did you see any photographs in the newspapers up there on Thursday, Friday or Saturday of me and another lad? Save them if you did, won't you? I'm hoping to be coming home next weekend, so cross your fingers and hope for the best. If I get up reasonably early, I'll call in, but don't expect me for certain.

On the Sunday night I have to slip over to Bill Bowes' home. I have something to see him about which is very important and then I've got to try and persuade him to show me the films that he has just completed on the Australian Tour. He gave a showing at Guiseley Town Hall last week and mum says they're terrific. However, that will only take up one night, but it must be Sunday. He'll be working on the others.

Well, Cheerio again. Hope to see you next week.

Yours

Brian

* * *

Brian managed to get home for a couple of days and, indeed, one of the highlights of his visit was watching the Bill Bowes cine films.

Brian and a few others had their private viewing at Bowes's

home in Menston. "There are three big reels and a small one which lasts nearly three hours," he wrote in a letter postmarked December 8, 1951. "Unfortunately, we only had time to run the first big one and the small one before Mrs. Bowes had got supper ready. I'll say it again, that it was smashing, and I'm certainly making a date sometime to see the rest. It shows our journey out on the ship, most big cities and the places where we visited and I'm simply longing to see the remaining two reels, this time on a full screen.

"He has his own projector, generator and sound piece – all superb pieces of workmanship costing well over £300 and we turned his sitting room into a small cinema. I sat back, deep in an armchair and just wallowed in the dreams of another Tour, which, I hope will come in the future (touch wood).

"If you ever hear of Bill giving a show of it, near at hand, do go and see it. Besides being interesting from the cricket and the Tour in general, it will also give you an idea of what Australia really is like. It's the best kind of geography lesson anyone could hope for except, of course, the trip itself, but do see it if you get a chance.

"Anyway, so much for that. I had a wonderful hour or so chatting with him and also spoke for a minute or so on the phone to London with some of our friends who came from Australia on the Strathaird with us. It was fun."

The show over, Brian got home about midnight and after a chat with his father and mother, he tried to snatch some sleep but couldn't manage it. At 3.0am, therefore, he got his stuff packed in the car and set off into Leeds and on to Doncaster.

"The streets were silent – a good job, too, because the roads began to get icy and the car was sliding about all over the place. Thankfully, I didn't hit any lamp posts or go through any hedges but whenever any vehicle came from the opposite direction I went very easy in case I skidded across the road. After a weary journey (my hands were frozen all the time) I arrived down at Muswell Hill just a little after 8.0am, just in time for some breakfast!!"

Back in London, Brian watched Leyton v Gorleston on the Monday afternoon, Leyton winning 5-4, but a couple of days later he was seeing the doctor again about his knee and was told he had adhesions between the tendon and sheath and that until he had broken them down he would still experience pain.

The doctor advised sprinting full out while at the same time warning that this could make his knee temporarily worse. "Well,

I did as he said and it didn't half hurt, I almost screamed, but I managed to stick it until I could get some treatment. Believe me, I certainly didn't believe in the Doc. That night it stiffened up and I could hardly bend it. Fortunately, it eased somewhat overnight and the next morning further treatment and training made it considerably better and now I'm feeling very fit. I've been doing lapping, sprinting and ball work without any worry today. Unfortunately, the Doc. hasn't passed me fit so I've got the chance of watching the Manchester United game tomorrow."

Brian had treatment and training throughout that week but he was looking forward to the following Wednesday when he was due to play in a game which Leslie Compton had arranged against a team from outside London.

A couple of days before that, said Brian, he was starting cricket practice at Mill Hill with Don Bennett and Alan Moss, the Middlesex fast bowlers. "It'll be fun," he predicted.

Asked by John what he would like for Christmas, Brian says: "A Parker 51. My pen, which I am using now, is 'going' and has no clip on it. It's OK for carrying it about in a writing case but I can't carry it about with me."

CHAPTER FOURTEEN

DECEMBER 14, 1951 – JANUARY 7, 1952

SOCCER SAGAS

Watches Man Utd beat Arsenal, and Harringay beat Brighton at ice hockey – Plays well in A team win over Brentford and gives their centre half a rough time – Strikes up a friendship with Cardew the Cad – Trauma of buying Christmas cards – Listens to Dai Rees talk about golf – Fury at attempt to break into his car – Gets stick from the crowd at Bury St Edmonds in 3-1 win – Two huge meals within two hours, recovers in time next day to play well in 1-1 draw with Wisbech – Delighted with John's Christmas present – Drives friends to Northampton and has blow out soon after doing 90mph – Forced to do 36 laps while training on New Year's Eve

In a letter postmarked December 14, 1951, Brian confirms having watched the Arsenal v Manchester United match the previous Saturday – after morning training and then lunch – but has to admit reluctantly that although it was a good game United provided all the football with Arsenal in bits and pieces until the last five minutes and then it was too late.

At night, Brian went to watch Harringay play Brighton in the last match before the circus takes over Harringay Arena for the Christmas period. It was a great match with Harringay winning 11-4 but the contest wasn't as one-sided as the score suggests. "It was wonderful stuff, the puck dashing from stick to stick, from end to end at lightning pace and lots of goals thrown in. We all had a sweep on the number of goals scored, but unfortunately no-one won as we didn't anticipate so many being scored, but we enjoyed ourselves, nevertheless."

In midweek, Brian was in home action for the A team against Brentford even though the ground was frosted over and 'as hard as hell'. Arsenal won 2-1 and Brian thought he played well at centre forward without managing to get either of the goals.

"Their centre half gave me a --- of a time, hitting me all over the place in the first half. However, he didn't have it all his own way and I kept hitting him as he turned, and occasionally when he was off balance I would just give him a 'helping hand' and down he would go. You can imagine what he was saying to me!!

"Anyway, in the second half, I came out with the intention to 'do' him. I got my chance soon after, when, between him and one of the full-backs, they were trying to pass the ball back to the goalkeeper. However, I had different ideas and went in like a 'ton of bricks', knocked them down like ninepins and then on into the goalkeeper who was diving for the ball. Unfortunately, the ball went wide when I hit it but I couldn't stop myself from going into the goalkeeper and he got his shoulder into my thigh and it didn't half hurt. At the moment I've got some fluid on my knee from it but I've got to run it off worse luck.

"I got the centre half again before the end and then, when the whistle blew for the close, I went up to him, offered my hand and said 'Well played. Tough game wasn't it?' I bet he felt like wringing my neck!!"

At night, by way of relaxation, the team went to the Supporters' Club dance and floorshow at Seymour Hall in the West End where he got introduced to 'Cardew the Cad'. "As he's a cricket enthusiast we got on very well, in fact well enough for him to leave his beautiful wife in my care whilst he went on the stage to do his turn...now I've got an invitation to call round at their home anytime I wish for a drink and a quiet evening!!"

Brian next writes to John a couple of days before Christmas, thanking him for his letter and card, also John's mother and Margery and others for their cards and Christmas present. But buying his own cards and sending them off is driving Brian frantic. "These last few days have been nightmares", he writes. "I got three dozen cards, sent every one off and then each day I look in the post to find a card from so-and-so whom I completely forgot so I've had to dash out and get a card and send it straight away so that they get it in time and don't get offended. I had one from Pauline – you know, the girl we met at Roundhay Park last summer. What was her surname? I couldn't remember it, so I couldn't send her one in return. It would look fishy addressed to Pauline ---- So-and-so Road, Leeds,

Centrespread of the Arsenal Christmas card which shows the Arsenal v Rangers floodlit match at Highbury – which Brian attended and described to John in an earlier letter

wouldn't it? However, anyone I've forgot now will have to 'leg' it."

Having no match the previous Saturday, Brian and his team-mates went to watch the Reserves beat Portsmouth 2-0 before heading into the West End to watch 'The Day the Earth Stood Still' at the Odeon and after more socialising over the next few days they went on the Wednesday to watch an Arsenal golf team play the South Herts Club. "We had a wonderful day out, a lovely Xmas lunch (five course) and tea and we stayed on in the evening for a social evening. We had a few drinks, an odd game of snooker and then Dai Rees gave a talk on his experiences during his visit to Pinehurst with the Ryder Cup team. They were very interesting and after a short break for supper, he began with an instructional talk on golf with references to his book which has just been published. We had a smashing time and finally got ourselves away just after 11.0pm."

Christmas cards were still causing him problems. After training in the morning he went to Highbury to see if he could get any more but they had run out and he had to search for them elsewhere.

Then a more serious situation on the Thursday evening when someone tried to force their way into his car and the handle was broken. "I could kill the person who did it. He didn't succeed in getting in and besides, there was nothing to take."

No envelope has survived from Brian's next letter which was written on Friday, December 28, 1951, and he bemoans the fact that he could not get home for the New Year. "....I guess they think that my training is far more important to me than a few days at home, so I couldn't do anything about it. Anyway, that's that, but I'm awfully disappointed about the whole affair, I was longing to get home to get my teeth in the turkey they sent home – it weighed 16lbs, the lucky devils, and of course to see you all again."

Brian reports that on the Saturday he was in the A team that visited Bury St Edmonds and came away with a 3-1 win from a tough encounter. "The ref and linesmen gave them everything and the crowd gave me the 'bird' and kept shouting 'How's that, Brian' and 'That's not cricket' and lots of other funny remarks. Of course, I didn't let them get away with it and kept putting my fingers up at them, and so forth."

With no match on the Tuesday, Christmas Day, Brian went to watch Arsenal play Portsmouth who they beat 4-1 after easing off in the second half. It was watched by a crowd of 51,241. Afterwards he and his friends dashed home for a 'huge Christmas dinner' with all the trimmings but when he was settling down to sleep it off on the sofa, Don Bennett and another 'lad' came calling with an invite to go to their digs for dinner! It was hospitality which couldn't be refused. "A couple of hours later I don't know how I could stand, I was that full of food, nuts and fruit etc and I went on eating all night. There were quite a few of us in the end – Jimmy Logie, Lionel Smith, Cliff Holton, Dave Bowen and a couple of others – and we sat round talking, watching television and finished up with a game of pontoon. It was a real day."

Hardly surprising that when Brian and the lads had to be up early the following day in order to play at Wisbech they were feeling the worse for wear. "Mind you, a few visits to the WC soon had us ship shape and we didn't do too bad to draw 1-1....I had a decent game and was feeling awfully tired

D. BENNETT

Don Bennett, Brian's team-mate and friend

when I got home so I went straight off to bed."

More training and nights at the cinema followed as the week wore on and Brian again expressed regret that he would not be able to get home for the New Year, but added in a PS: "Tomorrow we haven't a match and on Sunday I'm going up to Northampton with Dave Bowen to his home. They've got a pub, to put it bluntly, and there's every possibility of seeing Freddie Brown who is a great friend of the family."

Brian's first letter of the New Year – in which he reveals he is staying care of Mrs. Johnson at 12 Muswell Road – is postmarked January 7, and he thanks John profusely for having sent him the Christmas present he asked for – a fountain pen. "It's wonderful and a very good writer, too. Yes, it's already signed quite a few autographs and if you'd like to know you're getting the first letter I'm writing with it."

The previous Saturday, December 29, Brian watched Arsenal Reserves beat Norwich City Reserves 2-0 at Highbury and on the morrow he took three of the 'lads' in his car to Northampton on the planned visit to the Bowen family pub, the Plumbers Arms. The car journey, like many others during his lifetime, proved to be interesting to say the least.

"We set off early in the morning, filled the car up and off we went, through Hatfield and on to St Albans. Once past St A. we got on to the main road (Watling St.) and it goes for miles and miles, as straight as an arrow. It was on this road that I got the car up to 90mph and even then my foot wasn't right down. It was terrific and we almost flew along at times.

"Later when we turned off to take the road into Northampton one of my rear tyres blew up on me and we screeched to a stop. It didn't take us long to change the wheel and off we went again. We joked over the thought of what would have happened to us had we had the puncture when we were travelling at 90. It was horrible to imagine, the least of which would have probably turned us over (happy thoughts)."

After a huge lunch prepared by Mrs Bowen the party spent the afternoon reading and sitting by the fire with the occasional drink to fortify them. No mention of bumping into Freddie Brown but an invite to Brian to stay with the family during Yorkshire's match v Northants in the coming season. In between a 'smashing' tea and supper, Brian and Co. went to the cinema on what was turning out to be a memorable day.

It was back to reality the next morning, New Year's Eve, when Brian's training included about 36 laps which approximated to nine miles. "It was awful; I was that tired I'd hardly the strength to run after a ball when they asked me if I wanted a 'kick'. I kicked up a bit of a row about it but everything's settled now, I've got to do tons of sprinting and very little lapping." There was time for an hour or two's nap in the afternoon before dinner and then a visit to the cinema with a girl called Louise. After seeing in the New Year together, Brian returned to his digs for some much needed sleep.

Further details follow of his training and socialising in the latter part of the week and then the letter has to conclude because Mrs. Johnson's just laid the table for supper. How envious thousands of young men across the country would have been of Brian's lifestyle had they known about it in such detail.

CHAPTER FIFTEEN

JANUARY 13 – APRIL 1, 1952

COMING OF AGE

Home at 9.0am after party – Visits circus with brother – Buys new clothes in West End – Predicts Cup and League double for Arsenal – inflicts serious injury on opponent in 3-0 win at Kings Lynn – Cricket practice at Wandsworth – Complains about newspaper article on him 'going back to school' – Lose 3-1 to Fulham and resists retaliating after being floored and shaken – Beat Chelmsford in East Anglican Cup quarter-final – Learns of the King's death on way to match at Portsmouth – Game cancelled and returns to London – New digs – Watches Max Miller – Brings Don Bennett to 21st birthday celebrations – Arsenal agreement on some Yorkshire cricket practices – Socialises with Middlesbrough's Wilf Mannion and orchestra leader Billy Ternent – Farewell to The Gunners

With the season for celebrating still in full swing, the next letter to John, postmarked January 13, includes a lengthy description of an all-night party from which Brian did not return to his digs until 9.0am, sleeping until lunch and then kipping down again in the afternoon. No wonder he was tired – earlier on the day of the party he had travelled with the A team to Lowestoft which resulted in a hard fought 1-1 draw.

He seems to have regained his energy by Monday when he 'scrounged' a day off and went up to South Herts for a day's golf with Don Bennett, Dave Bowen and Lionel Smith. "It was a lovely day and to match the brightness of the day I played some smashing golf, both in the morning and afternoon. To crown all this, I found that I'd won half-a-dozen new golf balls in the Christmas draw, so the Gods really smiled on me that day."

In addition to the training and trips to the cinema, the week contained a couple of less routine diversions, Brian meeting up with one of his brothers for a visit to the circus at Harringay and later in the week going on a shopping spree in the West End and treating himself to a wool gabardine raincoat, a maroon corduroy coat, a couple of pairs of flannels and a pair of shoes – at a cost of well over £30!

A week later, Brian writes in high spirits chiefly because Arsenal have beaten Norwich 5-0 in the third round of the FA Cup and Brian believes his Club are 'the safest bet' for the Cup and League double, although it didn't quite work out that way, Arsenal losing 1-0 to Newcastle United in the Cup Final and finishing third to Manchester United and Spurs in the League.

At the fourth round stage, however, Brian is urging on Leeds United as well as his own Arsenal who have been drawn at home to Barnsley while Leeds are preparing for a visit from Bradford Park Avenue. "Yes, the draw's been nice and favourable for us," he says. "Our motto – 'Let the big

teams knock each other out earlier and then we step in at the end'!!" "There'll probably be a 'blood bath' at Elland Road in the fourth round, but they shouldn't find it hard, especially as John Charles is 'thriving' and playing well after his recent engagement." Brian was no doubt wrong about the bloodbath but he was on the money regarding the result, Leeds winning 2-0.

Brian's A team weren't doing too badly around this time, either, winning 3-0 away to King's Lynn whose side included Jack Howe (former Derby County and England), Ronnie Dix (former Bradford Park Avenue among many others) and Cliff Whitelum (former

Sheffield United and Sunderland).

"I had a very good game and scored a goal into the bargain. When I scored the goal I nearly 'scalped' the goalkeeper!! A ball was crossed from the right and I hooked it into the net as the goalkeeper dived to cover it. Unfortunately, he dived late and my studs went right through his scalp and made a gash which needed 12 stitches. It was awful. You could almost see his skull and when the trainer lifted his hair, his scalp came with it. It was purely an accident, but didn't they 'mix it' afterwards, especially when I had the ball and I had to fight for my life!! It was quite a match and I enjoyed every minute of it, except for, perhaps, the accident which occurred."

The following Wednesday, the A team were up against Norwich City A at Hendon. "We guessed as much, they were out to get their revenge on us for the Cup game and turned out a team which included six or seven Reserves. I was playing centre forward, and against me was supposed to be a centre half who had played for their first team and who was supposed to be a good player. However, I had a 'field day' and after I'd 'hit' him a couple of times when he came to tackle me early on, I never saw much more of him. We won 5-1, of which I managed to bag a couple and might have had a few more with a little luck."

Next day, Brian switched from football to cricket, going to Wandsworth for a spot of practice. "Did you read the Express last week? I don't know if there was anything in your edition up north, but there was something in ours about me 'going back to School again' (!!) meaning of course the Cricket School. It's all wrong, but Alf Gover and Andy Sandham asked me if I minded having my name put in the paper in connection with their Indoor Coaching School and that's what the silly devil of a reporter wrote 'Close goes back to School'. Granted Alf and Andy in general conversation gave me an odd hint or two to improve me, but to put the headlines as such was going a little too far. Anyway, as long as they're talking about you it doesn't matter whether it's good or bad. The time to worry is when there's no mention at all in the newspapers about you."

Come February, 1952, Brian is beginning to focus on how to celebrate his 21st birthday which is on the 24th of that month. He manages a trip home towards the end of January and takes a girl from Harrogate called Margaret to the Odeon to see James Cagney in 'Come Fill the Cup'. On his return to Muswell Hill he writes on

February 1: "I've invited her [Margaret] to come along to my party on the 25th and she will ask her father (who is evidently the boss at their home) and will let me know later by letter, so until then I cannot make any arrangements other than to say that the date (25th) is fixed and that you can invite anyone you like to come along with you. With regard to the party, could you enquire where there is a dinner-dance on that date? ....However, don't do any reserving as yet. We'll do that in the week before when we know how many are coming."

Back at Muswell Hill, Brian's next A game was against Fulham on a Wednesday afternoon. His side lost 3-1 but Brian was happy with his form despite being flattened on one occasion. "In the second half, late on, one of their players forgot he was playing football and tried to hit me 'over the stand'. He had no chance of getting the ball as I'd already slipped that past him and as I was on one foot he came in with everything and down I went. I didn't think much of it then except to get up and 'clock' him one but luckily I thought twice and ran down the field to wait for the free kick being taken. Since then, I've done nothing but wince every time anyone came near my side and my hands are almost void of skin, thanks to the icy ground. Unfortunately, I couldn't get anywhere near to the chap who 'did' me in, otherwise I wouldn't have been responsible for his condition – believe me, it would have been worse than mine."

Brian's team were soon back to winning ways, as he quickly points out in his next letter, their trip to Chelmsford bringing them a 3-1 win in the East Anglian Cup but things did not go quite so smoothly as the score line suggests. "It was a horrifying experience though as all through the first half we were theoretically the best side, but could we score? I had a couple of headers kicked off the line and the goalkeeper made a miraculous save off another shot, besides all the numerous chances that were almost goals but somehow were beaten out by their defenders. Then, all of a sudden, one of their forwards took a shot at our goal, caught the goalkeeper unsighted and we were one down. It knocked some of the sting out of our lads after that until half time when, after a pep talk, we came out determined to 'win or bust'.

"Another half hour past and we were gradually becoming desperate (although still playing the best football) and [we] were rushing things too much in front of goal instead of being a little more deliberate in our shooting. However, then a stroke of luck came our way and we fluked a goal. A centre from the right wing went underneath the goalkeeper's body as he dived and from then until the end of the game it was just a matter as to how many we would get. Unfortunately, I didn't score but I did make the last two goals... ."

Just before the end, Brian suffered a painful crack on the knee when a full back 'let fly' at him with his foot and he couldn't dodge the blow. It burst a blood vessel and before he had got off the field his knee had swollen to twice its normal size. Not that any of this lessened his general optimism. "We're now in the semi-finals of the Cup, so we might be getting two Cups at Highbury this year!!"

There was the chance to take his mind off football for a while early the following week when his Club organised a day out at Luton for a party of players so that they could look round the Vauxhall Motor Car Works. "It was a wonderfully interesting tour, as you might call it, and we enjoyed it very much. Our lunch and tea were provided by the Directors of the Works and everything was thrown open to us, including the testing department, hitherto closed to tourists. Unfortunately, no matter how much we were 'well in' it was impossible to wangle a new car but we came away with a very good appreciation of a Vauxhall car."

On the Wednesday morning his team got up early to go to Portsmouth and they were all assembled at Waterloo when someone broke the news of the King's death. "It was a great shock and took some assimilating before we believed the informant and then only until we had seen the stop press in the newspapers did we finally realise the truth. How was it taken up there?

"Everything went on as usual in London, except that all the cinemas and theatres closed down for the day and all sport except the cup-ties were cancelled."

The team continued on their journey to Portsmouth with Brian involved in a solo school and winning 10/- for his efforts. "But a funny incident occurred when we got out of the train. We had just got our feet on to solid ground again when this announcement came out over the loudspeakers in the station: 'Will the Arsenal football team kindly return to London on the train on the opposite platform as the match has been cancelled'." On the way back, Brian's winning streak at cards continued.

He urges John to speed up his search for a suitable venue for Brian's 21st birthday party but there is still uncertainty as to who he will be inviting and exactly who he will be escorting on the night.

Brian's letter in mid-February is from new digs at 61 Hornsea Rise Gardens and it confirms that he is still in goal-scoring form but also in the wars. In the Saturday match at Clacton-on-Sea he is prominent in his side's 3-1 win. In the first minute or so he barges through to score but the referee blows for a foul with Brian certain the foul was against him. Clacton score first but then Brian equalises before having two further goals disallowed and twice striking the bar after which he gets another knock on his knee.

Monday's golf at South Herts had to be called off at the 9th because of pouring rain and on the Tuesday afternoon he takes himself off to Hornsea Rise Gardens to look at the digs. "I was very pleased with them and the people and so I 'did a change' today. The house is a very nice one and I've got a lovely single room to myself."

Worthy of a mention is Brian's visit in the evening to the Empire Theatre to see Max Miller. "It was a smashing show and Maxie brought the house down with his cracks and dirty jokes. He was terrific. To show you what a draw he is, it was so packed out that people were standing four deep at the back of the theatre, both downstairs and in the balcony and that was in the first house!! We were told that there wasn't a seat to be had for the rest of the week and that we were very lucky to get in that night."

Brian is due home for his birthday celebrations the following week and he writes that he is bringing Don Bennett up with him and that Margaret will not be attending. Again, he urges John to get the event arranged somewhere and asks him to invite Margery and Esme to attend, the idea being that Don will escort Margery and he will look after Esme.

In the event it seems as if John's mother agreed to Don staying at their house because after returning to Muswell Hill Don writes to John and asks him to thank his mother for putting him up over the weekend. He asks John to give sister Margery a big kiss from him – "never got round to doing it myself. Ouch!!!"

His letter is postmarked March 3, as is Brian's next communication to John which mentions Brian's journey by train back to Muswell Hill with Don. The pair of them appeared still to be in a delicate state following the party celebrations. "We got into a sleeping compartment on our own and had quite a decent sleep, but even then we both woke up in a bad way!!!. Fortunately for us, we had made a mistake with the dates over the match and all we had

Brian's 21st birthday party with John, centre, Brian, seated, and Don Bennett, standing extreme right

to do that day was a few sprints in readiness for Thursday's match."

They recovered sufficiently to watch Arsenal Reserves play QPR at Highbury and beat them 4-1, Brian also picking up 'a couple of bob' for winning the sweep as to who would score the first goal.

Another thing Brian picked up was a very heavy cold and the Club rested him from a match on the Thursday but at the weekend both he and Don were playing at Gorleston – and each of them scored a goal in the 4-1 win.

Brian reveals he's just received a letter from Norman Yardley inviting him to play in a football and cricket match v Bradford Park Avenue on April 8 in aid of the British Olympic Fund. "I'd play quite readily but I've got to get permission from the Arsenal Club and then from the Association, so I don't know whether to bother about it."

Four further letters arrive for John from Hornsey Park Gardens with the last one postmarked April 1. His first describes 'a helluva game' at Norwich in the Eastern Counties competition which

Arsenal manage to win 3-2 despite seeming to be playing the first and second teams combined, so strong was the opposition. Brian got kicked 'all over the place' and one blow on the shin tore the skin right up his leg even though he was wearing a shin pad. "No wonder I could hardly walk off the field – however, it was worth it seeing we won and picked up a £1 bonus and two points into the bargain. We've got a chance for the league now, providing we win all our other matches, which of course will be a difficult task but not beyond the team's capabilities."

Too stiff and tired to do much training the next morning, Brian called to see "The Boss" in the afternoon to discuss how free he would be to get some cricket practice in with Yorkshire.

"He was very nice and friendly and we talked things over for a while. Eventually, he agreed to let me do my practising up in Yorkshire, providing I come down for my pre-match training on the Thursday, and any time that they wanted me to play. It will mean an awful lot of travelling and a very unsettled life for a month, but I'm very pleased with it. I shall do my [football] training each morning at Bradford PA with George and then dash over to Headingley for my practising in the afternoon. This will mean that I'll be up from Monday to Thursday and down here the rest of the week unless there are any midweek matches which they want me for. However, it will take care of itself." The 'George' referred to appears to be George Swindin, born at Campsall, Yorkshire, who played in goal for Bradford City (1933-36) and Arsenal (1936-54). Appointed Arsenal manager in August, 1958.

Another 'helluva tough match' soon followed the Norwich game, this time at Cambridge Town for whom former Huddersfield Town pair Bill Whittaker and Jack Percival were playing but Arsenal triumphed 2-0. "Percival was playing centre half against me, but I managed to give him a rough time and with a bit of luck I might have had two or three goals. Unfortunately, as it worked out, I didn't score but we won and that's all that matters. Now we are lying in third place in the league." The winning sequence continued with a 4-2 success against Portsmouth but Brian was rested from this match although he was at Hendon to cheer the lads on.

He was also present for the first-team match against Charlton which Arsenal won 2-1 but Brian was unimpressed. "Our side played as though the Cup Final was the next day and our passes were anywhere but the right place...but nevertheless we got two points and came nearer the Cup and League double."

Brian was picked for the Reserves against Brentford at Highbury and he viewed it with keen anticipation. "It's my chance again and I shall have to try like hell to grab it. If I do, well there's an opening right in front of me as soon as Reg Lewis passes out 'or doesn't want to play'. I've no fear of Cliff Holton, and Peter Goring is being made into an inside forward so touch wood and hope for the best."

The next letter reveals that Arsenal beat Brentford 1-0 and Brian admits the goal was a fluke and that the team in general played very badly. "....none of them seemed to 'want' the ball and as a result our teamwork was all at sea. I didn't do so bad as it sounds, in fact the times that I did get the ball (very few and far between) I used it quite well and made about four glaring openings from which we should have scored, even though I didn't get a chance myself."

Greater personal success followed on the Monday – this time on the golf course. "I had a big match on with Don Bennett up at South Herts. I was giving him eight shots in a match for 5/- and fortunately I was on top form and won 4&2. I had a marvellous round, going round in 78 (the bogey is 72) and enjoyed myself tremendously." Weary from his efforts, Brian went back to his digs and enthused about a new television programme he had watched called *What's My Line?*

At the weekend, Arsenal were at home to Middlesbrough and Brian's view was that his Club were lucky to sneak a win, knocking in three goals towards the end. "However, it doesn't matter how we won, we got two points and are now level with Manchester United. It probably won't be settled until the last match of the season when we meet them at Old Trafford. It wont half be a scrap."

In the evening, Brian went to the Arsenal Supporters' Club dance at Finsbury Town Hall to which some of the Middlesbrough players also called in and Brian bumped into their right half, Harry Bell, who was an old cricket pal. He called across Wilf Mannion for whom Brian had the highest regard.

"Wilf, who had played a blinder that afternoon, was 'well under' and kept trying to persuade me to have a drink, too. My will power's as strong as ever. On yesterday's showing, if there's a better inside forward than Mannion, I've yet to see him. He was superb, picking up all the loose balls in their penalty area and ours and never failed to use it."

Although Brian promises to write to John again 'next week',

there is no record of that correspondence and the last letter in the Collection from London is the one posted on April 1, 1952, with Brian explaining why his intended trip home had had to be cancelled at the last minute.

"On Sunday when I went to the ground for treatment the Boss asked me if I would put it off for another week as we have two matches this week, on Wednesday and Thursday. Anyway, I thought it wise to agree and stay down so here I am. He wouldn't have thought much of me if I'd said I wouldn't and I don't think I missed much as they [Yorkshire] won't be practising out of doors in this weather.

"Last Monday, instead of playing in the semi-final at Bury, I found myself playing at White Hart Lane against Tottenham. We managed to pull it off, winning 2-1 but it was a tough game. I managed to score the first, but shortly afterwards I collided with the goalkeeper and he put his knee right in my thigh. It just about crippled me but I kept on and my knee began to swell until at the end I could hardly walk, never mind run. I didn't do so badly and did one or two good things even while I was hobbling around in the second half."

After the match, with his thigh strapped, Brian and some of his team-mates went over to St John's Wood where Billy Ternent, the well-known orchestra leader, had invited them to his flat for drinks with his wife and friends. Then it was on to a club to play in a snooker match against Highbury Police. "We had tons of fun, lots to eat and drink and the snooker was enjoyable too. I won both my matches." The evening was still not complete because then it was back to Ternent's flat for a while and then on to Reg Arbiter's flat nearby where gin and sherry were served before a substantial meal was devoured. A taxi home arrived at 2.0am.

Brian writes that he had a long chat with Billy Ternent who said that he and his band would be playing at Filey during the summer and that he would call in at Scarborough when the cricket was on and invite the team to a night out in Filey.

The treatment on his knee continued throughout the week and on the Thursday he saw Jim Logie who had a huge carbuncle on his knee, the size of Brian's fist, and it had to be lanced. "No news of this leaked out or got into the newspapers except that 'Jim Logie has a slight strain in his leg' was mentioned." Brian's own fitness remained very much in doubt and he decided he could get through a game at the weekend but in the end was spared because blizzards caused everyone to be idle.

And so concludes Brian's accounts of life at Highbury. Plenty of hard work and hard knocks but these were balanced with a social life that would remain in his memory for the rest of his days.

As already mentioned, Brian's last letter from London was at the beginning of April and it was at the end of the same month that he failed to turn up for Arsenal Reserves' Football Combination Cup replay against Fulham. A month later he was told Arsenal would not be retaining him. He had played in 26 matches for the A team, scoring 13 goals, and in eight games for the Reserves he found the net three times.

As was to happen much later with Yorkshire and England, his parting with Arsenal was amid some controversy brought about by apparently poor liaison between Yorkshire captain, Norman Yardley, and wicket-keeper, Don Brennan, who was deputising for him in the match against MCC which began on April 30, 1952, at Lord's.

That was also the day of the Fulham game and Arsenal had given Brian permission to play cricket provided he could get to the soccer match in time for the kick-off.

Yardley had consented to Brian's request to leave Lord's early in order to fulfil his soccer commitment but Yardley did not play at Lord's and as Brennan seemed unaware of the circumstances he declined to release Brian early from Lord's. He was, therefore, absent at the start of the football match. As a result of this, he was given a free transfer at the end of June, 1952, and he went on to play for Bradford City until a torn cartilage ended his footballing career – as described in Chapter Seventeen.

CHAPTER SIXTEEN

MAY 15 – SEPTEMBER 23, 1952

BACK TO CRICKET

'At the double' again – Letter from Worcester with blunt advice for John – Stunned by John's illness – Advised to keep away – Mrs. Close's letter – A short return to Catterick – Wins shooting contest – Scores goals and makes runs – Hero of his Unit – Talks with Bradford City and others – Enjoys Pateley Bridge Show

With his Arsenal days behind him, Brian is free in the summer of 1952 to concentrate solely on his Yorkshire career and to try to re-discover the form that three years earlier had seen him achieve the double and a Test place in his first season of county cricket.

Still only 21 years of age, he lets neither himself nor Yorkshire down, completing the double yet again with 1,192 first-class runs for the county at an average of 33.11 and 114 wickets at 24.08 runs apiece. He played a big part in helping Yorkshire finish the Championship season as runners-up to Surrey.

Brian's letters to John are fewer around this time but one reason may be that 61 Victoria Crescent now has a telephone and communicating can be quicker and much easier than before. There are indications, also, that the demands on Brian's time with Yorkshire are such that he has realised he cannot go on writing to all and sundry as frequently as he did in the past.

Consequently, when Brian writes to John from Yorkshire's match against Worcestershire at New Road in June, 1952, he vents his anger at John demanding more telephone calls and letters, but in his next correspondence in early September he is stunned and distressed at the news that John is seriously ill in hospital with poliomyelitis. Brian admits that he was so shocked that he had 'cringed away' from writing much earlier.

At the end of the cricket season, Brian is back at Catterick for a fortnight to complete his required number of days service from being on the reserve list – and he does so in style, thoroughly enjoying the experience. He writes from there to John in Q Ward at Pinderfields Hospital at Wakefield where he continues his recovery from poliomyelitis.

LS PF 962   GTG 7.45   LEEDS T 15

GREETINGS = JOHN ANDERSON   61 VICTORIA CRESCENT HORSFORTH =

CONGRATULATIONS AND BEST WISHES ON YOUR BIRTHDAY =

BRIAN. ++

GREETINGS TELEGRAM

Brian's telegram to John congratulating him on his birthday

GREETINGS TELEGRAM   PF 962

JOHN. ANDERSON.

61 VICTORIA CRESCENT

HORSFORTH

Dear John

Thank you very much for your letter which I received at Lord's, although I was far from pleased on reading it.

Just because I haven't been down for a week or so you've no right to jump to conclusions....

At Chesterfield, I stayed on over the weekend and while I was at Harrogate I was otherwise engaged with a pretty young girl of whom you will be hearing very much more of.

I couldn't possibly ring you whilst I was at Harrogate [Yorkshire v Gloucestershire, June 11-13, Yorkshire won by seven wickets] for I had to set off fairly early in the morning and I didn't get home until well after 11.0pm each night. As for not ringing you when you sent me a telegram, well, I received it just before lunch when I was padded up ready to go in next. I couldn't ring you at lunch time and afterwards I was batting all the time until the end of the match [34*].

As we were leaving straight afterwards by car for London, I had such a rush on packing my bag and getting changed in time to get away with Don Brennan who was taking me down that I left a message with Bryan Stott to ring you. I couldn't possibly have asked him to wait without causing any ill feeling.

I don't usually write to anyone whilst I'm away on these trips, not even mum, Margaret or anyone and I wouldn't have written to you but I was very annoyed with you. For God's sake stop being so damned moody and enjoy life for a change instead of being sulky when things don't happen just the way you want them to. I was a great sufferer of that until a short while ago, but now I'm thankful to say that I've learnt my lesson. It can't go on always and things are bound to change for the better (my luck couldn't be worse at the moment in both batting and bowling).

However, it's about time you learnt your lesson too and if no-one else will correct you, I will.

When you go on your holiday on the continent, go there with the intention of having the best time of your life. Forget about everything else or everyone else and just think of one person –

Dear John,

Thank you very much for your letter which I received at Lords, although I was far from pleased on reading it.

Just because I haven't been down for a week or so you've no right to jump to conclusions like that, after all I'm not "counting" you.

At Chesterfield, I stayed on over the weekend and while I was at Harrogate I was otherwise engaged with a pretty young girl of whom yourself, and shake yourself out of this 'stupor' you're in. Believe me, it's the only way and if you don't enjoy yourself when you are young, you'll live to regret it for the rest of your life. After all, you can only expect back from life what you put into it, so come on John, pull yourself together and you'll be all the better for it.

When you come home again get stuck into your work and give your best to everything you do or put your mind to and you'll reap the benefit of it.

Well John! I haven't said half I would have liked to have said, but I hope it will make you think a lot, not only of yourself but of what other people think and see of you.

Don't think any worse of me for this, it's for your own good and if I'd have been your father, I would have done it a long time ago and given you a real shaking down.

At the moment you're not putting a scrap of effort into life so what can you expect in return? You expect people to run around after you, your mother and father to keep you for as long as you think fit and lots of other things. That's the wrong approach to life completely and it's now that you should be attempting to put something back into it in return.

I must close now as I'm in next to bat and I want to accustom my eyes to the glare [Brian made 78 and Yorkshire won by an innings and 26 runs]. However, if you think of all I've wrote I shall be only too pleased, because I know that once you think of it you're bound to change your line of thought to all things and it will be very good for us all besides yourself.

Anyhow, enjoy yourself on the continent. Give my best wishes to Don and tell him I was disappointed not seeing him at Swansea, but I'll see him again sometime − I'll look forward to seeing a rejuvenated John on your return with no exam worries or anything so Cheerio and Good Luck.

Yours Always

Brian

Friday, Sept 6 [September 5]

Dear John,

I really don't know how to start this letter, I'm almost stumped for words. However, I'll do my best.

I was very very sorry to hear of the dreadful happening which has befallen you. It was a great shock to me, one which I suppose I could not assimilate for a time because of the seriousness of it, and I can only say that I hope beyond hope that you will be cured and have a speedy recovery to your normal self.

I am very sorry not to have written before. I suppose you think me a heel for it, but I meant to write a thousand times and each time I cringed away from it and put it off. I feel worse for it now, so don't think too bad of me, please. Ever since I rung up home (yours) on the Sat. morning of the Surrey match to see whether you were coming to watch the match and your mother told me of your mishap, I have been wondering about you and Margery.

I intended calling down at your home to see your mother that week-end, but I just casually mentioned it to Mr. Broomhead (the Orth. spec.) who is a committee member of Yorkshire and he told [me] that in the interests of everyone, I should refrain from calling for a while, whilst there was chance of catching it. Later, Mr. Nash [John Nash, Yorkshire secretary] told me, so I decided to ring. However you know my powers of telephoning!!

Anyway, forgive me please and let's get on to a more cheerful note.

How's everything with you? Keep your 'pecker' up because everything will turn out OK and it won't be long before you're up and about again. How are the nurses there? Lovely and beautiful eh!

....How do you spend your days now, reading and what?

...What have I been doing? Not much in the cricket line I'm afraid – I can't do a thing right at the moment, no runs, no wickets. I reckon it's about time the season ended and none too soon neither.

We had a marvellous time on the Southern tour. We didn't pay much attention to the cricket and very rarely got to bed before the early hours of the morning. We had lots of parties, tons of talent and I increased my list of 'friends' in and around England by several. We went swimming in the sea at Clacton and it was lovely and warm. At Canterbury we popped into the Cathedral to see the Red Dean and watch the people troop out when he starts his sermon. At Scarborough, I've been dancing on the Spa, been to the Open Air Theatre to see 'The Desert Song', and to the Floral Hall to see a variety show. In fact, I've had a wonderful time altogether.

I'm selling my old car and getting a new one on Saturday all being well. I'm going home to fetch it, then I'm coming back to Scarborough to enjoy a holiday, playing golf, swimming, dancing.... Next week, I go up to Catterick to do my 14 days. 'Should be fun', I don't think, however it will be a change so I don't see why I shouldn't enjoy myself.

Well John, I guess I shall have to close for now – Len's just got his second century of the match [Yorkshire v MCC, Hutton 103 and 137] (100 more than what I'll get) [Close 14 and six, match drawn], so I'll say cheerio and good luck – write me and tell me all – I hope to come and see you when things have settled down and the season's finished, so until [then] keep your 'pecker' up, laugh at things which go wrong and they'll soon take a turn for the better.

Be seeing you.

Yours always

Brian

48 Hawthorn Ave
Yeadon
Sunday
[postmarked Sept 8]

Dear John,

I was pleased to hear from your mother that you are a little better and I hope the news of you both gets a bit brighter every day.

Mrs. Exley was up the other day and she sends her best wishes for you and Margery, for your complete recovery.

We haven't seen you since Brian's birthday, but we often talk about you, especially on Sunday nights, as you used to come up periodically when B [Brian] was away, and we haven't seen you at the matches, I expect you have been busy with exams etc.

Well the cricket season is all about finished and we shall have to settle down again to gardening and other jobs which we have put aside.

Peter was up from London in August and went with us to New Brighton for a week, we had a nice holiday and we all feel better for it.

I think this is all just now John, it has gone 12 o'clock (midnight). I have been getting the children's clothes ready for school and I am tired.

So Goodnight. God Bless you both.

Love from

Brian's mum

Mr. Close and the boys send their best wishes to you and Margery for your complete recovery.

48 Hawthorn Ave
Yeadon
Leeds
Tuesday
[postmarked Catterick Camp, September 23]

Dear John,
Just a few lines to let you know that everything's going OK up at Catterick.

How's everything with you? I hope that your legs are improving as they were when I came to see you just before I came up here.

I'm having a smashing time up here attached to the RASC Company. I came up here a week ago last Sunday and when I arrived there, there was no one expecting me until the following day so I went down to Richmond and stayed the night with some friends. It was grand to meet some of my old pals again and I had a pleasant time.

On the Monday, I reported to camp again and after having an interview with the OC I spent the rest of the day getting myself settled in and making friends with the officers and men whom I might have need to ask favours from. I didn't do too bad at all but even so they still got me out on to the range on Tuesday for the annual shooting classification. It was fun and after the counting up was done I found that I'd finished top with both rifle and Bren. Not bad to say I hadn't fired one for at least two years. We came back early and I got myself cleaned up and away I went again to see some more friends.

While I've been up here, I've been very busy with hardly a moment to reflect on how awful it can be up here. At night, I've met my old friends as well as lots of new ones and as a result I've enjoyed it tremendously. It's almost been like a tonic.

On the Wednesday they put me on to a three ton Bedford to act as a driver. Well, I'd had no experience at all with driving lorries and for a while I was crashing the gears and making a helluva din until I got used to it and then 'I went to town'. They put me on details here and there, popping down to Richmond, on to the Range and all over Catterick, making the damn thing go about 50mph when its only supposed to go 30. In between times I fiddled about with the engine etc and then used the Army's time, tools and oil to get under my car and grease that. I did all the springs, front suspension, steering and brakes, and she's going beautifully now. I enjoyed myself immensely rolling about in all the 'muck' and dirt and I've got so much grease on my hands now, it'll be weeks before I get them clean again.

I spent a day running blokes from 3TR backwards and forwards from the Range [and] a day running down to the Green Howards at Richmond and fetching rations for them. It's not so bad when you can stop outside a friend's house, pop in and have a cup of tea several times a day.

On Saturday morning after I had finished I dashed home and got there just in time to go and see the 'Derby' match between Bradford [Park Avenue] and Bradford City. I had to go along to see both managers to talk things over. They want me to play for them but before I commit myself they'll have to make it worth my while. Darlington and York are also wanting me, so between them I shouldn't do so bad!! I shall not decide until I get out of this mob at the week-end.

I had a couple of games at the unit last week. It's only a small unit and the team isn't so very good – they just kick the ball and hope but we played 2T Regt. Royal Sigs and beat them 6-1 and a day later we played the RASC Depot at Sedgefield and beat them 8-0. Each time I scored four goals, but at the expense of two bloody sore feet from wearing new Army football boots, scratched and bruised legs and a slightly sprained ankle. I'd have given anything for a pair of old boots but there weren't any in the Camp. The ones I was wearing damn near crippled me to walk in them let alone run. However, a good time was had by all and the Major who runs the team is nearly off his 'rocker' with excitement – they've never known such times before and at the moment I'm the unit hero – 'I could get away with murder at the moment'.

On Sunday, I set off to Ripon in the morning where I was playing in an odd cricket match. It was quite a nice day and I enjoyed it very much even though our side lost. I managed to sneak 50-odd runs before I decided to 'act the fool' and get out, but I only took one wicket. I didn't know whether I was holding a ball or a cabbage, it was that strange after three weeks without touching one. We had a bit of a party laid on for us after the match and we didn't arrive home until nearly midnight.

On Monday, we had to set off early again, this time for Pateley Bridge where they held their annual Show. We had another cricket match and this time I managed to get 65 runs before I was run out. After this I took no further interest in the match until nearly tea time and I went to have a look round the Show to see all the dogs, cattle, horses and pigs etc. It was a wonderful Show and I thoroughly enjoyed everything concerned with it and then I got back to the match again just in time to see them [us] all bowled out. This time I got two for about 15 and finished off a splendid day with a grand meal at the Lodge.

That was yesterday and this morning I got up early (5.30am) to come back to camp. As far as I can see I needn't have come for I've nothing to do for the first time since I came, not even on my own car.

Well John, I guess I shall have to close for the present. I shall be home on Saturday, I believe, so if I can possibly get over I might be over next week sometime. If there's anything you want particularly, let me know and I'll see what I can do. I haven't heard anything about my job yet, but I've got to do extensive work and enquiring as soon as I'm free from this.

Well John, Cheerio and Good Luck – see you soon.

Yours

Brian

CHAPTER SEVENTEEN

FEBRUARY 16, 1953 – MAY 6, 1954

MAJOR KNEE OPERATION

In BRI for cartilage operation – Describes driving to hospital in a blizzard – Severe reaction to operation – Fun with the nurses – Back home – Car will 'go like a rocket' – Oxford, 1954 – Rainy start to season – Cards but little cricket

At the completion of the 1952 cricket season, Brian was at the top of his form again but once more the fates conspired against him and very soon a serious knee injury was to end his football career and restrict him to just two Championship matches for Yorkshire in 1953.

After his release from Arsenal, several clubs expressed an interest in Brian's services, including Chelsea and Aston Villa, but he decided that with his commitment to Yorkshire cricket it would be in his better interests to play for a club nearer to home. Bradford City, Bradford (Park Avenue), Darlington and York City were all in touch with him but in the end it was Bradford City manager, Ivor Powell, who persuaded him to go to Valley Parade where he signed as a full-time professional.

Brian made his debut for Bradford City against Tranmere Rovers on November 1, 1952, and a week later he scored in his side's 2-1 win against Chesterfield, but soon afterwards he was badly injured while playing against Port Vale. The cartilage in his right knee was removed in an operation at Bradford Royal Infirmary in February, 1953, and although he returned briefly to play for the Reserves he suffered further swelling and decided to pack soccer in and concentrate solely on cricket.

John remains in Pinderfields Hospital around this time and Brian writes to him from Bradford Royal Infirmary giving details of his operation and then from home on March 1 during his recuperation.

There are no letters from this point until early in the 1954 season when Brian reports from Oxford to John at home and that is the end of the correspondence until Brian writes regularly on the highly controversial MCC 'A' team tour of Pakistan in 1955-56.

Ward 4
Bradford Royal Infirmary
Duckworth Lane
Bradford
Postmarked February 16, 1953

Dear John,

Thanks very much for your letter which I received the other day. Up to now I've had very little chance of writing back to any of the letters which I've received since I arrived here. You can perhaps tell by my writing that something's amiss. Well, I'll try to tell you it all since I came in last Tuesday.

Well, on Tuesday morning, the day that the snow blizzard was raging, I set off from home in my car, all packed and ready for the fray. First of all I had to dig my car out of the garage – snow drifts were piled up against the hut door – I couldn't call it off and disappoint the hospital staff. 'Big Head.'

Anyway, I got going and everything went okay until I got to the hill going up to Manningham Lane traffic lights. I got a good speed up at the bottom and went up like a bird, but as luck would have it, the traffic lights turned against me and I had to stop. When I came to start again, I couldn't and I had to wait five minutes before I could get any help. Later just going round Frank's end, I skidded on the icy road and went broadside along the street. Frank came and dug me out.

After a while, I arrived at the hospital and got settled down in the ward. Of course it didn't take long before I was the best of pals with all and sundry, including the nurses!! I wasn't confined to bed and I got up to play cards and one or two other things.

Margaret came in to see me on Tuesday night – she was determined I wasn't going to get lonely, and we had a nice little time chatting to each other. On Wednesday, Margaret came in again, and later mum came in to see me before the operation.

I had tons of stuff to eat and that night I 'gorged' myself, knowing I would have nothing at all the next day. Next day I was up at 6.0am taking the tea round, then at 9.0am they came to prick me for the first time. It was supposed to send me [to] sleep but it succeeded in doing the opposite and I was as gay as a lord when they took me off to the op. room.

I remember the anaesthetist sticking the last needle into my arm and saying 'now this will send you to sleep – he looks as though he doesn't believe it, does he'? About an hour later I awoke in the ward, a little dizzy but I could think quite clearly and I had a bit of fun with them all and when the Sister came to see how I was I started making love to her!! The rest of the day was OK. I had no pain and I surprised everyone by lifting my leg, moving my feet and contracting my muscles. Needless to say, since then I've paid doubly for being a 'feather plucker' as the reaction set in and has been going on for the last four days.

That night wasn't too bad, but the next morning it gave me hell. I get a nagging pain all down the inside and the back of my leg and it drives me mad at times. I keep taking pills every so often but they don't quell it for long and I'm back squirming again soon. All my nerves are on edge and twitching and I can't concentrate on anything for long. At nights, I take some pills (I'm dopey) and I manage to sleep till about 1.0am when the night nurse, with whom I get on very well, comes and chats with me and brings me a cup of tea. It has helped to pass along the nights which otherwise would've probably driven me frantic. I've had nightmares too.

Even amidst all this I've enjoyed myself with the lads in the ward – we have lots of fun and with the nurses too. I've had lots of visitors in every day, Margaret keeps popping up to see how I am and to see if I need anything and I find how she is and whether Frank's been in any of his tempers etc. The operation – well he has taken the inner cartilage out, tested the cruciate ligaments and then had a look at the outer. Here he found two bits floating around so he took them out and that was that.

I've got my cartilage in a little bottle and its got a big tear at the rear of it. At the moment they've just been doing me – the physiotherapist has been making me do my exercises. I can do them all quite easily at the time and they all think it's going along marvellously well. However, afterwards I get the pain in my knee and it nearly makes me writhe.

I don't know how long I shall be in here, but a rough guess is from two to three weeks. I can hardly move in bed – I've got a full plaster on right from my ankle to my groin and it doesn't half hold me down.

Well, so much for me. How are you and how is Margery? I hope you're both going on fine and having as happy and enjoyable a time as me apart from the pain and other things. At the moment my nerves are shot to bits and keep twitching every few seconds. It's a horrible feeling. I keep getting piles and piles of letters but they're going to have to wait until I feel a bit better. I came in hoping to catch up on my correspondence a bit but it seems to have got into a worse state – I shall have to stay in months to catch up now. Well, I must close now, so Cheerio and Good Luck until next [time].

Yours

Brian

48 Hawthorn Avenue
Yeadon
Leeds
[Postmarked, March 1, 1953]

Dear John,

Thank you very much for your letter, card and also the grand present which you gave me. You know how much I like my golf, don't you? Well John, I can honestly say that I shall get lots of enjoyment in playing with the clubs.

As you've probably seen, I'm out of hospital and at home now. My leg got strong very quickly and Mr. Naylor had a look at me and told me that I could go home on Thursday.

It wasn't until 8.30 on Wednesday night that they let me get up and at first I felt as heavy as lead!! The following morning I was up with the lark and was able to get washed in the bathroom once again. I felt grand. At the moment I've still got my plaster on (groin to ankle) and it ties me down a bit – I find it difficult to knock about, but you know me, I can't stay in one place longer than a few moments and so I've been managing the best I can.

I left hospital on Thursday morning after thanking the Sister and all the nurses for the 'good time' and all that they'd done for me. We really did have a wonderful time especially on my birthday [February 24] but I'll tell you of that later when I see you next – I hope it won't be long.

They brought me home by ambulance and I unpacked my stuff then went for a walk down town to see some friends and call at one or two places on the way. It was lovely to be up and about again but with the plaster on I was hobbling about like a lame duck – a short way in a long time. After a beautiful lunch of ham and eggs (I didn't half miss them in hospital) I had a rest and fell asleep.

That evening I thought to myself that I wasn't going to be caged in just because of a bad leg so Peter (he'd come up for a few days holiday) and I went out to the pictures in Bradford to see 'Trent's Last Case'. It was quite good.

Yesterday, I was up with the lark because I'd to get ready to go back to the Infirmary for exercise in the gym (three times a week) and worst of all I'd got to find my own way there by bus. Anyway, I got there early and went into the ward to find out 'if they'd missed me' – they sure had (big head), the ward was as quiet as ---- and I chatted for a few minutes with most of them. Later, I came home and spent the rest of the day quietly.

I don't know what I'm going to do today – if I feel strong enough I might go down to Bradford to see how the car's going on. I'm having it done up by a garage hand – a friend of mine. It's much cheaper that way and it gives him a bit of spending money too. It'll go like a rocket when I get it back. I've got to keep my plaster on until next Thursday to stop me bending the leg and to let the knee recover from the operation before I do any bending, otherwise I might get fluid on the knee and that will put me back a week or perhaps more. Anyhow, until then the car's no use so it's a good thing this chap could do it for me just now.

Once I can get about without the plaster and can use the car I'll be coming over to see you again. Perhaps a week on Tuesday. Let me know what you've been doing and how long you'll be in there, John.

Anyhow, I shall have to close now, but when I see you next remind me to tell you my experiences in hospital – they're quite funny but I'd fill a book with them.......

Anyway John, give my regards and best wishes to Margery and thank her for the card won't you please? Tell her I shall be coming over as soon as I am knocking about again. Also, thank your mother for the card and give her my regards and best wishes.

Until next, Cheerio and Good Luck.

Yours Always

Brian

Oxford University Cricket Club
Thursday [May 6, 1954]

Dear John,

Thank you very much for your letter which I got the other day at Lord's. I'm awfully sorry that I didn't see or ring you before I came down, but it wasn't because I didn't want to, because I did mean to ring you several times, but unfortunately I didn't get down to it – you know 'so much on my mind and one or two odd things'.

Seriously though, I never had a moment to myself. I had to get everything completed before I left, all my cricket clothes cleaned and pressed and numerous other jobs to get done, boots and cricket bag repaired – in fact so much so that I didn't usually finish and get to bed until 12 or 1 each night. What made it worse was that I had to do it all by "Shanks's Pony" as my car hasn't come through yet.

....We left for London just before lunch on Friday by train (the Committee wouldn't let us use cars) and arrived down about tea time. That night Ray Illingworth and myself went to Highbury to see Young England lose to Old England 2-1. It was my first night out for ages, or at least since Easter and I enjoyed it immensely. There was some lovely football on both sides but the Old'uns had a little more craft.

Saturday morning saw us all out at the nets early at Lord's but, just as we were about to start playing, the rains came. Just like the weather – we have a perfectly dry April and then when the cricket comes, down comes the rain to spoil it.

However, we did manage to start before lunch and we played the rest of the day without interruption. We didn't do too bad at all, bowling them out for 162 on a wet slow wicket. I did well with getting two cheap wickets after lunch, but when it was good to bowl on after tea I never got chance and Wardle nipped in for the last four tail enders. Still the season's young!!

Well, as you know, we didn't play again in that match so we

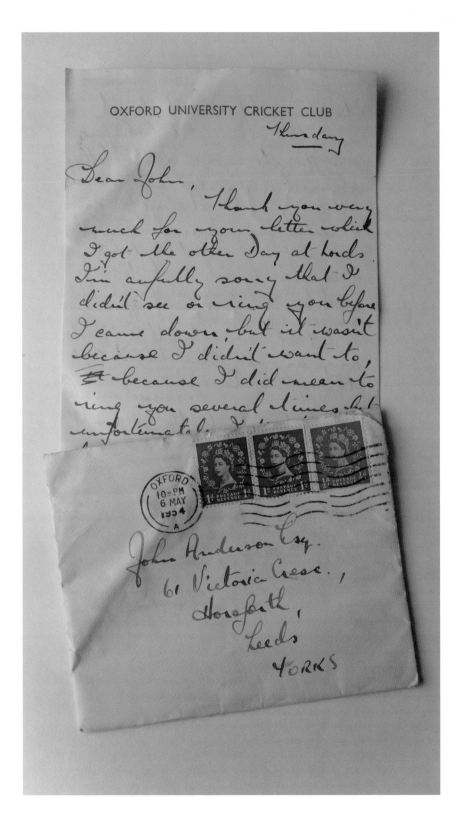

spent our time playing solo in the dressing room. Sunday was a bleak, rainy day so we had to cancel our golf and go to the pictures instead. I saw 'King of the Khyber Rifles' starring Tyrone Power.

....On Tuesday lunchtime, the game was called off and we got packed up and came along early to Oxford. It was raining here as well when we got here, but the 'pub' or hotel whichever you may call it is a lovely cosy place and we settled down to a game of solo again and didn't pack up till after 11.0pm. Yesterday, we were rained off again and back to the hotel we went again for another session of solo.

Well as you can see we haven't 'broke any pots' yet. I seem to have got used to this life of quiet restfulness rather than dashing around after this and that.

Well, John, that's that up to date – at the moment I'm just waiting to go in next but one. The weather's fine but windy and the wicket just like a sponge so if I get in I shall just have to take it steady.

....Well, John, I must close now as there's been another wicket fallen and I shall have to go and watch the game just in case, so I'll say Cheerio and Good Luck. [Close scored 22 not out and Yorkshire went on to win by 235 runs on the first innings. Match drawn.]

Yours

Brian

CHAPTER EIGHTEEN

DECEMBER 13, 1955 – FEBRUARY 6, 1956

TO PAKISTAN

*Airmail from RMS Circassia – 'The Final Test' remake –
Photographers on board – Avoids sea sickness – Fit as a fiddle –
Bad umpiring decisions – Golfing success – Filming and touring
in Lahore – Hanif's 'stupid batting' – Touch-down in Delhi –
New Year's Eve dance – Hunting in Hyderabad – Team 'water
battle' truce*

With the telephone now a part of everyday life and a means of
instant communication, Brian's letter from Oxford in May, 1954,
was his last to John until Brian was on board s.s. Circassia in
December, 1955, on his way to Pakistan on the MCC's first 'A' tour.
The postmark is unclear but probably 13 December, 1955.

The conclusion of the 1954 season left Brian with 822
Championship runs for Yorkshire and 47 wickets, the team finishing
second in the table to all-conquering Surrey. In all first-class matches
for Yorkshire he scored 1,287 runs and took 66 wickets.

The following season Yorkshire again finished second to Surrey
in the Championship, Brian scoring 941 runs in the competition
and taking 74 wickets while in all first-class matches for Yorkshire
he hammered out 1,131 and captured 90 wickets.

Brian also made his England comeback in the fifth and final
Test against South Africa at The Oval, England having won the
first two games in the rubber and their opponents the next two.
The match was won by England by 92 runs and Brian played a
significant role, opening the batting with Jack Ikin and top scoring
in the first innings with 32 out of a total of 151.

He had done more than enough to be included in the party for
Pakistan which was a mix mainly of emerging players and a few
others with considerable county experience. Only three of side were

Brian, playing for MCC v the South Africans, takes a low catch to dismiss J H B Waite off a ball from Fred Titmus

over 20 years of age.

It was a happy band of players which set sail, little knowing that they would become involved in deep controversy and acrimony through an incident which led to MCC President, Lord Alexander of Tunis, offering to call off the Tour and send the players home. It did not lead to this but on their return to England in March the Tour manager, Geoffrey Howard, issued a long statement in which he acknowledged 'The folly of the Peshawar incident' and its serious repercussions, and that 'our young team are bitterly sorry about it and have suffered a good deal as a result'.

'The incident' occurred on the evening of February 26, 1956, after the third day of the third Pakistan v MCC Representative match and involved one of the umpires, Idris Begh, receiving the 'water treatment' in a high-spirited rag-type piece of japery which resulted in the immaculately dressed Begh getting a cauldron of

Surrey County Cricket Club 3D.

KENNINGTON OVAL

ENGLAND v. SOUTH AFRICA
Saturday, August 13th, 1955 (5 Day Match)

	ENGLAND		First Innings		Second Innings	
1	Ikin, J. T.	Lancashire	c Waite, b Heine	17	c Goddard, b Heine	0
7	Close, D. B.	Yorkshire	c Mansell, b Goddard	32	b Goddard	15
3	P. B. H. May	Surrey	c Goddard, b Fuller	3		
4	Compton, D. C. S.	Middlesex	c Waite, b Goddard	30	c Waite, b Fuller	30
2	Watson, W.	Yorkshire	c Mansell, b Tayfield	25	b Fuller	3
5	Graveney, T. W.	Gloucestershire	c Fuller, b Goddard	13	b Tayfield	42
6	T. E. Bailey	Essex	c Heine, b Tayfield	0	lbw b Tayfield	1
8	Spooner, R. T.	Warwickshire	b Tayfield	0	b Tayfield	0
9	Laker, J. C.	Surrey	c & b Goddard	2	b Tayfield	12
10	Lock, G. A. R.	Surrey	c McLean, b Goddard	18		
11	Statham, J. B.	Lancashire	not out	4		
			B 2, l-b 5, w , n-b	7	B , l-b , w , n-b	
			Total	151	Total	

FALL OF THE WICKETS

1—51	2—59	3—69	4—105	5—117	6—117	7—118	8—123	9—130	10—151
1—5	2—30	3—95	4—157	5—165	6—166	7—170	8—188	9—	10—

BOWLING ANALYSIS   First innings   Second Innings

	O.	M.	R.	W.	Wd.	N.b.	O.	M.	R.	W.	Wd.	N.b.
Heine	21	4	43	1								
Goddard	22.4	9	31	5								
Fuller	27	11	31	1								
Tayfield	19	7	39	3								
Mansell												

Score-Board Indicators. For the convenience of the public during FIRST CLASS MATCHES, indicators have been installed on both Score-Boards, from which fieldsmen will be easily identified by lighted numbers, corresponding to those on the score-cards. Letter S—Substitute.

NEXT MATCH AT THE OVAL, SAT., AUG. 20th (2 Day Match)
SURREY II v. ESSEX II

	SOUTH AFRICA		First Innings		Second Innings	
1	D. J. McGlew	Natal	c Spooner, b Statham	30		
2	T. L. Goddard	Natal	lbw b Bailey	8		
3	H. J. Keith	Natal	b Lock	5		
4	W. R. Endean	Transvaal	c Ikin, b Lock	0		
5	R. A. McLean	Natal	b Lock	4		
6	J. H. B. Waite	Transvaal	c Lock, b Laker	28		
7	J. E. Cheetham	W. Province	not out	12		
8	P. N. F. Mansell	Rhodesia	lbw b Laker	6		
9	H. J. Tayfield	Natal	b Statham	1		
10	E. R. H. Fuller	W. Province	c Spooner, b Lock	6		
11	P. S. Heine	Orange Free State	run out			
			B , l-b 7, w , n-b		B , l-b , w , n-b	
			Total	112	Total	

FALL OF THE WICKETS

1—22	2—29	3—33	4—33	5—	6—77	7—86	8—91	9—98	10—112
1—	2—	3—	4—	5—	6—	7—	8—	9—	10—

BOWLING ANALYSIS   First Innings   Second Innings

	O.	M.	R.	W.	Wd.	N.b.	O.	M.	R.	W.	Wd.	N.b.
Statham	15	3	31	2		1						
Bailey	5	1	6	1								
Lock	22	11	39	4								
Laker	23	13	28	2								

*Captain   ‡Wkt.-keeper   Toss won by—ENGLAND   RESULT—

Umpires—Bartley, T. J. & Davies, D.

HOURS OF PLAY—ALL DAYS—11.30—6.30   LUNCH 1.30

Printed on the ground by the Surrey County Cricket Club Printing Department

Official scorecard for England v South Africa at The Oval,
multi-signed by both teams

Brian walking out to bat
with Jim Parks on the tour

water poured over his head.

Begh had initially taken this initiation ceremony with much good humour but when other Pakistanis came on the scene he began to feel that his dignity had been pricked and was offended. The controversy was further fuelled by suggestions that the 'ducking' was a consequence of several umpiring decisions which had gone against MCC in previous matches but this was strenuously denied by the manager and players on their return home.

The MCC captain on the Tour was Donald Carr and he was very much to the fore in what happened. He later accepted full responsibility for what had gone on.

It would, perhaps, be a surprise, if Brian had not been in the thick of boisterous activity of this nature and Carr would go on to confirm that the Yorkshireman had, indeed, been a major player in the escapade, escorting Begh in a tonga – a light two-wheeled Indian vehicle – to the team's hotel where the 'ducking' occurred.

Well over 60 years after the event, Brian's letters to John recall something of what happened at the time and they also describe in detail other water battles involving the MCC squad.

MCC lost the four Representative games with Pakistan 2-1 with the other drawn and their sole victory did not come until the final encounter in Karachi but there was some excellent, if at times slow, cricket played on the Tour. Brian and Peter Richardson were in fine form and they got the MCC innings off to a good start on several occasions. Brian was MCC's leading scorer in first-class matches, playing in 12 of the 16 games and making 684 runs at an average of 36 with a top score of 92.

Brian also shot two fascinating 16mm cine films of the Tour which survive to this day and Brian's reels are now with the Yorkshire Film Archive in York. They show the team enjoying themselves on board ship to Pakistan and then visiting various tourist sites in that country as well as some cricket action and nice film of Pakistan life and famous places, temples and mosques. Brian was no doubt inspired by Bill Bowes' film of the 1950-51 Tour to Australia.

Billy Sutcliffe, Brian's county captain from the start of the following (1956) season, was the Tour's vice-captain in Pakistan, and also included in the party was their Yorkshire team-mate, Mike Cowan, but he was plagued by back trouble and returned home after playing in just four matches.

And so Brian's final batch of letters to John set the seal on the early part of a career which was never less than astonishing. John's admiration for Brian – he went on to become best man at Brian's wedding to Vivien – never wavered and Brian, for his part, always went out of his way to fill autograph books for his friend and he would make sure that there was a Yorkshire or England ticket available whenever John wanted one.

Throughout their lives, Brian and John lived only a few miles apart and when Brian died on September 14, 2015, John followed him to the grave a few weeks later. The funeral services of both men were at St Chad's Church, Headingley.

Brian's tumultuous career had already been well documented by then but his 'Just a Few Lines' letters to John have applied extra colour to a life that few can match in the world of sport.

[December, 1955]

Thanks very much for your present, John

Dear John,

Just a short line to let you know what's been happening up to press.

First of all, I had a nice and quiet trip to London with not even one disturbance and from Kings X I made my way over to the Imperial Hotel where I had a lovely Turkish Bath and a nice sleep. They woke me up with tea and toast at 8.0am and after washing I set off for Slazenger's.

There I met Mr. Hadingham and everything went according to plan and from there I was 'chauffeured' across to Broadcasting House. Here it turned out that they were making a rebroadcast of the film 'The Final Test' which we saw. Several of the film cast were the same – the barmaid, the young boy, but Jack Warner's part was taken by that TV star of 'The Teckman Mystery' fame [John Justin] and Robert Morley's part being taken by another stage actor with a very similar voice. It was quite amusing, really, especially when we had to say our 'piece'.

In the evening we had a dinner at the hotel with one or two MCC officials and that was that.

The following morning we set off very early and after an uneventful train journey up to Liverpool we boarded the ship after a lot of 'fuss and palaver' with the customs and passport officials. We got on to the ship and were immediately surrounded by photographers etc including a TV cameraman whom we had to parade in front of.

Eventually we were 'set free' and then it wasn't long before we set off on our voyage. There was nothing much doing the first couple of days as there was a heavy swell on the sea and the ship rolled like hell. Of course, nearly everyone was either in their cabin trying to sleep it off or moving around holding their tummies or something like it. I was one of the very few who wasn't the least bit troubled – mind you, I took things carefully as there was no point in risking matters too much.

It wasn't until we got thru' the Bay that people began to move around and we got playing the deck games. The weather has been fair but not really sunny until a couple of days ago and it was only yesterday that they filled the pool up and we were allowed to swim.

Ever since Monday morning, I've been doing a spell of training at 7.30 each morning, lots of laps, sprints and exercises and now I'm feeling as fit as a fiddle with 11 days to go.

We have had Housie-Housie, a racing game, and dancing etc at nights but the latter's not much good with what we have on board!! I won a few bob each time on the races, every time I've played cards I've always won (we play most afternoons when the sports are stopped so that the older people can get some rest) and the other night I even won the treasure hunt we had, much to my surprise – I always seemed to be two or three clues behind everyone else so it hasn't been a bad trip for me so far. Well John, I haven't much more room so you'll have to wait till next time for more, so Cheerio

Brian

Chittagong, Friday
[January, 1956]
Dear John,

Just a short line to let you know that everything is going OK – I don't know when you're going to get this letter?? The postal service out here is awful and when we were in West Pakistan our delay many a time was several days so no-one knows what it'll be now

Brian in blazer and whites before the first unofficial Test in Lahore

we're in East Pakistan. All the mail has to come and go via Karachi and there's only two services across here a week.

Well, we've completed one Test [Representative] match now [MCC v Pakistan, Lahore, January 20, 21, 22, 24, 25, 1956. Match drawn.] and we're still living!! We had one or two bad umpiring decisions against us but we managed to keep their rate of scoring so low that they nearly batted the rest of the time after they had bowled us out for 204. I was bowled out with a full toss just when I was beginning to see the ball. In the second innings, I was given out lbw to a ball which pitched about six inches or more outside my leg stump. I was annoyed, but I couldn't do anything about it.

Well, you've probably read about the match so I don't see why I should give you a detailed description of it all.

Our stay in Lahore was very nice indeed – I met a relation of my friend from Hyderabad whose job was a film producer and actor – he helped me to get something for my camera when I arrived there and from then on I went all over the place with him. He had a couple of cars, a Mark VII and a Triumph Sports (not the TR2) and he let me drive and borrow them whenever I wanted.

We went out to dinner several times at the Gymkhana Club and out to the Golf Club (bit of a rough one) for a drink or two. On the day between the University match and the Test match, [January 19] I fixed 12 of the lads up with a game of golf. It was great fun even though it was certainly unorthodox golf. Not having swung a golf club since leaving England and playing with borrowed ones, I topped the first one about 20 yards but afterwards I played very well. Roy Swetman [Surrey] and I beat Maurice Tompkin [Leicestershire CCC. He died later that year following an operation, aged 37] and Steve 3&2 ['Steve' was the nickname of Somerset's Harold Stephenson].

Also, in what little time I managed to get spare whilst I was there, I went around the beauty spots of Lahore. I went to see the Badshahi Mosque, supposed to be able to accommodate 100,000 people when praying – it was really a beautiful spot and I took many shots with my camera. Next door was the fort, a remnant of the Mogul Empire.

Afterwards, we went to the Shalimar Gardens and later to Jahangir's Tomb. They were all lovely places indeed, both built by Shah Jahan around about 1640 (the man who built the Taj Mahal).

We went to the Races a couple of times during our stay in

Brian picking a winner at the races with team-mate Alan Moss

Lahore, but I'm afraid I didn't fare too well!! It was most enjoyable though and it was good fun to get away from the cricket atmosphere for a while.

The Test match [drawn] finished in a bit of a farce, a result of Hanif's stupid batting, [142 in ten-and-a-half hours] and that night we all went out on the 'binge'. We arrived back late and found that we had to be up at 4.0am to fly at 5.0am from the airport. I don't think many of us went to bed and by the time we got on the plane we were nearly dead!!

We were travelling on a PAF Bristol Freighter converted (speed of 160) and we had so much luggage our main worry was whether we would get off the floor or not!! We dropped down in Delhi for refuelling and breakfast and from then we were flying in broad daylight. We flew over many well known city, town and river – Lucknow, Ganges etc – but our best sight was passing over the Delta of the Ganges and the Brahmaputra. Must close, Best Wishes. I'll write again soon.

Brian

I'll write again soon. Give my regards to all at 61.

Dear John,
Just a short line to thank you for your letter which I received today and to let you know how things are up to press.

Last time I wrote to you I believe I was a little bit down in the dumps. Anyway, now things are much better and I feel as fit as a fiddle and on the whole we're enjoying ourselves. After a very enjoyable Xmas, during which I made several influential friends, I went out to my friends' homes nearly every evening and had some English-made food for a change.

I went swimming a couple of times in the sea and on New Year's Eve these friends took me to The Boat Club dance (fancy dress)!

Well, after three or four very miserable days in Karachi to start with it all changed and I was disappointed at leaving when we had to. However, better was to come but let that wait for a moment. Karachi must be the ugliest place in Pakistan, what with all the refugee camps, filth etc. and all this amidst a sandy and dusty background. There's only a little green vegetation in an odd private garden or so but apart from that it's nothing but dull and drab surroundings.

I went to see 'The Rains of Ranchipur' starring Lana Turner whilst I was there. It was quite an enjoyable film.

Since I landed, I've been taking some lovely cine films of our Tour and when I get back I'm going to have it made into a film and then you'll be able to see for yourself.

We left Karachi by train for Hyderabad. Hyderabad in the Sind, not in the Deccan as you think, so you see we won't be able

The DVD of Brian's cine film. The cover shows Yorkshire team-mate Mike Cowan who started out on the Tour

to meet the Nizam. [The Nizam of Hyderabad was a monarch of the Hyderabad State; also know as Hyderabad Deccan. The state was ruled from 1724 until 1948 by the hereditary Nizam who was reputed to be the richest man in the world in 1948.]

We landed in Hyderabad at mid-day and after lunch we were all taken by bus for a run out to see the great Ghulam Mohammad Barrage Dam across the Indus. It was quite a formidable construction and we enjoyed the run out. After, a few of us went over to the Gymkhana Club for a game of squash until darkness fell.

The following day we were all up early and boarded Jeeps for a shikar (a hunt). We drove down narrow sandy roads, cart tracks, and out of camel trains, mule trains and carts pulled by oxen for 30 miles or so, then we left the road for the bush. After a few miles of this − clouds of sand and dust hung in the air for miles behind − we stopped and got out on foot. We distributed the six guns (three to each gun) and off we went. The Pakistani bearers walked ahead of us to disturb the partridge and quail out of the grass and bushes and we were supposed to do the rest!! I had the first kill of the day with a quail but I'm afraid that after that every time I had the gun we saw nothing. It wasn't a successful shoot − the birds didn't show up but we did see a large wild boar which we had to leave alone because we hadn't a rifle, only shotguns which would have just maddened it!

I wasn't playing in the match at Hyderabad so I went for a run in my friend's car (a huge Pontiac). It was the young lad who took us on the shikar the previous day. That night we took part in the 'Battle of Hyderabad'. We were split up in two Government Rest Houses and the lads in ours (two miles from the other) pinched the toilet kit of the six in the other for a bit of a lark. Just before dinner we received a phone call saying they had found out and were coming over by truck to raid us. Well, we locked all our doors and windows and barricaded ourselves in with buckets of water ready for them. No sooner had we done this than they came. They tried everything they could, including pouring water down the chimney to smoke us out. However, we were master of that by putting the fire out. Later, when the siege was at its height, I sneaked out and ran over to their place and ransacked it. Then I came back, sneaked in again but not before I'd had a 'romp' on the lawns with four of them. You ought to have heard them when we told them where I'd been and what I'd done. However, we forced them into a truce after

Brian on safari. He is on the right looking over the shoulder of team-mate Peter Sainsbury

this (they couldn't do a thing) and we finished the night off with a lovely dinner, a few drinks and a toast to the victors!!

One of the days of the match I went out with my friend and the Pir of Pagaro (a spiritual leader – they call him His Holiness) on another shikar the other side of town towards the mountains. After a 50-mile drive in the latest Chevrolet (the Pir's) we boarded an open Jeep and with guns at the ready we set off. We must have covered 80 miles at least over the bush and mountains before we saw anything – then the Pir shot a fox, I shot three sand grouse and my friend a few more. Later we gave chase to a few deer but we lost them when they went across a ravine.

Due to our match being rained off, we agreed to play a one-day match against the Pir's XI. I scored 95 not out. Our time in Hyderabad came to a close – I'd enjoyed it very much.

Best wishes

Brian

CHAPTER NINETEEN

FEBRUARY 12 – MARCH 7, 1956

Oh! Calcutta

In praise of Lahore – 6-0 soccer win v Bahawalpur locals – Amir's magnificent palace – Pillow rugby – 'Shocking umpiring' – Out for a duck – Oh! Calcutta – Water frolics galore -The water ragging incident – Songs on the bus – Threatened with rifles – Ready for home

Dacca, Wednesday
[Postmarked February 2, 1956]

Dear John,

Thank you for your letter which I received a few moments ago and as I've nothing to do until after 7.0pm (it's now 6.0pm) when we've to go to a cocktail party at the High Commissioner. What a bore, but I guess we can't do anything about it!

The last letter I wrote to you I don't know whether you found it interesting or not, but I wasn't in the mood when I wrote it in Chittagong and I don't think I put much into it at all. However it seems that there's a 'helluva' delay on our letters getting home so in future you'd better keep your fingers crossed.

Well, you ask me which place was the best? I think I enjoyed Lahore the best. There seemed to be much more happening and I made several friends, one of which was an actor and producer of Pakistani films (he was an uncle of Imdad whom I'm sure I told you about in Hyderabad). Anyway, he had a Mark VII and Triumph Sports which he loaned me whenever I needed any transport. He took me around to see all the historic and beauty spots, fixed me and the rest of the lads up with clubs and a game of golf so it wasn't bad at all.

The town on the whole was cleaner, more modern and greener

than any of the previous places. In Bahawalpur there was a lovely stadium and ground with squash courts, swimming bath and football ground adjoining it. After the 2nd day's play, many of us were quite fresh so we went over and took some of the locals on at football. We had a smashing game and ran them off their feet to win 6-0. It brought back memories!!

One of the first days in Bahawalpur we went to a reception in the pavilion of the ground. It was a lovely building with a huge central hall with carpets covering the whole of the floor – we finished up the evening playing games and tricks before it all developed into a mixture of soccer, rugby and all-in wrestling!!

At the reception I met a retired General who was in some way connected to the Amir of Bahawalpur. Well, with a little quiet persuasion he agreed to fix us up with a visit to the Amir's palace if we managed to finish the game off early (we had no free time at all allowed and the palace was 30 miles away). It was a truly magnificent place, too wonderful to describe in this short space, so you'll have to wait until I get back home soon.

Now we come to Chittagong which, on our arrival and drive through the town, we thought was the end of the world. However, when we got to the Club we found that hotels were non-existent in Chittagong and that the English people had offered to have us individually.

I stayed with a young fellow from Edinburgh who had a small three-year-old daughter, but his wife was away in Calcutta expecting an addition. He was a grand chap, the house was a lovely huge one and the food we had was terrific.

At night we went out to dinner or parties and what a time we had?? On the Saturday night we finished up at the Club and at 2.0am the MCC were taking on the locals at rugby with a pillow – several had their shirts torn off and one finished without pants but the MCC triumphed 4-0. Then we reluctantly said goodbye to them all [having reached the end of his space on the Airmail, Brian concluded his letter on a scrap of lined paper] after a most enjoyable stay – we'd had a couple of games of golf on their pitch and putt course (holes 90 to 160 yards long) and even had a trip down to the beach.

Anyway John, I must close now, so Cheerio and Good Luck.

Brian

I'll write again soon.

Brian

Sialkot – Monday
[Postmarked February 14, 1956]

Dear John,

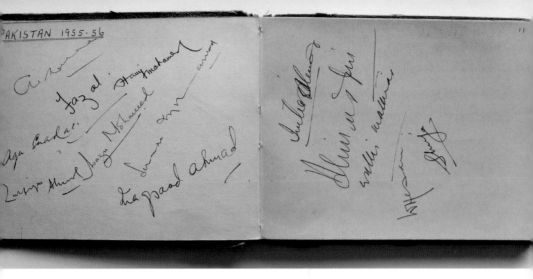

Just a short line to let you know that we're going on OK in spite of our defeat in the [Second]Test.

Granted we played badly compared with usual, but the umpiring was shocking. On the whole, we've reckoned that in each pair of innings we start [with] three or four wickets disadvantage. It's quite true what was printed in one of the Brochures 'that they would win by fair means or foul'. The finishing touch came after lunch on the last day. We had five wickets left and with Jim Parks in with Peter Richardson batting there was a chance that if they could play themselves in again we could draw the match.

However, in the very first over after lunch Fazal [Mahmood] bowled one down Jim's legside and, rather than risk hitting it to one of his short legs, he just watched it and let it hit his leg. There was an appeal and up shot the umpire's finger like a rocket. It looked almost as though it had been pre-arranged but it was the finishing point for us. The others soon went and left Peter carrying his bat [59 out of 105, MCC lost by an innings and 10 runs]. He batted better than ever before on the tour and if he'd have had someone to back him up we'd have easily pulled the match out of the fire. I got out first ball to a shocker. It was so bad and slow, I think the surprise of it got me out.

Anyway, it hasn't dampened our spirit any. Certain we're annoyed – who wouldn't be – but we go to Peshawar for the next Test [Representative match] where there is a responsive turf wicket. With a little luck and God's blessing, I think we might turn the tables on them.

In the celebrations they had afterwards, the umpires were in the thick of it – they needed to be too, they're the best two 'bowlers' we've come across. To them it seems that whether the ball is going to hit the wickets or not is a secondary consideration and we can't catch them out off the edge of the bat, it's got to be the middle or not at all!!

Well, so much for that. After the Test we had a couple of days to spare so half of the team went over to Calcutta by air to spend a couple of days having fun. I was one who stayed back in the Shahbagh Hotel (nicknamed Shagbag) and spent the time relaxing in the sun on the balcony outside my room. It was lovely and peaceful and as a result I think I look fairly brown now.

In the afternoons, a few of us went over to the Dacca Club where we played an odd game of tennis or so, and after getting a sweat on we went for a swim in the bath there. It was rather lovely. My tennis wasn't too bad at all considering my last game was in Australia in 1950. I managed to win my games without losing a set. It was good fun. In the evenings there was nothing to do, except go over to the Club for a drink and a game of snooker.

After leaving Dacca, we flew via Calcutta and Delhi to Lahore where we stayed the night and then came on to Sialkot by bus the following morning. It was a nice run out and not too long either. We arrived in time for lunch and then had a bit of practice in the afternoon.

Today we managed to bowl their side out for 147 [Combined XI first innings] and then we made about 160-3. I managed to get off the mark again with 82 then in trying to get the last 18 in 15 minutes I got caught out at long on.

Well John it won't be long now thank goodness so I'll say Cheerio and Good Luck. See you soon. Give my regards to all at home (61).

Brian

Peshawar Tuesday
[Postmarked February 29, 1956]

Dear John,

Thanks very much for your letter which I received yesterday. It was nice to hear all the news of what's happening back home. We're cut off from everything out here and all we learn of what is going on in England is what we read in our letters and in a 'fortnight-old' paper we occasionally get. I'm sorry to hear of your grandfather's illness – give him my best wishes for a good and swift recovery.

Well John, a lot of things have happened out here in the last day or so [the water jape on Idris Begh during the third Representative match in Peshawar] and unfortunately I can't write everything down in a letter for several reasons – you'll just have to wait (16 days to be precise) until I get home when I can tell you the lot!! However, don't believe all the newspapers say as I'm sure they will be all contorted as not one of the Pressmen were present until long afterwards.

It was our 'greatest night' and so funny we burst our sides with laughing. Unfortunately, it was an incident, a joke or piece of ragging which fell on stony ground. They've no sense of humour out here, although every one of their players except [word crossed out] Kardar [Pakistan captain Hafeez Kardar] (this letter might be censured) nearly ------ themselves with laughing and the other umpire did too.

Anyway, what was blown up into a political and international situation by Kardar and their hopelessly exaggerated Press (anti British) seems to have quietened down at the moment. We were almost ready to pack our bags there and then and be flown out ('much to our disgust', we haven't needed to but we were all for it). Anyhow, so much for that, wait for the minor details until the 16th or 17th.

Since I wrote last, we haven't had a bad time really. At Sialkot – the place itself was dull, dirty etc., but one morning we were shown around one of the few Sports Factories there. It is quite a big sports manufacturing centre, in fact the only one.

They make tennis, squash and badminton racquets – hockey sticks, footballs and lots of things entirely by hand. They set young lads 10 years old to work doing odd jobs and by the time they're a 'decent' age they can do almost anything.

One of the nights there, when the match was as good as won, we were all having a few drinks and chatting – it was Mr. Howard's [C.G. Howard, manager] birthday and he was full of the devil after a glass or two, when all of a sudden we started our aquatic sports.!! Someone splashed a little water about and before long everyone was in shorts or trunks and buckets were flying around all over the place. I was writing, but realising what was going to happen I hastily put it all away and beat it.

As each person got wet, they joined the 'mob' chasing the rest. They even broke into the rooms and 'drowned' one or two sleepers including the Press. It was great fun. I got changed into a pair of trousers and dark shirt so that I would be camouflaged in the darkness and laid low for a while in some bushes. There were three of us who escaped that night – Jim Parks, Pete Sainsbury and I – and eventually we took to the trees and watched in comfort all the goings and comings of everyone. They were dashing about all over the place with buckets or jugs but could find us nowhere. Later on, when they couldn't find us, they 'wrecked' our rooms and upset everything – I slept that night with half my bed missing, I had it supported on two armchairs. We had a great time and I might say that if we didn't do things like this at some of these places we'd go nuts. [This water ragging occurred before the Begh incident match.]

There's nothing to do at night time except sit around in each other's company all the time, and of course the subject of conversation is always cricket. We have to find some diversion somehow and those are the things we do to let our 'hair down' (we can't let it down on the cricket field!).

After our game at Sialkot we played a game of soccer on the lawn outside our hotel. It was grand fun and good exercise and the North just managed to beat the South 10-9.

At night we had an awful trip to Lyallpur by train and arrived but I can't waste space on that except that it took us 12 hours to cover 110 miles!! At Lyallpur our living quarters were quite good, being new bungalows in the compound of a large cotton factory (four of us to a bungalow). The boss of the factory gave us his huge, most beautiful house at our disposal and after the match was finished we had two free days, both of which we spent playing football in his garden and bathing in his Pool. He filled it up specially for us and we relaxed in armchairs in the sun all day, occasionally going in for a dip to cool off. He (our host) put a huge radiogram at our disposal at the side of the Pool and we listened to a lot of Doris Day, Howard Keel, Ava Gardner records etc. It was great fun and was voted one

Cooling off. Brian about to go into the pool

of the best places we had been to in spite of the smells, flies and filth of the town.

After leaving there it took us 24 hours to get up to Peshawar!!! and one of the free days we had before the Test we went through the Khyber Pass right to the Afghan border. It was a great experience and one we shall never forget. However, wait a little and you'll hear more. Give my regards to everyone – see you soon.

Yours

Brian

[On the flap of Page One of his letter, Brian wrote: "The cheating ------have done it again on us. It works out that about 12 of our wickets are taking on about 30 or more of theirs."]

Multan
[Postmarked March 7, 1956]

Dear John,

Just a brief line before I arrive home. The 'fuss' seems to have died down, but even the mention of Idris Begh's name puts us into fits of laughter. Anyhow, wait until I get back and I'll keep you laughing for days!!

Since I wrote to you from Peshawar we lost the Test match, which was inevitable considering about 11 wickets of ours 'took on' 34 wickets of Pakistan, at a rough guess. Anyway, it can't be helped 'it'll all be the same a hundred years from now' as <u>our</u> song goes. We've got one or two songs going about the Tour and when we get into the bus we nearly lift its roof off!!

After the Test match was finished we found we had a couple of days free before travelling on to the next place. On the first day we went out for a trip into the hills to Warsak to see the beginning of the Canadian Hydro Electric project given to Pakistan under the Colombo Plan. There wasn't very much but preparations going on at the time, excavating, tunnelling and one thing and another but we did have quite an interesting morning out there. We were entertained very well.

The following day, in amongst our packing etc., I managed to get an Australian couple with whom I had made friends to take three of us out to the Kohat Pass. It was a lovely trip and the Pass, if not quite as rugged as the Khyber, was equally picturesque. We stopped at the village of Darra at the mouth of the Pass and popped into some of the weird houses and shacks at the side of the road. They were miniature 'arms factories' turning out rifles, revolvers and sten guns etc. which were exactly like British, American and other foreign makes, even to the stampings and markings on them. It was amazing the amount of arms there were to see or buy and even an expert would have had difficulty in differentiating between them and the real thing.

We continued up the Pass and took some film shots. Of course all these places are in the Tribal areas where no law exists except that of a gun and so everyone you see carries a rifle and bandolier or some such weapon. Up in the Khyber we were taking some snaps of women in purdah carrying huge loads on their heads. Our action infuriated the men with them and they slung the rifles at us and would have shot us had not our liaison officer been alert and told them we meant no harm.

We also had a nice game of golf whilst we were there and enjoyed the change immensely, even with a couple of armed guards trailing a few yards behind us (Governor General's orders in case the tribesmen and students enraged by the local Press to take the law into their own hands). When the G.G. heard the true facts he was rather amused but detailed a 24-hour guard on us for safety (like an adventure story "Battle of Peshawar").

Anyway, that night we left Peshawar to travel overnight by train to Sargodha. We arrived the next morning and our first official thing was lunch at the RPAF [Royal Pakistan Air Force] College officers mess. Here we arranged a soccer match that night with the College team and gave them a horrible beating (8-0).

At Sargodha, we again stayed individually with the teachers from the PAF College (British people) and the place where I stayed was very nice indeed. At night after the game, we popped across the road and joined the lads in a swim in the College Baths. It was smashing.

Apart from the usual run of parties we saw a film, believe it or not!! It was an old one which I had seen several years ago called 'Green Dolphin Street' starring Lana Turner and Donna Reed. I enjoyed it very much when I first saw it. Do you remember it?

Anyhow, our stay in Sargodha came rapidly to a close (as we hope the rest will) and on Monday morning we had to get up at 5.0am to fly to Multan at 6.0am!!! Fortunately, I'm having a rest this match for I felt like anything but cricket that day. Actually, I've been fed up of the cricket for a long while – how I'm longing to get home again and see some lovely fresh English grass. Well John, I shall have to close. I'll give you a ring when I come up home (don't know yet) so until then I'll say Cheerio and Good Luck. Best wishes to all.

Yours

Brian

This was the last of the 'Just a Few Lines' sequence of letters that Brian sent to John. Two days after Brian's letter had been posted, the fourth and final Representative match began in Karachi and MCC were able to end their tour with victory by two wickets. Although Brian was desperately homesick by now he was still able to make a significant contribution to the narrow win by top scoring in each innings – 71 out of 184 in the first and 30 out of 126-8 in the second.

CHAPTER TWENTY

FRIENDS TO THE END

Less than two months after Brian had penned his last letter to John from Pakistan, Yorkshire were back in action at the start of a new season and although injury kept Brian out of Championship action until early June, 1956, he was on the merry-go-round of constant cricket from which he never stepped off until his full-time retirement from the game over 20 years later. Even then, he continued to play in first-class representative matches, charity games and even captained the Yorkshire Academy for a while in his early 60s.

That letter to John from Multan was the last that either survived or was written to him, the latter being the more likely in view of how religiously John kept hold of everything that Brian sent to him for the remainder of their lives.

As mentioned at the start of Chapter Eighteen, communication by telephone was rapidly becoming a part of everyday life and was even more the case come the 1956 season which produced a soggy summer and a much below par performance from Yorkshire.

There can be little doubt that Brian would have continued his epistles to John out of friendship and a perceived sense of duty had the telephone not made the time-consuming task of writing on sheet after sheet of notepaper totally unnecessary.

No need now for Brian to compose with his pads on while waiting to go out to bat, with one eye on the play waiting for a wicket to fall and the other on his pen and paper. Or to burn the midnight oil at home or elsewhere as he collected his thoughts and attempted to shrug off tiredness.

There must have been times when committing pen to paper was a huge burden but one which he felt compelled to carry out in the name of friendship – never 'Just a Few Lines', as he liked to start off his letters, but page after page of detailed description.

The drying up of the letters, however, did not bring about a complete cessation of written communication because even after Brian's marriage to Vivien there were infrequent postcards from Mr. and Mrs. Close from holiday destinations around the world

Montreux

Brian and Vivien with best man John and Brian's sister Mary who was one of the bridesmaids

for several more decades and these, like the letters had been, were stashed away by John.

And if any further evidence were needed of Brian's loyalty to John it could be seen at Ottery St Mary in March, 1966, when Brian and Vivien were married and John was the best man. By now Yorkshire captain and soon-to-be England captain, Brian was at the peak of his career and many a famous name would have been honoured to be his best man, but he chose his old school mate.

John, for his part, continued to cut out and keep every scrap of newspaper upon which Brian got a mention and this was virtually on a daily basis. When both of them had passed on, Vivien received a battered old suitcase from John's family and it was stuffed with newspaper cuttings, stored but not forgotten and hiding autograph books filled with famous names around the cricketing world that Brian had collected for his friend.

John may well have gone on to carve out a name for himself as a tennis player of some repute had he not been cut down in his youth by poliomyelitis. Perhaps in Brian he saw something that might have been in himself had fate not dealt him a cruel hand.

Perhaps, also, John was finally at ease in passing away only a couple of weeks after Brian, no doubt having left specific instructions that the funeral service and the wake should both be at the same places as his lifelong buddy.

Before closing this narrative, I should make it clear that Brian not only wrote scores of letters during his cricketing lifetime but also received hundreds of letters and telegrams from the famous and not so famous; from royalty and prime ministers, from actors and entertainers, and from former players including the likes of Len Hutton, Herbert Sutcliffe and several Yorkshire captains. In addition, he was sent through the post many more messages from a miscellany of clubs, organisations and individuals, the majority of whom Brian probably didn't know or hadn't ever heard of. All of the above wanted to congratulate or commiserate with him during the various stages of his unique career.

But that is another story...

Tailpiece:

Baildon Town Council have made sure that the name of their esteemed sporting personality will live on in perpetuity. During the winter of 2019, a new housing development was opened in the town off Otley Road and just a couple of hundred yards from where Brian and Vivien lived for all their married life. It was named Brian Close Walk and the picture shows Vivien having just performed the unveiling ceremony, watched by daughter, Lyn, and Yorkshire CCC Chairman, Robin Smith.

STATISTICS

DENNIS BRIAN CLOSE

FIRST-CLASS CRICKET FOR YORKSHIRE 1949 TO 1970
FIRST-CLASS CRICKET FOR SOMERSET 1971 TO 1977

Left-hand batsman
Right-arm pace and off-break bowler

Born:	Rawdon, Leeds on February 24, 1931
Died:	Baildon on September 14, 2015
Yorkshire debut:	v. Cambridge University at Cambridge May 11, 1949
Last played:	v. Somerset at Hull on September 12, 1970
Somerset debut:	v. Leicestershire at Leicester on May 1, 1971
Last played:	v. Worcestershire at Worcester on September 7, 1977
Final First-Class:	for D B Close's XI v. New Zealanders at Scarborough on August 31, 1986
Yorkshire Cap:	August 31, 1949

LIST A CRICKET FOR YORKSHIRE 1963 TO 1970

LIST A CRICKET FOR SOMERSET 1971 TO 1977

Yorkshire debut:	Gillette Cup v. Nottinghamshire at Middlesbrough on May 22, 1963
Last played:	John Player League v. Somerset at Harrogate on September 13, 1970
Somerset debut:	John Player League v. Leicestershire at Leicester on May 2, 1971
Last played:	John Player League v. Gloucestershire at Taunton on August 28, 1977

FIRST-CLASS MATCHES FOR YORKSHIRE
BATTING AND FIELDING

Season	M	I	NO	Runs	HS	Avge	100s	50s	Ct
1949	26	42	8	958	88*	28.17	0	3	16
1950	1	2	0	39	22	19.50	0	0	0
1951	2	4	0	64	39	16.00	0	0	0
1952	33	45	9	1192	87*	33.11	0	8	27
1953	2	2	1	14	10	14.00	0	0	1
1954	30	41	7	1287	164	37.85	2	7	23
1955	28	45	5	1131	143	28.27	2	4	35
1956	27	37	5	802	88	25.06	0	3	23
1957	29	48	3	1315	120	29.22	3	4	32
1958	32	49	4	1335	120	29.66	1	7	30
1959	31	54	3	1740	154	34.11	4	8	32
1960	36	51	3	1699	198	35.39	3	8	44
1961	34	58	7	1821	132	35.70	5	8	44
1962	28	45	6	1438	142*	36.87	3	7	29
1963	24	36	3	1145	161	34.69	1	7	24
1964	33	50	7	1281	100*	29.79	1	7	46
1965	30	46	7	1127	117*	28.89	3	2	31
1966	30	50	9	1259	115*	30.70	3	6	44
1967	15	20	2	643	98	35.72	0	8	21
1968	25	31	7	599	77*	24.95	0	3	32
1969	20	27	4	812	146	35.30	1	4	10
1970	20	28	2	949	128	36.50	1	6	20
	536	811	102	22650	198	31.94	33	110	564

Centuries (33)

1954	123*	v. Somerset	at Sheffield
	164	v. Combined Services	at Harrogate
1955	114	v. Cambridge University	at Cambridge
	143	v. Somerset	at Taunton
1957	108	v. Derbyshire	at Bradford
	120	v. Derbyshire	at Chesterfield
	103	v. Sussex	at Hove
1958	120	v. Glamorgan	at Swansea
1959	144	v. Oxford University	at Oxford
	154	v. Nottinghamshire	at Nottingham
	128	v. Lancashire	at Sheffield
	128	v. Somerset	at Bath
1960	102	v. Hampshire	at Portsmouth
	198	v. Surrey	at The Oval
	184	v. Nottinghamshire	at Scarborough
1961	132	v. Surrey	at The Oval
	111	v. Lancashire	at Manchester
	103	v. Glamorgan	at Leeds
	103	v. Somerset	at Hull
	100	v. Cambridge University	at Cambridge
1962	121*	v. Somerset	at Taunton
	140*	v. Warwickshire	at Sheffield
	142*	v. Essex	at Sheffield
1963	161	v. Northamptonshire	at Northampton
1964	100*	v. Surrey	at Bradford
1965	115	v. New Zealanders	at Bradford
	117*	v. South Africans	at Bradford
	101*	v. Surrey	at Bradford
1966	103	v. Cambridge University	at Cambridge

	105	v. Gloucestershire	at Bristol
	115*	v. Nottinghamshire	at Worksop
1969	146	v. New Zealanders	at Bradford
1970	128	v. Northamptonshire	at Northampton

BOWLING

Seasons	Matches	Overs	Mdns	Runs	Wkts	Avge	Best	5wI	10wM
1949	26	1089	291	2703	105	25.74	6-47	6	0
1950	1	50.2	14	132	7	18.85	4-66	0	0
1951	2	39	16	74	2	37.00	1-22	0	0
1952	33	1107.4	331	2746	114	24.08	6-69	6	0
1953	2	45	19	105	3	35.00	2-61	0	0
1954	30	519	136	1428	66	21.63	6-38	4	0
1955	28	804.4	244	2002	90	22.24	7-62	5	0
1956	27	266.5	75	674	24	28.08	4-27	0	0
1957	29	259	84	682	30	22.73	5-29	1	0
1958	32	324.1	82	856	32	26.75	4-30	0	0
1959	31	726.2	206	2031	81	25.07	8-41	5	0
1960	36	611.3	207	1493	64	23.32	8-43	3	0
1961	34	568.2	214	1426	58	24.58	6-49	2	0
1962	28	392.5	156	885	29	30.51	3- 4	0	0
1963	24	388.2	127	1038	42	24.71	6-55	1	1
1964	33	539.5	195	1243	52	23.90	6-29	1	0
1965	30	527.2	202	1217	58	20.98	6-49	4	1
1966	30	502.3	192	1118	54	20.70	6-27	2	0
1967	15	250.1	96	565	18	31.38	3-28	0	0
1968	25	316	136	694	29	23.93	4-87	0	0
1969	20	115	47	282	7	40.28	1-4	0	0
1970	20	34	10	95	2	47.50	1-15	0	0
	536	9476.5	3080	23489	967	24.29	8-41	40	2

10 wickets in a match (2)

1963	10-74 (6-55 and 4-19)	v. Glamorgan	at Sheffield
1965	11-119 (6-52 and 5-67)	v. Kent	at Gillingham

5 wickets in an innings (40)

1949	5-58	v. Essex	at Leeds
	7-47	v. Worcestershire	at Worcester
	5-73	v. Sussex	at Leeds
	6-87	v. Surrey	at Bradford
	6-130	v. Lancashire	at Leeds
	6-105	v. Gloucestershire	at Huddersfield
1952	5-64	v. MCC	at Lord's
	5-40	v. Oxford University	at Oxford
	5-36	v. Lancashire	at Leeds
	6-69	v. Nottinghamshire	at Nottingham
	5-24	v. Leicestershire	at Leicester
	6-94	v. Hampshire	at Scarborough
1954	6-68	v. Gloucestershire	at Bristol
	6-45	v. Gloucestershire	at Sheffield
	6-38	v. Northamptonshire	at Bradford
	5-32	v. Hampshire	at Bournemouth
1955	5-32	v. Kent	at Hull
	5-88	v. Northamptonshire	at Northampton
	5-95	v. Nottinghamshire	at Nottingham
	7-62	v. Essex	at Bradford
	6-63	v. Derbyshire	at Bradford

5 wickets in an innings *(Continued)*

1957	5-29	v. Cambridge University	at Cambridge
1959	5-12	v. Warwickshire	at Sheffield
	5-75	v. Middlesex	at Scarborough
	8-41	v. Kent	at Leeds
	6-87	v. Somerset	at Bath
	5-47	v. The Rest	at The Oval
1960	5-64	v. Sussex	at Middlesbrough
	6-59	v. Derbyshire	at Chesterfield
	8-43	v. Essex	at Leeds
	5-36	v. Somerset	at Hull
	6-49	v. Kent	at Dover
1963	6-55	v. Glamorgan	at Sheffield
1964	6-29	v. Kent	at Bradford
1965	5-69	v. New Zealanders	at Bradford
	6-52	v. Glamorgan	at Swansea
	5-67	v. Kent	at Gillingham (1st innings)
	6-49	v. Kent	at Gillingham (2nd innings)
1966	6-47	v. Surrey	at Bradford
	6-27	v. Surrey	at The Oval

FIRST-CLASS MATCHES FOR SOMERSET
BATTING AND FIELDING

Season	M	I	NO	Runs	HS	Avge	100s	50s	Ct
1971	25	41	10	1388	116*	44.77	5	6	33
1972	19	31	5	1299	135	49.96	3	6	17
1973	21	32	5	1096	153	40.59	3	3	21
1974	23	38	7	1099	114	35.45	1	5	23
1975	21	36	6	1276	138*	42.53	1	8	14
1976	17	28	4	971	88	40.45	0	7	13
1977	16	25	2	438	87	19.04	0	2	19
	142	231	39	7567	153	39.41	13	37	140

Centuries (13)

1971	104*	v. Leicestershire	at Leicester
	116*	v. Northamptonshire	at Northampton
	102	v. Yorkshire	at Taunton
	114	v. Surrey	at Taunton
	103*	v. Indians	at Taunton
1972	108	v. Glamorgan	at Swansea
	108	v. Warwickshire	at Weston-super-Mare
1972	135	v. Gloucestershire	at Taunton
1973	114	v. Essex	at Taunton
	153	v. Middlesex	at Lord's
	108	v. Glamorgan	at Neath
1974	114	v. Leicestershire	at Weston-super-Mare
1975	138*	v. Gloucestershire	at Bristol

BOWLING

Seasons	Matches	Overs	Mdns	Runs	Wkts	Avge	Best	5wI	10wM
1971	25	32	9	124	4	31.00	3-20	0	0
1972	19	35	10	128	3	42.66	2-77	0	0
1973	21	159.5	29	560	10	56.00	2-3	0	0
1974	23	97	29	255	13	19.61	5-70	1	0
1975	21	290.1	87	906	29	31.24	4-22	0	0
1976	17	163.1	36	605	15	40.33	3-35	0	0
1977	16	0.2	0	8	0	—	—	0	0
	142	777.3	200	2586	74	34.94	5-70	1	0

5 wickets in an innings (1)

1974   5-70   v. Lancashire at Taunton

TEST MATCHES

BATTING AND FIELDING

Season	Versus	M	I	NO	Runs	HS	Avge	100s	50s	Ct
1949	New Zealand	1	1	0	0	0	0.00	0	0	0
1950-51	Australia	1	2	0	1	1	0.50	0	0	1
1955	South Africa	1	2	0	47	32	23.50	0	0	0
1957	West Indies	2	3	0	89	42	29.66	0	0	2
1959	India	1	1	0	27	27	27.00	0	0	4
1961	Australia	1	2	0	41	33	20.50	0	0	2
1963	West Indies	5	10	0	315	70	31.50	0	3	2
1966	West Indies	1	1	0	4	4	4.00	0	0	1
1967	India and Pakistan	6	9	1	197	47	24.62	0	0	8
1976	West Indies	3	6	1	166	60	33.20	0	1	4
		22	37	2	887	70	25.34	0	4	24

BOWLING

Seasons	Matches	Overs	Mdns	Runs	Wkts	Avge	Best	5wI	10wM
1949	1	42	14	85	1	85.00	1-39	0	0
1950-51	1	9.2	1	28	1	28.00	1-20	0	0
1957	2	2	1	8	0	—	—	0	0
1959	1	16	1	53	5	10.60	4-35	0	0
1961	1	8	1	33	0	—	—	0	0
1963	5	25	5	88	0	—	—	0	0
1966	1	12	3	28	1	28.00	1-21	0	0
1967	6	87.4	30	209	10	20.90	4-68	0	0
	18	202	56	532	18	29.55	4-35	0	0

ALL FIRST-CLASS MATCHES

Matches	Innings	NO	Runs	HS	Avge	100s	50s	Ct/St
786	1225	173	34994	198	33.26	52	171	813/1

Overs	Maidens	Runs	Wkts	Avge	Best	5Wi	10Wm
11661.5	3602	30947	1171	26.42	8-41	43	3

LIST A: YORKSHIRE 1963 TO 1970 AND SOMERSET 1971 TO 1977

Yorkshire debut:	Gillette Cup v. Nottinghamshire at Middlesbrough	May 22, 1963
Last played:	John Player League v. Somerset at Harrogate	September 13, 1970
Somerset debut:	John Player League v. Leicestershire at Leicester	May 2, 1971
Last played:	John Player League v. Gloucestershire at Taunton	August 28, 1977

YORKSHIRE BATTING AND FIELDING

Season	M	I	NO	Runs	HS	Avge	100s	50s	Ct
1963	2	2	1	58	29*	58.00	0	0	0
1964	1	1	0	1	1	1.00	0	0	1
1965	4	4	1	128	79	42.66	0	1	1
1966	1	1	0	29	29	29.00	0	0	0
1967	1	1	0	1	1	1.00	0	0	1
1968	1	1	0	10	10	10.00	0	0	0
1969	12	12	0	263	96	21.91	0	2	8
1970	10	9	0	141	28	15.66	0	0	3
	32	31	2	631	96	21.75	0	3	14

YORKSHIRE BOWLING

Seasons	Matches	Overs	Mdns	Runs	Wkts	Avge	Best	5wI
1963	2	30	3	102	6	17.00	4-60	1
1964	1	11	1	35	2	17.50	2-35	0
1965	4	17	6	47	2	23.50	1-12	0
1966	1	12	6	22	1	22.00	1-22	0
1967	1	2	0	8	2	4.00	2-8	0
1968	1	12	1	30	0	—	—	0
1969	12	48	11	162	7	23.14	3-36	0
1970	10	20	3	69	3	23.00	3-27	0
	32	152	31	475	23	20.65	4-60	1

4 wickets in an innings (1)

1963   4-60   v. Sussex   at Hove

SOMERSET BATTING AND FIELDING

Season	M	I	NO	Runs	HS	Avge	100s	50s	Ct
1971	16	15	4	467	89*	42.45	0	3	2
1972	20	20	1	484	88	25.47	0	2	8
1973	18	17	1	313	76	19.56	0	1	6
1974	24	24	0	630	131	26.25	2	0	2
1975	23	21	0	308	55	14.66	0	1	9
1976	19	18	1	391	69	23.00	0	1	8
1977	6	4	1	65	28*	21.66	0	0	2
	126	119	8	2658	131	23.94	2	8	37

Centuries (2)

1974   128   v. Gloucestershire   at Bristol
        131   v. Yorkshire at Bath

SOMERSET BOWLING

Seasons	Overs	Mdns	Runs	Wkts	Avge	Best	5wI
1971	55	8	206	11	18.72	3-17	0
1972	66.4	10	273	11	24.81	3-25	0
1973	96.4	5	440	19	23.15	4-9	1
1975	3	0	21	0	—	—	0
	221.2	23	940	41	22.92	4-9	1

4 wickets in an innings (1)

1973   4-9   v. Glamorgan   at Taunton

ENGLAND BATTING AND FIELDING

Season	M	I	NO	Runs	HS	Avge	100s	50s	Ct
1972	3	3	0	49	43	16.33	0	0	1

ENGLAND BOWLING

Season	Matches	Overs	Mdns	Runs	Wkts	Avge	Best	5wI
1972	3	3	0	21	0	—	—	0

ALL LIST A MATCHES
BATTING, FIELDING AND BOWLING

M	I	NO	Runs	HS	Avge	100s	50s	Ct	Overs	M	Runs	Wkts	Avge	Best
164	156	11	3458	131	23.84	2	11	53	376.3	54	1436	66	21.75	4-9

SUBSCRIBER LIST

John P Adams
Norman A Alvin
Ken Beanland
Phil Beaver
The Bellamy family
Geoff Binks
Ken Blackburn
Eric A Blakey
Anthony Bradbury
John Briggs
John Brook
Rupert Brown
Mr Derek Burley-Emmerson
Tony Burnett
Phil Burrow
Michael Burton
Pamela Burton
Gaynor Buttle
David Byrne
Lucas Chambers
Martin Chandler
Tony Clarkson
Howard Clayton
Lance Close
Vivien Close
David Ian Coldwell
Mr J Trevor Constantine
John Conyers
Dorothy Cook
Geoff Cope
Kathleen Crawshaw
Jeffery Dalton
Tony Debenham
Jonathan Dicks
Paul Dyson
Duncan Eccles

Harold Vaughan Edmondson
David Exall
Jack Fahey
Mike Farrow
Malcolm Ferguson
Mr Malcolm Ferguson
Peter Ford
C J Fox
Henry Free
Alex Michael Gatt
Michael C Gibson
Jim Goodman
Malcolm Graham
Martin Grayshon
Stephen Greaves
James M Greenfield
Pete Greenwood
Lyn Close Hainsworth
Keith Hamilton
Bob Hammond
Kevin Hardisty
Chris Hardy
Ian Michael Harrison
John Harrison
Richard Harrison
David Heard
John Helm
Geoffrey E Hill
David Hird
David Hirst
Shirley Hodgson
Barry Hood
David Hornsby
Housemans of Guiseley
Trevor Howe
Roy Humbles

John Christopher Hunt
Peter Ingle Britton
Richard Ingleby
Andrew Jacob (Somerset admirer)
Johnny Kennedy
Colin Johnson
Martin Kirby
Barrie Leadbeater
Vanessa Lee
Ian Livingstone
Tony Loffill
Anthony Hugh Lupton
Steven M
Mr Edward Peter Matthews
Kevin McCabe
Chris Metcalfe
Ralph W Middlebrook
Alex Mills
Lewis Mills
Roy Milnes
Captain Martin John Moore
J Richard Morton
Mel Neary
Tony Ogley
Mr D W Pae
J. Michael Parkinson
Robert Pearson
David Peel
Richard Pennell
David Perry
John Pickering
Mr Cyril Pickup
Nigel Pullan
Jack Quarmby
Tom Ralph
Howard Ray
Geoff Relton
Brian Richards
Mr Tony Robson
Katrina Rook
David Ryder
R C Scruton

David Sewards
Bob Shackleton
Russell Short
Richard Shutt
Phil Sissons
Robin Smith
Mr John Spencely
Roy Stafford
David Stead
Chris Stephenson
Mr James Stewart
Kevin Sutcliffe
Peter Swabey
Brian Tempest
Robert Thompson
Gwyneth Todd
Nicholas P Tubbs
Ian Vertigan
Peter Warner
Harvey Watson
Jeff Watson
Peter Watson
H M Way
John Wells
Paul White
Peter Wigglesworth
Eric Wild
Peter Wildsmith
Steve Wiles
John S Williams
Gerry Wright
Jez Wright
Bob Yardley
Edward Yardley
Zig Zwierzewicz
Sydney Porter
Christopher
Martin
Paul
Sydney
Tina & Dave